Praise for *The Six Attributes of a Leadership Mindset*

The Six Attributes of a Leadership Mindset is an engaging book of great relevance to anyone with responsibility for leading others. The six key attributes of leadership that Joe delves into will help any humane leader become even more effective. He makes it clear that while there aren't magic answers, there are plenty of ways in which we can all improve our leadership – and who doesn't want that?

Dave Harris, Business Director, Independent Thinking Ltd, author and education consultant

I must admit that I am not a keen reader of books on leadership, yet I found myself totally immersed in *The Six Attributes of a Leadership Mindset*. Writing in a refreshingly humble, thoughtful, and humorous style, Joe gives due attention to what he calls the obvious and points out some subtle yet fundamental differences between various concepts – for example, being a leader versus demonstrating leadership, and the difference between establishing connections and developing collaboration. The book also touches on one element I found particularly interesting: the notion of world view and the ability of the leader to change it.

The book's content is not only grounded in solid research and the author's rich experience, but is also brought to life with inspiring stories and practical exercises. The special emphasis on the behaviours related to these attributes also further contributes to making *The Six Attributes of a Leadership Mindset* a very useful companion for leaders.

Dr Jean-Claude Pierre, CEO, Scott Bader Group

D0377702

In *The Six Attributes of a Leadership Mindset*, Joe Britto provides a resource that will support many leaders in reviewing and reflecting on their leadership. He offers a range of insights and opportunities to challenge existing practice and explore alternative ways forward, and shares a rich range of stories and anecdotes to illuminate and inform his model.

John West-Burnham, Honorary Professor,
University of Worcester

In *The Six Attributes of a Leadership Mindset*, Joe Britto provides an intriguing and exciting new dimension to the journey of leadership. The insight, clarity, and applied stories and challenges he shares offer an accessible foundation of opportunity to every reader – and his wonderfully structured, powerfully reasoned, and convincingly developed framework brings to life the attributes of a leadership mindset. Furthermore, Joe's message goes beyond the world of work and challenges us to refresh our mindset in order to get more from life in a refreshingly easy-to-follow flow.

The Six Attributes of a Leadership Mindset should be a compulsory handbook for all those in or aspiring to any leadership role.

Neville Pritchard, founder of People in Flow Ltd

The Six Attributes of a Leadership Mindset is one of the few development books that will sit next to me on my desk and serve as a working reference and reminder of things to practise on a daily basis. I would definitely recommend it to anyone who is interested in enhancing their leadership mindset.

Zena Knight, Director,
Advanced Behavioural Capabilities Ltd

The Six Attributes of a Leadership Mindset

The Six Attributes of a
Leadership
Mindset

FLEXIBILITY OF MIND
GENUINE CURIOSITY RESILIENCE MINDFULNESS
RESILIENCE ENTERPRISE THINKING
ENTERPRISE THINKING GENUINE CURIOSITY
CREATING LEADERS
MINDFULNESS RESILIENCE
ENTERPRISE THINKING

Joe Britto

Crown House Publishing Limited
www.crownhouse.co.uk

First published by
Crown House Publishing
Crown Buildings, Bancyfelin, Carmarthen, Wales, SA33 5ND, UK
www.crownhouse.co.uk

and

Crown House Publishing Company LLC
PO Box 2223, Williston, VT 05495, USA
www.crownhousepublishing.com

First published 2019. Reprinted 2019.

British Library Cataloguing-in-Publication Data

A catalogue entry for this book is available from the British Library.

Print ISBN: 978-178583406-6
Mobi ISBN: 978-178583430-1
ePub ISBN: 978-178583431-8
ePDF ISBN: 978-178583432-5

LCCN 2019937537

Printed and bound in the UK by Gomer Press, Llandysul, Ceredigion

For Ruth. Friend. Confidante. Teacher.

Foreword by Gill White

History has given us many leaders who have no power, no team, no title, no money – nothing. Yet they motivate thousands to follow them, and to change laws, beliefs, countries, and governments. The list is long: Mahatma Gandhi, Martin Luther King, Jr., Nelson Mandela, and Mother Teresa, among many others. What do these leaders possess that drives them to such greatness, and how do we all get some of it?

In this book Joe Britto helps us to understand that leadership is a mindset. It's not a title, a role, a rite of passage, or something that's bestowed or inherited. Leadership is a way of behaving and a way of thinking. It's a way of being in the world. Once we understand this, we can lead from anywhere – in any situation. Benjamin Zander, in *The Art of Possibility*, teaches us that an orchestra needs a "leader in every chair", because a lack of ownership for one's own notes, and not holding other musicians to account, could lead to the entire piece being played off key.[1]

Joe helps us to practise and build a mindset that enables us to lead better. But reader be warned: just reading this book will not turn us into awesome leaders. This takes work, practice, effort, and consistent application. And like anything worth having, it will take time and we will fail along the way. An old boss of mine used to say, "Failure is glorious because it means you were reaching further than you ever have before. And it comes with a beautiful jewel – a new pearl of wisdom." So, as you'll hear Joe say soon, treat this book as a manual: dip in, try it out, and explore what the six attributes mean for you both in your professional and personal life.

Before you continue with the book and follow Joe's explanation of the six attributes, a word on what those attributes have come to mean to me.

Mindfulness is a particular passion of mine. As Joe suggests, mindfulness is effective in "slowing down the world" – and it's true. I began to study transcendental meditation in 2008 and it was transformational for me; I

---

1   Rosamund Stone Zander and Benjamin Zander, *The Art of Possibility: Transforming Professional and Personal Life* (London: Penguin Books, 2002 [2000]).

had more time in my life than I had dreamed was possible. I know it's not easy to find the time to devote to gaining mindfulness, but I've found that if we do, we feel more in control, calmer, and less anxious about everything.

I love the fact that Joe emphasizes the "genuine" in genuine curiosity, the kind of curiosity we had as kids: not seeking information to necessarily gain something, just being "genuinely curious". As parents, how many of us have been driven to the edge by our children's charming yet insatiable curiosity? "Why is the sky blue?" "Why is the sea green here and blue there?" Why, why, why …? Somewhere in the process of growing up we can lose the innate desire to seek to understand for no other reason than because it's fascinating.

Thinking differently, flexibly, isn't easy – but it is a choice. This is where flexibility of mind comes in. So if mindfulness helps us to wake up and become conscious, and genuine curiosity leads to interesting answers, it's flexibility of mind that helps us to creatively combine ideas into a bigger one.

I read the chapter on resilience first because I've always been worried that I won't have what it takes when my mettle is truly tested. I once went on a week-long fitness bootcamp, and on the third day we were running around a field pretending that we were in a war zone: saving imagined victims and hauling them to safety. My "victim" was a baby, and on the third round of the course I couldn't breathe any longer. But I kept going. When we focus on what we truly believe is important, we often find we are capable of much, much more than we might at first think.

The chapter on creating leaders reminded me of the advertising tycoon David Ogilvy, who used to send every new office manager a Russian doll with a note inside that read, "If each of us hires people who are smaller than we are, we shall become a company of dwarfs. But if each of us hires people who are bigger than we are, we shall become a company of giants."[2] As Joe says, great leaders "know that those they lead will come up with bigger and better ideas than they ever could. And they understand that that's a good thing."

---

2   David Ogilvy, *Ogilvy on Advertising* (London: Prion Books, 2007 [1983]), p. 47.

My favourite chapter is the one on enterprise thinking. Thinking for the whole company and setting personal interests aside is not easy. Perhaps because enterprise thinking can seem counterintuitive it is one of the toughest of all the attributes. The challenge is to understand and not just know the old adage *a rising tide raises all boats*. That's possible when we feel the connection to our business that Joe talks about. If we, as leaders, can take the step toward enterprise thinking, we can then help our teams feel connected too.

It's my sincere hope that, as you turn the pages, you'll find as much to gain from the insights Joe has shared in this inspiring manual for leadership and life as I did. Enjoy the ride.

Gill White, Director of Business and Markets Development, Chartered Institute of Personnel and Development (CIPD)

Preface

An Insight

2009 wasn't a good year for me. While the rest of the world was reeling from one of the biggest financial meltdowns in recent history, I was dealing with a meltdown of my own. I'd been a psychological coach, trainer, and management consultant for nine years by then, and I was in the middle of a nervous breakdown. It wasn't a lot of fun – in fact, it's not something you'd wish on your worst enemy – but for me it was a turning point.

I re-evaluated everything in my life and one of those things was what I was doing professionally. You know that old adage *if you give a person a hammer, every problem they come across is a nail*? Well, I saw clearly how that applied to training and management consulting and, in doing so, I began to lose faith in the ability of both to create long-term change. I began to lose faith for the simple reason that training gives people hammers in the form of techniques, and although those hammers may work in some instances – when your problem is a proverbial nail – they aren't flexible enough to work beyond the situation they're designed for. I lost faith in consulting because it's mostly about imposing a business model on an organization. That works for the immediate problem, or for as long as the consultant's there, but tends to slip when the consultant goes or the circumstances change.

So I stopped working for a while and tried to find an approach that would create long-term change. One that would be flexible enough to address not just current challenges but problems coming down the road – ones my clients couldn't even see yet.

What I did during that time was think. A lot. I thought about what clients really want. About why, in a multibillion-dollar training and consulting industry, clients are willing to accept that their investment won't create long-term change.

I began to think about successful change in all its forms. What makes some people successfully quit smoking, get fit, or pivot quickly into a new career? I wondered what happens before a business can create a culture change, or before a senior team can align around a common strategy.

So there I am in the middle of a nervous breakdown, thinking that this was the worst thing that ever happened to me, cursing the circumstances that led me to it, and wondering how to make what I did for a living work better. In case you're wondering, the irony did elude me at the time. But eventually I saw it: the question I was asking of my work was the answer I needed in my personal life. I saw clearly that before I could get out of the breakdown, I needed to think differently. The thought was as simple as it was obvious: that before we can make any change – personal, professional, or organizational – we need to think differently about the challenge we're facing.

Enter leadership mindset stage left.

Mindset because before anything can change, we need to think differently. *Leadership* because before something can change, we need to be willing to take personal responsibility for making that change happen. Because mindset can be a nebulous concept, I worked to identify the attributes of a leadership mindset – the qualities and behaviours that embody this way of thinking. Looked at like that, solving personal or professional challenges becomes a two-step process:

1   Grow the six attributes of a leadership mindset.

2   Apply that shift in thinking to the challenge you're facing.

By doing that, we not only develop a new way of thinking; when we apply the six attributes to our challenges, we come up with revolutionarily different solutions because we see different possibilities in those challenges.

It would be disingenuous of me to say that it's easy to embed the six attributes. It happens with effort and practice over time. For some it may be an easy shift to make, for others it may require a 180-degree change in perspective.

The point of this book is to share the ideas that make up the six attributes: what they are, how they work, and how to use them to grow our own leadership mindset. I've developed these ideas through observations of the people and businesses I've worked with. I've used this approach in the consulting work I do, helping leaders shift their thinking to address the challenges in their teams or businesses. But because I started thinking about the approach in the middle of a personal breakdown, I'm also offering it as a way to navigate through life. Maybe that's not so different. After all, businesses are run by people.

The promise of the six attributes is that we can create real, meaningful, and self-sustainable change. But the benefits don't end there. Perhaps the real gift of the six attributes is that we can all grow our mindsets. Do that, and as we lead our way through life, we make a difference to ourselves and to the lives we touch.

My hope is that this becomes a handbook of sorts. In the following pages I'll begin by defining a leadership mindset and looking at some of the challenges to living the six attributes. From there I'll go over the behaviours of each attribute and offer a few challenges you can use to grow them. That's what I mean about it being a handbook: it doesn't have to be read in order. Each chapter explores a different attribute. Begin with the one that most interests you, try out the challenges and develop that attribute in yourself for a while. When you feel you're making headway, pick another one. Read that chapter and give those challenges a go.

There's no rush. Like I said, the six attributes build with effort and practice over time. This book will still be here, so feel free to take it at your own pace.

Take care,

j.

Acknowledgements

Books aren't a one-person endeavour. I'm grateful for the help of the whole team at Crown House Publishing, especially David and Karen, without whom this book wouldn't be what it is. Tom did a great job on the cover, and Louise's edits gave the book a much-needed polish. Daniel's proofreading made everyone's reading experience much better. Thanks also to Rosalie for her marketing prowess.

A big thanks to Ruth, Murray, and Chad for reading early drafts and for the suggestions that followed.

These ideas were honed in conversations with the team at Innate Leaders – Sarah, Louise, Gizem, and Katherine, you guys rock. And of course, Ruth.

Thanks to Amy – love comes in many shapes. And to my family for their support.

Contents

Introduction:
On Mindset

What Does Mindset Have to
Do with Leadership?

The Toquaht First Nation of British Columbia, Canada, have a word for the traditional territory overseen by their Chief: *Hahulthi*. It includes the land, the ocean, the people, and everything living and non-living that exists within that territory. Historically, the Chief would have seen clearly that, on behalf of his people, his responsibility was to care for his *Hahulthi* for generations to come.

Armed with a version of leadership like that, the Chief had a clear purpose and goal. His mindset was that of a steward. And every decision he made took place against the backdrop of the thousands of people who would come after him.

He thought that way not because he was an enlightened individual – although who knows, maybe he was. I'd suggest he thought that way because of the cultural environment he grew up within. The Chief grew up in a place which taught him to see his role as a caretaker of the land, people, and things in his territory.

What this points to is the importance of how we come to view leadership, because how and what we learn about leadership determines how we lead when it comes to our turn.

When I'm in session with a group of leaders, we begin by defining a leadership mindset. I often offer them the chance to do that by representing their ideas as a piece of art. It's a tough ask because it can be uncomfortable for some. And that's the point. Often a leadership mindset means being willing to operate on the edge of our comfort zone. So the challenge is a chance to live the attributes of a leadership mindset while defining a leadership mindset.

After that work of art is made, we'll have a go at defining what we mean in words. Somewhere in that conversation I'll offer a definition that's something like this:

A leadership mindset is a way of looking at the world borne out of our experiences that leads to a set of behaviours.

That's what the Chief has. In his case, that world view is informed by his culture and history. For us, it can be informed by our personal experiences growing up, our environment as we make our way through life, or the examples of leadership we've seen in our jobs over the years. Either way, just like the Toquaht Chiefs, our ideas of leadership are forged in the crucible of environment and experience.

If we're lucky, we'll have had positive experiences of leadership; but it's just as likely that our leadership world view is informed by domineering leaders who want everything done their way, head-strong leaders who believe that because they're the leader they're always right and need to be seen as such, or well-intentioned leaders who know no other way to lead than by telling people what to do. These behaviours are all attributes of something, but not of a leadership mindset.

The useful thing about the above definition is that from it we can isolate the specific attributes that demonstrate a leadership mindset. Think about it like this: if someone lived a leadership mindset, there are certain qualities they'd likely have. And here they are:

- Mindfulness
- Genuine curiosity
- Flexibility of mind
- Resilience
- Creating leaders
- Enterprise thinking

It's easy to look at these attributes and see them as separate qualities. That might lead us to approach each attribute as a task to complete. But if we did that we'd be missing the point. The attributes aren't a skill, they're a way of thinking. And the attributes aren't tasks to tick off a list, they're behaviours that emerge from a way of looking at the world – from a leadership mindset, you might say. In fact, each attribute leads to certain behaviours. We'll focus on those in the next chapters, but, for now, the point is a simple one: when we're talking about a leadership mindset, we're talking about a way of leading that's informed by our world view.

We hold that world view not because we learnt it in a book (even this one), but because we've lived the experiences that gave rise to it. These experiences can be anything from the difficult times we've gone through, or the great times we've had. What matters is that the experience presents us with a choice about who we are, what we want to be in life, and – for us in this context – what that means for how we lead.

If we haven't had the chance to live the kinds of experiences that point toward the six attributes, it doesn't mean all's lost. If we want to lead from a different world view, it means finding the courage to put ourselves into situations where we can experience a different way of looking at the world. Because of that shift in perspective, we begin living the six attributes, and that means a leadership mindset emerges.

The Foundation of Leadership

Perhaps now's a good time to think about where the six attributes fit into that familiar question: are leaders born or are they made? There are camps on both sides, each defending their point of view. Those who feel leaders are born stress that learning how to lead is not only impossible but pointless. Instead, we should make the most of the qualities we have – let ourselves off the hook for not leading because, well, if you don't have it, you don't have it.

And then there's the other camp. It's this camp that churns out book after book dissecting the skill of leadership and offering an eager audience the distilled wisdom on how to lead. This camp isn't content to line our shelves with books; they've also developed skills-based courses that reveal the hard skills of leaders and package them into systems and processes. In their most lucid moments they develop metrics for how to measure the skills they've identified so that their followers can chart their leadership progress.

As you may have guessed by now, I don't side with either camp – for the simple reason that any debate that's been going for as long as that one is self-evidently unwinnable. Instead, I'd suggest there is another way to think about the nature versus nurture argument. What about if both the leaders-are-born and the leaders-are-made camps are built on the common ground of mindset? What I mean by that is, if we feel that leaders are born, then we're saying they have some special quality that allows them to lead. A quality, that I'd say, grew the six attributes and was honed by the environment and experiences the individual has lived through.

If we're saying that leadership is a skill we can learn, then I'd suggest we can learn all sorts of techniques – but if we don't have the attitude to go with it, our skills and techniques become formulaic and that rarely breeds a following.

Like I said earlier, not all of us have had the experiences that may cultivate the six attributes. Not all leaders have had those experiences. But that doesn't mean we can't all develop them. Whether we do comes down to the answers to two very simple questions:

1 Am I willing to challenge my world view – to see its limits, and allow it to be stretched?

2 Am I willing to reshape my world view and allow that perspective to change the way I behave?

These are personal decisions, and if you answer in the affirmative you'll stand out. Leaders living the six attributes encourage people to be the best they can be. They speak to the best in people and empower them to be their best. The six attributes help people to think; not like the leader, but for themselves. They know that those they lead will come up with bigger and better ideas than they ever could. And they understand that's a good thing.

That's the kind of standing out you can expect when you live the six attributes. And, no, it isn't easy. Where does the courage to stand out come from? Where does the ability to bring others together come from? What's the mysterious quality that allows a leader to take charge of a situation, make a decision, or stand in opposition?

Whatever that quality is, it's my premise that it's borne out of the decisions a person makes. After all, it's a choice to stand out, to bring others together, and to lead. So that quality isn't really mysterious: it takes an initial decision and an ongoing commitment.

That quality isn't demonstrated by answering "yes" to these two questions once – after all, the six attributes are a journey not a destination – but rather by answering "yes" to challenging our world view consistently over time, even when we think we're right (but we'll get to that).

And that's why growing the six attributes is a personal decision. It's the decision we make sitting in a meeting when the topic on the table makes no sense to us. Do we go along, or do we decide to stand out and say we don't understand? What about when it's clear to us that a plan isn't going to work? Do we stand by and watch it fail or do we decide to speak up?

Of course, making that decision begins with the view we take of ourselves and of our abilities. If we're positive about ourselves, and confident in our abilities, we're more likely to speak out than if we're not. One way to think of that is to ask ourselves, "How can we become confident if we're not?" That isn't a road I'm walking down here because there are lots of other books on the subject, and also because I think it's a red herring in terms of leadership. For me, leadership isn't about being confident in what we're doing. Leading when we have all the information is not only rare, it's pretty easy. It's easy to stand out and say difficult things, offer an inspiring vision, or stand in opposition if I have all the information to prove that I'm right.

In the real world we'll more often have an incomplete picture of what we're trying to achieve. The unknowns are many, and our ability to offer a vision, or garner the support to try something, is the challenge of everyday leaders. And, to come full circle, that's why answering "yes" to our two questions is what allows the six attributes to grow. Answering "yes" means we understand that we don't have all the answers. It means we understand that there's more for us to know and that there are greater possibilities than we can imagine. And answering "yes" means we're open to seeing what those possibilities are, knowing full well that the answer will come from outside of us.

Answering "yes" comes from a place of humility. So, if the road to hell is paved with good intentions, the road to living the six attributes is paved with openness. We're all capable of making the choice to answer "yes", but that doesn't mean walking the road is easy.

Why are the Six Attributes of a Leadership Mindset Needed in Business?

Since you know this isn't going to be an easy journey, perhaps now's a sensible time to ask why we should take the first step. Along with a shift in mindset comes a change in behaviour. That's important because thinking differently with no change in behaviour, or tangible effects in the real world, is a purely intellectual enterprise – which, although interesting as a thought experiment, isn't the thread we're pulling on. The shift towards the six attributes of a leadership mindsct gives us a different way to look at the challenge in front of us *and* a willingness to do something different because of that shift.

If we're talking about a leadership team that isn't a cohesive unit, that may be struggling to agree and implement a business strategy, one option is to offer them the skills to conduct better meetings. What they'd get from that is a set of tools they may or may not use. Another option might be to tell them what's possible for the business and offer a plan detailing how to get there. The thing is, if the solution were as simple as telling people to listen to each other or providing a strategy, my guess is they would have worked that out already.

So another approach is to think about why the team isn't doing those things already. That could be for a whole bunch of reasons, all of which (as we'll see) have their core in what we're calling the six attributes of a leadership mindset. If that's true, helping the team grow the six attributes means they can develop their own way to solve their challenge. And if they developed their own solution, it'll make sense in their business context – because they know their business better than any consultant would. And because they developed their own solution, they'll be more inclined to put it into effect. And because they've put it into effect, they'll be invested in that solution succeeding.

What the team will get from the process of developing that solution is a different way to think about how they interact, and about what it means to lead, which leads to a change in the way they behave. That change in behaviour leads to different ways of doing things. It means teams don't tend to rely on the same approach and the same solutions they've always tried, and it means they come up with revolutionary ideas to the challenges they face. And they can apply that different way of thinking to any challenge down the road again and again, which means long-term, self-sustainable change becomes possible.

And all that happened because we invested in growing the six attributes in our team.

So the simple answer to the question, "Why are the six attributes of a leadership mindset needed in business?" is because – in an uncertain economic climate and a fast-changing world – we need leaders who can pivot and flex quickly. And that requires a flexible world view.

Before we unpack the attributes, let's think for a second about what might make it difficult to cultivate them.

The Drive to Conform

We're social animals. We like fitting in. Leading often means standing out, which can leave us isolated and alone. Who wants that? The drive to conform is a real and tangible reason why we find ourselves doing and saying things we don't agree with.

Conformity is a human trait American social psychologist Stanley Milgram highlighted in a series of experiments he performed in the early 1960s. The premise was this: Milgram recruited volunteers and told them they were taking part in a study on memory – on whether punishment improved it, to be precise. The truth was, it was an experiment to see how far subjects would obey an authority figure who asked them to act in conflict with their conscience.[1]

In the experiment, volunteers would visit the basement of Linsly-Chittenden Hall at Yale University, where Milgram was a professor. They were met by the experimenter – dressed in a white coat for added effect – and a second person, who they were told was a volunteer but who was actually in on the experiment. The experimenter asked the two "volunteers" to draw names out of a hat to decide who would be the learner and who the teacher. Of course, the ballots were rigged and the real volunteer always came out as the teacher.

Then the rules would be explained: the teacher and the learner would be situated in two different rooms. The teacher would be given a list of word pairs to teach the learner. The teacher would recite the first word and four possible pairs. If the learner got the pair wrong, the teacher was told to punish them with an increasingly severe electric shock. The shocks were mild to begin with but went all the way up to 450 volts – enough to kill someone. Of course, the learner never actually received any shocks, but

---

1   Stanley Milgram, "Behavioral Study of Obedience", *The Journal of Abnormal and Social Psychology*, 67(4) (1963): 371–378.

they did scream in pain and angrily demand to be released from the experiment.

If, on hearing the screams of the learner, the teacher got cold feet, they'd be prompted by the experimenter with standardized phrases that increased in urgency.

At a certain point, the learner would stop making noises, giving the impression they may have been killed. The experiment was stopped when the teacher had administered three consecutive 450-volt shocks or refused to continue.

Milgram's question was this: how many people would go all the way to 450 volts?

The answer may surprise you, and it's why mindset is so important. What Milgram highlighted is that when the authority figure – the experimenter in the white coat – promoted people to keep shocking the learner, 65% of people gave a stranger three 450-volt shocks.[2] Don't forget, at this point the learner would have gone silent and might be dead.

If you're thinking, "That's fine, we've changed a lot since the sixties," then I've got bad news. The experiment was repeated by British mentalist and illusionist Derren Brown in his 2006 TV show "Derren Brown: The Heist"[3] and again in 2009 for the BBC 2 *Horizon* documentary.[4] The result? Over 50% and 75% of participants respectively went all the way to 450 volts.

I'm describing the experiment to illustrate just how willing we are to conform. Milgram discussed his findings in his book *Obedience to Authority: An Experimental View* and the title gives us the clearest lens through which to view his work.[5] What

---

2   Milgram, Behavioral Study of Obedience, 377.
3   Channel 4, "Derren Brown: The Heist" (Original broadcast date 4 January 2006). Available at: https://www.channel4.com/programmes/collections/63-money-money-money/41020-001.
4   BBC 2, "How Violent Are You?", *Horizon* (Original broadcast date 12 May 2009).
5   Stanley Milgram, *Obedience to Authority: An Experimental View* (New York: Harper & Row, 1974).

Milgram is showing us is that, when confronted with an authority figure, most of us tend to choose deference. Of course, it doesn't feel like we're making a choice. And that's the point: we're following, not leading.

In the real world that authority figure isn't an experimenter in a white coat. It could be the perceived authority of our peers, it could be our boss, or it could be as abstract as a rule which we think is unbreakable. The drive to conform could be to avoid the potential for conflict, or just the risk of losing our job or losing face. It's easy to not conform when we have nothing to lose, but it pays to be compliant when what we value is at stake.

It's because it's so hard to break the status quo that many of us would just as soon give up on the decision to lead and follow along with whatever might be on offer at the time. Which is great if what's on offer moves a team, a business, or humanity forward in a useful way. But what if it doesn't do any of those things? Should we stand up against it? Of course the answer is "yes", but how can we do that while experiencing such a compelling drive to conform?

A Lesson from Recent History

Perhaps anti-apartheid activist Stephen Biko said it most clearly: "the most potent weapon in the hands of the oppressor is the mind of the oppressed."[6] In Apartheid South Africa, the struggle was life and death. Biko died in police custody in 1977, detained under the Terrorism Act for leading students in rebellion against systemic racism. Biko understood the power of mindset and the power of personal leadership. He knew that apartheid worked because, alongside an institutionalized racism that privileged

---

6   Steve Biko, Black Consciousness and the Quest for a True Humanity. In Aelred Stubbs (ed.), *Steve Biko: I Write What I Like* (Oxford: Heinemann Educational Publishers, 1987 [1973]), pp. 87–98 at p. 92.

whites while removing all opportunity for non-whites, it accomplished something far more powerful.

During apartheid in South Africa it was customary for black men to doff their caps to white people they passed on the street. There was no law that required them to do so and it wasn't a custom enforced by the police. Biko saw clearly that, by following the custom, black men were buying into the system of their oppression. Biko argued that for black South Africans, liberation could only be achieved by coming together as a unified group, but to do that they first had to liberate their minds. He was talking about a change in mindset.

Thankfully our struggle isn't so stark. We're not breaking the chains of institutional or governmental oppression. But developing the six attributes is a revolution nonetheless: a quiet revolution in which we have the chance to liberate ourselves from our self-imposed limits – and that includes our willingness to conform.

Leadership offers the freedom to decide who we want to be, what our teams can be, and what our businesses are all about. As uncomfortable as the last two examples may feel, acknowledging the power of the drive to conform can – if we're willing to look it in the eye – allow its power over us to fade.

Nothing Worth Having Was Ever Easy

"OK," Phil Follower might say, "it's hard. Fine. How many people would agree they're deciding not to lead?"

Few, I'd guess. Many of us might see leadership as a skill to hone. Others might see it as an ability we're born with, while some might see leading as something they very rarely have the chance to do. Not because they don't want to, but just because the chance doesn't come up. If living the six attributes really is a decision, then the idea that we don't have a chance to lead – or don't have a leadership role – is one of the subtle ways I think we can abandon the decision to lead.

"But how am I abandoning leading?" Phil says, "You've just said some people don't have a role where they can lead! Well, how do you do," he offers his hand in a mock introduction. "That's me!" Phil's annoyed, but that's not a surprise; the surprise is that he's taken three steps toward me and he's a big guy. Not Hulk big, but I-could-knock-you-out-with-one-punch big.

I continue cautiously – after all, he's a figment of my imagination. "See, the thing is, Phil," I begin.

He grunts but stands his ground.

"The thing is," I continue, "you lead yourself every day."

He cocks his head and folds his outstretched hand into a fist. I know I've got maybe five seconds to make sense before I get a close-up of that knockout punch.

"You got yourself out of bed on time this morning." He says nothing but I keep going. "And how about what to wear, what to eat for breakfast, the pearl of wisdom you gave the kids this morning? How about navigating yourself to work, prioritizing your day? Heck, what about the word of advice you gave your colleague?"

He drops his head (but not his fist) and thinks for a moment.

"These are all decisions you made to lead. And if you can do that, doesn't it mean you can look at your job and think about what could be done better, faster, and more effectively there, if only you took on the mantle of leadership?"

It seems like hours before his fist finally lowers to his side.

As I'm sure you see, the opportunity to live the six attributes is in front of us every moment of every day. The question isn't, "Why are the six attributes of a leadership mindset needed?" It's, "Are we willing to develop them?"

I'd say we abandon leadership in other ways too. It could be that we think we can only lead if we have great ideas. It could be we think leaders must have a big following. It could be that we have a role as a manager or supervisor and see our place as implementing someone else's ideas rather than looking for efficiencies ourselves. These positions all amount to the same thing: a willingness to abdicate leading.

That might sound harsh (I can see Phil warming up his fist again), but I truly believe that, in the times we live in today, we all have an obligation to lead. Excusing ourselves isn't a luxury we can afford anymore. The world needs your leadership mindset.

Messiah Syndrome

Before we leave this topic, there's one excuse we use to get out of leading that I hear more than any other, and it's one I'd like to think about now. Phrased in different ways, and with different examples of great leaders as its focus, the point goes something like this: "Sure, Martin Luther King/Margaret Thatcher/Steve Jobs/my first boss was a great leader. They had this – I don't know – this *thing* that really set them apart. They were amazing."

Although it'll be phrased differently each time I hear it, the core of the point is always the same. I call it the messiah syndrome. It's frustrating to hear because it's the kind of thinking that allows people to keep themselves small. Looking to anyone else as a guru, a messiah, or just plain amazing is another way of giving ourselves permission not to try. After all, if [insert your favourite leader here] is such a guru how could you hope to be like them? How could anyone?

As Annie Abdicator might put it, "It's so cool that Nelson Mandela/Joan of Arc/Arianna Huffington achieved X, Y, or Z but they're amazing, right? And there's no way I'd achieve anything close because I don't have that magical thing that they have. I'm just, well, you know, me."

But here's what Annie Abdicator's missing: seeing our heroes as more than us means we have the perfect excuse to not try. That doesn't mean we shouldn't admire people. It means it's worth pausing to acknowledge the hard work and effort they've put in to get to where they've gotten.

Most great leaders have gone through personal and professional hardship. They developed their mindset because of the environment and experiences they lived through. They came out the other side of those hardships better because of them. Often we don't hear about the challenges faced by people who form great companies, political movements, or small-scale social change. Sometimes that happens because we don't ask. We compare ourselves to the myth that these leaders become, and see ourselves falling far short. And because we fall short, we tell ourselves it's not our place to lead.

But anyone who ever did anything worthwhile worked hard to get there. Which isn't to say that some people didn't get lucky to achieve what they've got, but that's how the world is: success is a mixture of hard work and luck – and not always in equal parts.

My point is that if we don't acknowledge the hard work that goes into being good at anything, it's easy to let ourselves off the hook of actually putting in the hard work to do it ourselves. And that's just as true of developing a leadership mindset.

So remember this: the six attributes I'm going to talk about aren't "magical" – they're all qualities you already have. That doesn't mean you can't develop them further and it doesn't mean they're easy to develop. I'm still working on it myself, and it's still hard work. It's something I practise every day. Some days I do well; others, I fail miserably. Before every client phone call I make, I feel nervous; every time I consult I'm nervous before-hand. You know what, I'll go one step further: I'm not just nervous, I'm scared. Why? Because we can never really know how what we say will be perceived. But that doesn't mean we don't try. Leading is scary and difficult, and that's the reason why we need to practise it. Every day. And that's true whether you're a CEO or a teenager who's left school with no qualifications.

Chicken and Egg

To repeat: the process of cultivating the six attributes of a lead-ership mindset isn't "magic" and doesn't involve joining a cult or becoming a guru. Before we look at what makes up the six attrib-utes, you might be wondering what comes first – do behaviours create the mindset, or is it the other way around?

We could debate that one for years to come, I'm sure. Ultimately, though, I don't think it's a helpful way to approach a leadership mindset. Chicken-and-egg questions like that can send us career-ing off the path, into weeds that are easy to get lost in. More importantly, I'd suggest that debating which comes first is just a way to put off actually doing anything. For me, the twin poles of a leadership mindset and the behaviours of the six attributes are symbiotic; they feed off and reinforce each other. You can start with either one of them – consistently practising the behaviours will affect our mindset, if we let it; insight into a leadership mindset is likely to affect our behaviour. It really doesn't matter where we start. It just matters that we do.

A Word on the Challenges

In each chapter we'll consider what each attribute means in detail and, because everything is meaningless without action, I'll offer a few practical challenges that you can use to develop that attribute. To be clear, these challenges aren't simply leadership skill-building techniques. The main difference is that these challenges aim to create a shift in mindset.

The graphic that follows shows the interplay between our mindset and how we think, act, and feel. Everything in the box on the left affects the other aspects, so if we effect a change in one area – how we feel, let's say – it has an effect on other aspects – how we act, for example. It's as simple as this: when I feel good I'll behave differently than when I feel sad or depressed.

But it isn't a one-way street. Those things affect our mindset, and our mindset affects how we think, act, and feel. In fact, any change to either of the elements on the left changes our mindset.

The challenges in this book have the potential to do that. Choose challenges that push you out of your comfort zone. If you practise the challenges often – make them part of your day – it can affect the way you think, what you do, and how you feel. And that will lead to a different way of seeing the world. Your perspective will shift, and you'll begin to see the challenges you face in your suitcase-packing dilemmas/personal life/business differently.

The thing that makes the six attributes worthwhile is that they can be operationalized. Each time we grow an attribute we grow our leadership mindset. The goal isn't just to grow the six attributes. It's to apply that shift in mindset to the very real challenges your teams and businesses face.

As I said in the preface, feel free to use the following chapters like a handbook. Flick through the pages and pick an attribute that most intrigues you; try out the challenges and develop that attribute in yourself as much as possible. Then, when you feel you're making headway on that attribute, pick another. And so on and so on. Each time you master a challenge you're growing your leadership mindset.

Chapter 1
Mindfulness

Mindfulness is a buzzword these days. Google it and you'll get hits advocating mindfulness for everything from spiritual development to a cure for depression and anxiety, and a de-stressor for modern life. Mindfulness is big business with mindfulness schools and a plethora of books all vying for our attention and money. But despite being a buzzword and a fast-growing cliché, mindfulness has very real and practical applications that are neither abstract Eastern mysticism nor new-age hippy-dippy. So, mindfulness is important, but it's not a golden bullet to save us from all ills. In our context, mindfulness is one of the six attributes. Nothing more, nothing less.

Have you ever walked out of a meeting wondering what was just said? Have you ever sat in a meeting so engaged in the conversation that later, when a colleague says you seemed defensive, angry, or quiet, you're genuinely shocked? Have you ever been so caught up in the banter of pundits and colleagues – or so sure of your own direction – that you were bowled over by a challenge you didn't see coming? I'd say what we're all missing in those situations is an understanding of the direction of the conversation – and of the impression we're leaving – and a failure to read or anticipate where our team or business is at. I'd say we're missing the ability to be present in the moment and see, really see, what's unfolding in front of us – which is where mindfulness comes in.

To be mindful isn't magical or spiritual, though it can have a touch of both. Being mindful is just what it sounds like: being aware of what's happening now. It means being free from the thoughts in our heads; concerns about what we should or shouldn't say, a preoccupation with how we might look if we spoke up, or any number of other thoughts that do a good job of keeping us, well, small.

We only have so much brain power, and if that capacity is being used up worrying about [insert your current preoccupation here] it means we don't have space to focus on what's really important. Mindfulness gives us that space. Being mindful liberates us from the small and mundane and lets us elevate our perceptions and our conversations – and see what's happening beneath the surface.

Mindfulness is central to a leadership mindset because the stillness of mind that it brings creates a fertile landscape in which to grow the other five attributes. From that stillness and presence, genuine curiosity, flexibility of mind, and even enterprise thinking all become possible.

So let's begin by understanding where mindfulness came from.

A (Very) Brief History of Mindfulness

Meditation, the practice of training the mind, is most often associated with Eastern religions – such as Hinduism and Buddhism – and has been practised for thousands of years. Though there are others, its two most popular forms are concentration meditation and mindfulness meditation.

Concentration meditation encourages attention on an object in order to develop a discipline of mind. This kind of meditation mostly consists of sitting comfortably and bringing our focus back to the object of our attention when it drifts. That object could be a statue of Buddha, a candle, a point on the floor, the wall, a rosary, a chant, or even our breath. It's referred to as concentration meditation because it trains the mind through concentration on an external or physical reference point.

Mindfulness meditation has also been practised for thousands of years in the Buddhist tradition and has moved into Western culture mostly through Vipassana, which means *to see things as they really are.* Ten-day Vipassana meditation retreats are becoming increasingly popular throughout the world. It teaches us to train our minds to be fully aware and present when meditating.

Unlike concentration meditation, mindfulness doesn't train the mind on an object. It focuses on an awareness of our bodies and surroundings. The intent is that when we "end" our meditation, our mindfulness is still there, slowing down the world as we notice the small things around us. That leads to a deep awareness of our surroundings and of our relationship to the world.

With practice, we don't just see the world for what it is, we come to see ourselves for what we are too. Not more than we are, not less than we are, just what we are. We become aware of our prejudices, egos, agendas, and our own wishful thinking that prevents us from honestly seeing events unfolding in front of us for what they are. Normally, as we notice the world around us, we can't help but notice our own reaction to it. That awareness can breed a calmness that acts like a buffer against life.

Why Mindfulness Matters in a Leadership Mindset

But how does that relate to a leadership mindset? Well, the reason why I'm counting mindfulness as an attribute of a leadership mindset is because clarity of mind is the best way I know of making astute observations and informed decisions. If I can't, or won't, see what's right in front of me, if I'm blindsided by events I should have seen coming, or if I'm trying to wrestle the world and everyone in it to do what I want, then I may be doing a lot of things, but living a leadership mindset isn't one of them.

Let's think about that for a moment. For me, one of the benefits of a leadership mindset is that it allows us to move beyond reacting and allows us to start anticipating. It's about trying to see down the road as far as we can with as much clarity as we can. It's about seeing our successes and the challenges that lay ahead of us and it's about making decisions with the best available data and the clearest possible insight that allows us to pivot to accommodate the twists and turns that await us.

That's what makes mindfulness so important. Because none of that is possible if we lack the ability to see the situation unbiased by what we think should happen or what we really want to happen. Expectations keep us holding on to a version of reality that may not be true, and that's a poor window through which to look at our team or business.

Practically speaking, if we're trying to wrestle the situation to the ground to push our agenda forward, we could be missing things that might make our idea work better. We might miss the article that shoots our idea down but offers us a chance to see the holes in our thinking. We miss an insight because we're so fixated on making the plan work as we first conceived it. We miss … [fill in the blank]. The biggest clue to that way of thinking is saying "should" or "ought to". If we catch ourselves becoming annoyed because something *should* have happened or someone *ought to* have done something, we're ignoring why those things didn't happen, and what we can learn from the situation.

But mindfulness isn't just about strategy planning. The attribute of mindfulness relates to seeing the people around us clearly. It takes mindfulness to see the subtleties in people's reactions during a meeting, to notice resistance or openness, to take a clear look at the facts. If we don't see these things, we charge ahead – bull-in-china-shop-like. We don't try to phrase our ideas carefully, meaning that others struggle to really understand what we are saying, we don't admit the change is tough, and on and on the problems run. Because we haven't noticed what's happening for our audience, we run the risk of losing the support we did have and losing any chance of gaining new support.

That ability is a long way from the idea in neurolinguistic programming (NLP) of looking at people's eyes to see if they're lying. It's a leap from Dale Carnegie's *How to Win Friends and Influence People.*[1] That's because mindfulness isn't about using techniques on people. Mindfulness is about seeing a situation for what it is. Like a leadership mindset, it's a way of looking at the world that's borne out of our experiences. If mindfulness hasn't been part of your life experience to date, it's about trying the idea on, adopting the behaviour, and seeing the effect it has on you and those around you.

---

1 Dale Carnegie, *How to Win Friends and Influence People* (London: Vermilion, 2006 [1936]).

The Behaviours of Mindfulness

I mentioned in the introduction that every attribute of a leadership mindset has a corresponding set of behaviours. Perhaps now's a good time to think about what the behaviours of mindfulness are. I say behaviours because, although we'll all wear mindfulness differently, we'll also be able to see commonalities in the way that somebody with mindfulness – as an attribute of a leadership mindset – holds themselves. These are some of the behaviours we can expect to see:

Attribute of a leadership mindset	Behaviours
Mindfulness	Self-awareness Seeing

Challenge: An Experience of Mindfulness

We could talk about mindfulness forever and get no closer to living its behaviours, so before we go any further, let's have a go at experiencing it. Before we begin, let's remind ourselves that it can take years to develop the kind of clarity that comes with mindfulness. Monks dedicate their lives to it, and although we don't all have the desire or resources to do that, mindfulness practice can be a good idea for everyone.

Of course, sitting on a cushion on the floor – as is customary in the practice – isn't for everyone and that's why I'll offer a few different approaches before the end of this chapter. For now, let's just get a taste of what mindfulness is. We'll begin with a fairly traditional take, so that way we know what we're digressing from if we choose to. But, like I said, if this doesn't work for you, just hold on; there's another bus coming.

First off, find a place where you can be uninterrupted for ten minutes. Read this section through then set the book down and give it a go. Set a timer beforehand, if you like, so you don't have to keep checking the time.

Sit on a chair, with both your feet flat on the floor. Place your hands on your lap, palms down. Hold yourself upright as much as possible. Try not to slouch forward. Close your eyes if you like, or leave them open. If they are open, find a spot about six feet in front of you on the ground and keep a loose focus on that spot, i.e. not an intense stare, but a relaxed gaze.

Then listen and notice. Listen to the sounds around you. The wind outside perhaps. The drone of traffic. Listen to the footsteps around you if there are any. A neighbour's dog barking. Listen to these things without a story line. Try not to run into a dialogue of how the wind's kicking up the leaves and making a mess on the lawn or pavement. Try not to tell yourself the story of how you used to love running through the leaves in autumn when you were a kid. Give up the story about how cruel the owner of the barking dog is to keep it locked up while she's at work.

Instead just listen.

Notice your breathing. And notice the gentle rise and fall of your stomach as you breathe in and out. Notice the gap between the in breath and the out breath. Notice how you're feeling. Your reaction to the sounds around you. Notice if the dog barking annoys you. And with everything you notice – good, bad, or indifferent – let it go with every breath out.

If it helps, imagine the things you notice are clouds drifting by on a summer's day. It's as if, sitting there on your chair, you're on a hillside watching these clouds float by. And just like watching clouds pass, you're not attached to the thing you notice. It's just there. Drifting by. A temporary feeling, or thought, or thing. And when you don't hold onto it, it just goes on its way. Drifting away with every breath. Leaving you free and unaffected.

If a thought or a feeling does take a hold, notice that it's done that. Don't beat yourself up, don't tell yourself you've wasted three, five, or nine minutes of your practice. When you notice that your mind has wandered, breathe out and let that thought go. Then go back to hearing the sounds around you. Noticing you and the world around you without creating a story around any of it.

Keep doing this for ten minutes. And after ten minutes, stop.

Mindfulness and the Gap

It could be that this exposure to mindfulness was a challenge. If it was your first experience it may have been hard to keep from storytelling for more than a few moments at a time. Or it may be that you've had lots of experience with mindfulness and it was a familiar experience that you can maintain for longer than ten minutes. In either case, mindfulness isn't about how long you sit for. It's about the quality of your practice. And the thing we're practising is what I call living in the gap.

The gap is the fraction of a nanosecond in which you're just noticing. When there's no story, no words running through your head. When you aren't self-conscious of your breathing but just aware. Breathing in and out without forcing either. The gap is the space between sensory input and your conscious reaction to that input. In terms of a leadership mindset, the gap is the space in which you can truly see before judgement and emotion clouds your thinking, and before you feel pressured to act.

I like to think of the gap as a place of potentiality because what we think or feel after the gap determines what we'll do.

Think about it like this:

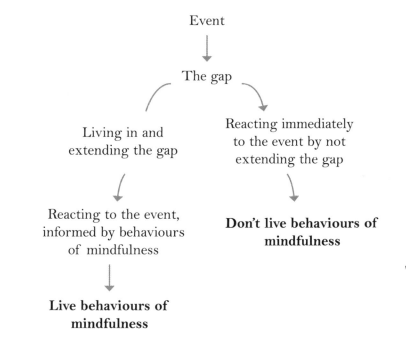

Event

↓

The gap

Living in and extending the gap

Reacting immediately to the event by not extending the gap

Reacting to the event, informed by behaviours of mindfulness

Don't live behaviours of mindfulness

Live behaviours of mindfulness

With practice, mindfulness helps us to extend the gap. And extending the gap allows for clarity. It's almost like the world runs in slow motion and we can clearly see what's happening in front of us. That takes effort, of course. But put in that effort and, as we grow our awareness, we grow the behaviours of mindfulness. Then self-awareness and seeing come together to allow us to make a conscious choice about how we want to respond to the events around us.

The Behaviours of Mindfulness: Self-Awareness

Self-awareness may be the first quality that grows as we develop mindfulness, and it's the quality that allows us to notice the effect of being present. It's possible that the first thing we notice is ourselves. If we're willing to see clearly, our mindfulness allows us to see our own biases. Although it's not easy, we notice our ability to see people and situations for what they are. And because of that we can make choices rooted in wisdom, not in emotion or manipulation. That practical realization changes how we see the world. That's the power of self-awareness: it means that we can see the effect of our behaviour and make the changes we need in order to speak to people in ways they'll listen to. It means we can adjust our behaviour to have a useful effect on the people and things around us, to move our agenda forward.

More than that, self-awareness helps us to notice our own reactions. Are we being agitated or impatient? If so, why? What's driving that attitude? That's an important question because attitude is loosely informed by our emotional state and, if we can see that, it means we can put off making a big decision until we've addressed whatever may be stressing us out. Self-awareness makes for better decisions.

Before we start thinking about self-awareness, a word of warning: developing the level of self-awareness that I'm talking about puts us in a position to manipulate people. Being aware of what's happening for ourselves and them, and being able to adapt a message to increase its chance of being heard, does mean we could manipulate others. But it's a short-term strategy. All the work we've put in to gaining others' trust comes tumbling down as soon as they spot that they're being manipulated. And they will. Maybe not the first time but definitely the second. That's what makes it a short-term strategy – we only get to use it once. And not just once with each individual, because that person will speak to anyone who's willing to listen about how we used them or double-crossed them, which will make everyone else suspicious enough of us that we won't be able to manipulate them. In fact, think of everything in this book in that same way: the behaviours are like the force in *Star Wars*, except if they get used for the dark side, they melt away.

Self-awareness is the act of being present with ourselves. By present, I mean being in the moment. Zen Buddhism has a lot of great proverbs and one of my favourites is this: "When you get hungry, eat your rice; when you get sleepy, close your eyes."[2] It could be the definition of being present. In our modern world we're always thinking about what we should do next or what we've just done. Said another way, we're usually either living in the past or in the future.

We get pulled in so many different directions that it's hard to focus on the here and now. Being present encourages us to do just that: focus on what we're doing *now*. Self-awareness gives us the thing to focus on: ourselves. Not in an egotistic or narcissistic way, but in the sense of being honest with ourselves in terms of what we're feeling and how we're behaving.

It's self-awareness that allows us to see if our plans are based on wishful thinking. And it's self-awareness that allows us to separate ourselves from the treadmill of everyday life and stand apart from the people, conversations, and events in our team and business to notice our honest reaction. That's important because it's only when we can be honest about how we feel that we can begin to think clearly about a situation.

---

2 Burton Watson (tr.), *The Zen Teachings of Master Lin-Chi: A Translation of the Lin-Chi Lu* (New York: Columbia University Press, 1993), p. 77.

Just then another figment of my imagination strolls into my office. The room is filled with sunlight on an autumn day. It's cold outside, but in here it feels as cosy as the wool jumper Angie Agitated is wearing. "OK, enough of the hippy-dippy stuff," she says, eyes darting around the room searching for the crystals and dowsing rods she's sure are there. She looks momentarily offended when she doesn't see them, but then decides only a fool would leave them laid out. Probably hidden in a drawer, she thinks. "Cut to the technique already. How do I get to a leadership mindset level of self-awareness?" There's a pause for dramatic effect and then, "What's the down-low?"

Well, that's the thing, there isn't a technique, there's practice. And by practice, I mean mindfulness practice. Taking the time to notice what's going on around us, and what's going on for us. And although that is exactly the hippy-dippy stuff Angie wouldn't like, it can be useful to notice what's happening within us. We can do that sat on a cushion. Or, if that feels a bit hippy-dippy, there are other ways to practise, but they all have at their core a willingness to see the world for what it is, rather than as it appears in whatever story we tell ourselves about it.

The Behaviours of Mindfulness: Seeing

Mindfulness has a real and practical purpose. You might be thinking, sure, it's great to develop mindfulness and see people and things as they really are, but so what? Maybe you've taken time to sit on your mindfulness cushion every day for years, maybe you've done a ten-day Vipassana course and practised every day since, or maybe you've developed mindfulness in other ways. You see things clearer than you did before. Great, but what use is that?

A leadership mindset is a challenge because its many attributes are working in concert. Seeing people and situations with clarity is only useful if we understand what we're seeing, and – as we'll explore in a bit – if we know what to do with what we've understood.

"Seeing" is a simple word to refer to a larger idea: understanding what's going on under the surface. It's what I'd like to think about now. I don't want to present this to you as some kind of magic woo-woo. (I can see Angie nodding her approval.) It's not. Understanding what's going on under the surface is something we do hundreds of times a day. I'd suggest that 90% of the time we see what's going on and understand enough of what we see to make a clear and accurate assessment of the situation. So perhaps 10% of the time we don't do these things: maybe we're hot under the collar about something, feeling a time pressure, or just plain old-fashioned distracted. It could be for these or many other reasons, but the outcome is the same: we miss what's happening under the surface and, as a result, whatever call we make about what to do next doesn't benefit from our understanding of all the information that was available to us.

Though there are lots of books to teach us techniques for how to see, the truth is we already can. Not sure if that's true? I'd suggest you've proved it by virtue of the fact that you've navigated hundreds of challenges to have survived to this point in life. In fact, you do it so quickly you may not even notice it. The challenge isn't seeing; it's slowing down a process that you normally do automatically so you can do it intentionally. What we often think of as emotional intelligence is really just the ability to see what's happening in a social setting. Seeing is useful in any situation – social, strategic, whatever.

Up until now, mindfulness has been an internal concept. Self-awareness by its very nature involves focusing on ourselves. With seeing, mindfulness takes a step into the outside world and allows us to think about a different way to lead. Taking that step means we extend the gap.

Seeing Agendas and Motivations in the Gap

If someone says, "I don't understand why you said that," what do they mean? That might sound like an odd question. On the surface the answer's obvious: they don't understand me. But what could it mean *under* the surface? The words could mean a raft of different things. For example, "I can't believe you said that" could mean:

> "I'm surprised you said that, because I wouldn't have in the same situation."

> "I'm hurt that you said that."

> "There was no reason for you to say that."

> "Saying that just caused a problem that you could have avoided."

These are just a few examples. In normal conversation – with friends, let's say – we hear what is said and infer meaning from the context that being friends gives us.

Here's an example: I'm sitting with a group of friends – let's call them Sue, Jamie, Carol, and Ron – in a pub in south London. A week before, Sue told me over the phone that Jamie and Carol are in danger of losing their house because of a few bad investments they'd made. She was wondering aloud about how we could help them.

Sitting in the pub with the group, I throw out an off-hand comment about how I'm buying new hardwood floors for my place and how I can't wait to get the new furniture I ordered. Then, without thinking, I say how cool it is that in these difficult financial times we're all lucky enough to own property.

Sue shifts uncomfortably in her chair. Jamie and Carol force a strained smile and Ron raises a glass and says, "To my financially savvy friends."

Jamie doesn't raise his glass; he pushes his chair back and mumbles, "I just have to go to the little boy's room."

As he heads off, Carol watches him walk away. She watches until he disappears into the crowd. When he's gone her gaze falls to the floor. She doesn't look up.

Ron shrugs, gives up on his toast and takes a drink from his glass.

Sue leans toward me and says, under her breath, "I can't believe you said that."

I'm momentarily puzzled then throw my head back. In that second I recall the phone call and become aware of the mistake I've made.

Here it takes just moments to understand what Sue means. In truth, it takes no time at all. I don't have to run through the possible meanings because Sue's remark, in the context, shows me that I've hurt my friends by highlighting the difficult time they're going through in the most callous way. I'd forgotten the phone call Sue and I had, but context provides me the "quick-key" reference to understand what's gone wrong. I instantly understand what she meant because I could infer the agendas and motivations of my friends. I can do that by replaying the scene in my head and understanding the implications of each step.

To be clear, that mental recap might look like this:

1 I replay what I just said.

2 I realize Sue's tone of voice suggests she's disappointed in me.

3 I flick through my memories to figure out why.

4 I recall the conversation Sue and I had a week before on the phone.

5   I see Sue's comment as evidence that she's worried about the effect of what I said on Jamie and Carol.

6   I infer her motivation: she might also be annoyed with me for forgetting our phone call.

7   I infer Jamie's motivation for walking away: he's either hurt or anxious about his house and his poor investments.

8   I spot that Carol's eyes lingering on Jamie shows her motivation: her affection for him and her understanding that my comment took a toll on him. Her agenda is to support and protect him.

9   I understand by Carol's look at Jamie that the bad investments were his, and see that as the reason why he's taking it harder.

10   I see that Ron doesn't have any agenda because he doesn't know anything about the problems that Jamie and Carol are facing.

11   And finally, Jamie and Carol's agenda is to keep their situation secret. Their motivation is possibly that they feel they'll be judged harshly for making bad investments or because they don't want to look less than capable.

Because I'm "tuned in" to the agendas and motivations of my friends, I know what's going on under the surface of Sue's comment. And I know what to do about it. In this case, say sorry to Jamie and Carol and help them if I can. So although I've just made a mistake, seeing it means I can salvage the situation.

That's an example of the 90% of situations in which we can clearly see what's happened. But what about the remaining 10%? What happens when we fail to see?

The answer is much the same, but with a few key elements missing. I'd suggest that in that 10% of the time, I might see what's happening: that Jamie has left, that Carol is looking at the floor, that Ron took a drink, and that Sue said she "can't believe I said that", but it all means little to me because I can't see what's happening under the surface so I'm not aware of the agendas and motivations that are playing out. In which case I'd respond with, "What do you mean?" to Sue's comment. I might even brush off the remark as unimportant.

The nub of seeing the agendas and motivations of others is, unsurprisingly, to recognize that something is happening under the surface. In our example, on the surface, Sue calling me the week before might just have been to catch up. If that's true then her comment could be seen as a reflection of mild annoyance that I've forgotten something she said. But if I'm aware that Sue has an agenda and a motivation then I'm more inclined to look for it. I could infer that because Sue talked to me and not Ron, she may feel closer to me than him; she may feel I'm the sort of person who'd want to help Jamie and Carol; she may have been overwhelmed by the situation and hoping that I'd bring a new insight or plan; she may even like me romantically and, as a result, hope that I'd recall the conversation as a sign of my interest in her.

What I'm doing here is twofold: I'm using mindfulness to see and then I'm acting to explore the agendas and motivations that could underlie my observations. I could just as easily do this for a business deal, or in thinking about how stakeholders might receive a strategy, or how to get ahead of the competition. In all cases there may be agendas and motivations, or there might not be. It's like looking for gold during the Klondike gold rush: it might be out there, but I'll never find it if I don't start digging.

Being Present with Others

Since we live in this world with other people, seeing hinges on being present with others. If self-awareness is the act of being honest with ourselves, being present with others is about putting our focus onto other people when we interact with them. It means placing our attention on them so that we hear the subtleties of what they're saying; we notice the frustration or reassurance in their voice, and we notice the signals their body language is sending. Combined with self-awareness, being present with others gives us the chance to notice how we feel about what's being said and then respond openly and honestly. And that allows us to see how to have meaningful conversations about everything from a course of action to the fallout from a mistake; from designing a process, to developing a strategy for a business.

Being present with others is so important, and for that reason it's the focus of the next challenge I'd like to offer you.

Challenge: Being Present with Others

Like I said, there's more than one way to practise mindfulness. In the previous challenge we focused on the world around us and the physical sensations in our bodies. This time we're practising noticing what's happening with other people. Just as we're unlikely to master the first challenge in a few days, this isn't something we'll get good at right away either. Just like the sitting mindfulness we tried before, this takes practice and conscious effort. What I'd like to offer you now is a way to practise the behaviour in the moment when you're speaking with someone else.

That's right, you can only practise being present with others *with others*. So think of this like practice without the training wheels. What might be helpful is to practise with someone else who's reading this book. If that's not possible, pick low-risk conversations. Perhaps in the weekly catch-up meeting at work, or with friends in a bar, or with your partner over dinner.

Rather than trying to be present with others for the entire conversation, try to maintain this during short chats or for part of a conversation to begin with – the first ten minutes of a meeting, for example. The point of doing that is to give yourself a break and acclimatize yourself. As I said at the start, none of this is easy. Setting the bar too high when you're practising is the best way that I know of to fall below your goal. Do that often enough and giving up isn't far behind. Think about doing any new thing – going to the gym, let's say. When you go for the first time you don't lift the heaviest weights you can find, go to the hardest class, or set the treadmill on max. You start off gentle and slow. The same applies here.

There are two sides to being present with others. The first, when they're talking; the second, when you're talking. Of course you can be present with others without speaking at all, but for this practice, we'll focus on these two aspects. In this challenge I'm treating them as two practices, but of course, feel free to combine them into one if you want.

Let's start by practising being present when someone else is talking.

Just like before, after reading the challenge through, put the book down and think about a conversation – or part of one – that you feel would be a good opportunity for practice. Remember to go for a low-risk conversation. If the person you're practising with is unfamiliar with this book, and with mindfulness, you can tell them that you're practising being present in what you're doing. Letting people know what you're doing helps take the pressure off sometimes. If that isn't possible or appropriate that's OK too; just pick a conversation that's as low-risk as possible. Set a goal of being present with others for ten minutes. Short practice is your friend if you're starting out.

When you enter the conversation, place all of your attention on the other person.

Notice their facial expressions.

Notice their hand movements.

Listen to the words they're choosing to use.

Notice the tone of voice they use to deliver those words.

Notice sighs, pauses between words, and how words may or may not trail off.

Just like in our first mindfulness challenge, notice these things and notice any reactions you may have. Notice if you start to build a story around the meaning of their behaviours or language. That the sigh you just heard means the person is frustrated, or angry. And how that leads you to think they're angry at you, that they are hard to deal with, or how you've heard people talk about this person's temper and now you're going to get a front row seat, or whatever else. None of that might be true: they could just be tired after all.

If you find yourself building a story, notice you've done that and direct your attention back to the person.

Notice if you're jumping ahead because you think you already know what they're trying to say. Notice if you cut them off, or are preparing what you're going to say when they stop talking.

Focus on the message the person is trying to convey. Ask yourself, *what is this person actually trying to tell me?*

There'll be room for interpretation later, but, for now, your goal is to just hear and understand the person in front of you.

If you need to, check with them that you're understanding what they're saying. This isn't a silent practice, but it also doesn't give you licence to jump in and take over. What I'm suggesting is to check any gaps in your understanding with them and then allow them to make their point as clearly as they can.

What kinds of things might you want to check? Well, if you find yourself filling in a blank because you're sure you know what they mean, that's one thing to check. If you hear a clue that this person may think differently about something you regard as obvious, check what their take is. And if checking your understanding shows that they do feel differently to you, notice if you feel the need to defend your view.

Since the goal of this practice is to truly hear what someone else is saying, after your ten minutes is up – and if the situation allows – reflect back to the person what you think you understood. Give them the chance to either verify their point or clarify further.

If there's a need for them to clarify, notice how or why you may have got the wrong impression. Was it because your mind wandered? Because you missed something in their tone or body language? Or that you assumed you knew where they were going so didn't check your understanding? Whatever the reason, try not to beat yourself up. This is practice. It's a lifelong pursuit you'll get better at, but no one can expect to catch everything.

Being present when you're talking is different.

It means making your point as clearly as possible while, at the same time, noticing the effect your words are having. If that sounds hard, it might be reassuring to know that it involves the same approach as being present when others are talking — so if the prospect of being present while talking sounds daunting, practise the first version we discussed for a while. Of course, if you'd like to start with this one, there's no reason not to.

Here's how this challenge goes. Once again, give yourself a time frame.

When the person has said what they need to say, pause and take a breath. If you're starting the conversation, begin by taking a breath. As you exhale, allow any tension to drain from your body. Notice any tightness in your shoulders, your neck, or your throat.

Notice how you're holding yourself. If you're sitting, notice the seat against your body; if you're standing, notice the muscles in your legs.

Focus on the person you're about to speak to. Notice what they're doing. Are they busy at their computer? Did they just get off the phone? Look them in the eye and begin to speak. Notice their reaction to what you're saying. Notice if they agree or disagree. If they agree, that's great.

If they don't, try not to build a story around it. What might a story be? Well, that they don't agree with you because they have something against you, or they're stupid, pig-headed, or not very nice, or any other possible stories you might tell yourself.

Instead, hold onto the notion that the person disagrees with the idea you're raising, not with you. If that's the case, it could mean that you haven't explained it fully, or that they see the same situation differently. Once again, notice if you feel the need to defend the idea. If so, breathe out and imagine that need drifting away. Instead, ask why they see the situation differently and listen to their perspective.

And, having done that, you'll be back to being present as they speak.

Being present with others while speaking is hard. It's hard because we have a point of view that we want to express, and if someone doesn't share that point of view, we tend to want to convince them. The goal here is to express yourself as clearly as you can. Notice how you're delivering your message and how what you're doing could undermine it: either by what you say, how you say it, or by failing to see how it's being received.

Seeing Before Acting in the Gap

I'm sure it won't surprise you to hear that seeing before acting in the gap is about taking the time to reflect before we do something. Too often we think that when something happens, we need to act there and then. If someone says something, we need to respond right away; if there's a problem, we need to fix it now. Since the gap is the space between the event and what we do as a result, we can extend it by doing nothing at all. If we're in conversation, we can extend the gap by pausing before we speak.

That's the gift of mindfulness. When we practise mindfulness, we can notice when we feel an urge to act immediately. We might notice a pressure to say something, to make a decision, or just to go and talk to someone. All of those things close the gap. I'd suggest that when we're feeling pressured to act, eliminating the gap is the very last thing we want to do.

Seeing before acting in the gap is about more than noticing how we're feeling. It's about using the space and the clarity that mindfulness gives us to take effective action. I'd say an effective course of action is a considered one, and that's what using the gap is all about.

But how can we do that? It begins with the mindfulness we've been practising. To spread our options before us and look at each without a story; to just see them for what they are; to use our mindfulness to notice if we feel pulled toward a course of action and why. Is it because it'll make us look good to our boss or colleagues? Is it because it's the easy, short-term option? Are we shying away from a course of action because it might mean defending it in a meeting? Or because it'll be a challenge to implement, which we'd prefer not to take on? Or is the best solution a new direction that means we have to admit to being wrong before?

The gap gives us the chance to explore all of these possibilities. It means that we get to understand the motivations and agendas behind the decisions we make – and determine whether those motivations and agendas are things we want to base a decision on. If we decide not to pursue a new and better direction because we don't want to admit the route we've been following so far isn't working, is that what we really want to do?

That's one kind of clarity that comes from seeing in the gap – the kind where we see the courage that we'll need to pursue a course of action. But seeing in the gap gives us something else: the space to consider the consequences an action may have versus the outcome we hope for.

We make multiple decisions every day. And if we think of decision-making like a tree, some of those decisions are made on the outermost branches: they're small, have limited points of intersection with anything else, and have a limited long-term effect. An example could be deciding what to eat for lunch: it may influence what we eat for dinner in that we don't want the same thing twice in one day, but beyond that the decision has a limited long-term effect and no meaningful consequences. (Unless we happened to eat poison for lunch.)

Of course, there are other decisions that have more points of intersection – where we relocate the office to, or who we merge the business with. If we're a manager, what about who we bring into the team, the key performance indicators (KPIs) we set, or the team restructuring we have in mind? The points of intersection we're referring to are the consequences those decisions might have. Those kinds of decisions are at the tree trunk level: they have the ability to influence every branch.

Truly seeing means looking for the unintended consequences of a course of action. For example, fallout we haven't anticipated during the implementation of a plan. Take moving to remote working as an example: it's a great idea and means we can be more responsive to clients, so we line all our ducks up to make it happen. We talk to IT and make sure they have the gear they'll need. We talk to staff and make sure they have a workspace to use when they're in the office. We ensure they know that the goal is to be mobile, so we work out a rate they can charge for personal car use. We train managers on a new KPI system so they can rate people knowing that just because someone isn't there, it doesn't mean they aren't working. We do all of those things and think we're ready to go. It's only when we go live that we work out that the great IT system we signed up for – the one the supplier said was so intuitive that training staff on it wasn't necessary – is so foreign that staff don't know how to use it.

Seeing in the gap is about having the clarity and presence of mind to stress-test our own ideas, using the space that the gap affords to really explore what's going on. It's about being able to be so unattached to our ideas that we can become their worst enemy.

Typically, when we come up with an idea we believe in, we treat it like a fortress – believing that our idea is so solid that there's no need to step out of it. But instead of sitting in the fortress convinced we're safe, seeing in the gap means stepping outside and ordering our (mental) troops to attack it. In doing we find our idea's weak spots. I call this breaking the idea, and it's an idea we'll come back to again. For now, it's enough to say that breaking an idea helps us to see its unintended consequences. And because we've done that before putting any wheels in motion, we have the luxury to adapt the idea – to strengthen its fortifications.

Breaking ideas might be hard to do for ourselves to begin with. If we're really attached to an idea, we can't see where it might fail. If that's the case, we can enlist the help of others; we can share the idea and invite them to shoot holes in it. And then, holding the tatters of the idea, we can see if it's worth putting back together. If it is, we can patch it up, only this time with the knowledge of how to fill the holes. It may be that the idea isn't worth any more work, but the thinking you've done could lead to another idea.

It's the ability to remain unattached to the idea that allows us to see its unintended consequences. Using the gap to explore the implications of a course of action offers us the chance to live considered lives. It's like looking at a map and checking out the terrain before we head out on a journey. And, because we've done that, it means we can pick the route most likely to get us to our destination.

This kind of mindfulness isn't the same as the forms I've described so far, because it involves action on our part: that's why I call it purposeful mindfulness.

Purposeful mindfulness is just what it says on the tin: using mindfulness. In the Buddhist tradition, active meditation ranges from the martial arts to flower arranging (*ikebana*) and calligraphy (*shodo*). In each example, there are specific actions to be made in a specific order. It's a ritual that helps the practitioner focus their attention, acting with full consciousness and intention. Purposeful mindfulness is different. It draws on what it notices in the moment – a hole in an idea, for example – to adjust what it does next. No rituals or sequences of actions. Purposeful mindfulness is working with the other five attributes to allow its thinking to flex. It's like asking ourselves, "Now that I've noticed that, what will I do differently?" Adaptability is at the heart of purposeful mindfulness, and it's the focus of our next challenge.

Challenge: Purposeful Mindfulness

The beauty of this challenge is that you can try it during any activity. For me, driving is a good chance to practise purposeful mindfulness, because noticing and adapting to what's happening on the road is a big part of driving.

Before we jump behind the wheel, though, let's start out small. In this challenge we'll practise purposeful mindfulness with a common action most of us do every day: walking to pick something up – in this case a piece of paper. If you use a wheelchair this will still work; and if you're not mobile, begin with another everyday activity, such as eating.

In this challenge I'm going to focus on walking. So if you're ready, let's go.

Maybe try this out for the first time in your living room or any quiet space where you're unlikely to be uninterrupted. Begin by getting into loose-fitting clothes. Maybe take your shoes and socks off. Place a piece of paper on a table or on the floor on the far side of the room.

Make sure the room is well ventilated and at a comfortable temperature. If you'd like to light a candle, that's no problem. If you want to burn incense, that might be nice too.

When you're happy with the room, set a timer. For this challenge we're going to avoid walking in a straight line – walk around the furniture if you like, or just on a winding path. Change direction every few steps. If you'd like to set an interval timer that beeps as a reminder to change direction, that will work too. If this is your first purposeful mindfulness challenge, start out with ten minutes.

Choose a place to begin and stand there. Hold your hands in front of you, palm up with the back of your left hand sitting in the palm of your right hand.

Then breathe.

Set your intention to go and pick up the paper. Intend to notice everything that happens between now and when you pick it up.

Then when you're ready, begin. Notice the floor against your feet. If it's wooden or tiled, notice the temperature, the smoothness of the surface. If it's carpet, notice the texture on the soles of your feet. Notice the warmth, the pile of the carpet as your toes sink in or sit on the surface.

Notice your clothes against your body. Notice the sounds around you and any breeze in the room. Notice the weight of your body on your feet. Notice any thoughts running through your head and notice how you don't engage with that dialogue but instead redirect your attention to the task at hand.

When you feel still and grounded, lift your right leg in preparation to take a step. Notice how your clothes feel when you move. Notice the other leg balancing you as it takes the weight of your entire body. Notice the adjustment you make as your ankle moves slightly and you rebalance. Then extend the raised leg forward. Notice how your body accommodates the change as you do so. The sense of leaning forward slightly as your leading leg takes a step. And notice your foot: the heel landing on the ground, and the ball joining it as your foot comes to rest flat on the ground. Notice shifting your body weight. And notice the stretch in your other leg and how that stretch sees your other foot rising, your toes bending as you prepare to move that leg to take your next step. And notice all of those sensations and all your adjustments again.

Notice what happens when you change direction. How your foot angles to allow that direction change. Notice how your body adapts to walk in the new direction. Keep your attention on the small individual movements, accommodations, and feelings that make up one change in direction. Notice each action separately and pay attention to each one until you notice every stage of shifting direction.

Don't rush. Go slow and give yourself the chance to notice every movement and every adjustment you make and every sensation that comes with it.

Notice how the breeze changes as you move around the room. Notice your breathing, the rise and fall of your chest as the air comes in and drifts out. Notice where your eyes fall. And do all this without a story, without a narrative, without judgement on how well or how poorly you're doing. Just notice the small and subtle changes as you walk toward the paper.

Keep walking. If your attention drifts, focus on your next movement, on your next step, on the paper.

The point here is to be fully present as you walk. Fully present means noticing everything that's happening within you and without you.

As you get near the paper, notice the change in your thought process. At what point do you think about picking up the paper? Do you consider which side to pick it up from? How high to raise it? Notice how this change in thinking leads to a change in your actions as you decide how to pick up the paper. Notice how your body goes about the task. Notice how you change from the motion of walking to the movement of picking up the paper.

As I said, purposeful mindfulness is about using mindfulness to see and adapt to the information the world sends us as we work toward a task – picking up the paper, in this challenge. In the real world, we're adapting to people's reactions, or information that highlights blocks to our plans. Purposeful mindfulness allows us to remain still and calm as we see new information and adapt to it. In fact, if life can sometimes drop us in quicksand, purposeful mindfulness is a rope we can use to pull ourselves out.

I imagine the goal is to live in a way that is fully mindful, as if our whole lives are purposeful meditations. It's a noble but probably impossible goal, but that doesn't make it any less worth pursuing.

Mindfulness as an attribute of a leadership mindset is a willingness to be open to what's happening around us. It gives us the chance to be fully present, and that means we get to make conscious choices about how we'd like to be in any given situation.

If we make the choice to practise mindfulness, we create room to make the choice to live the other attributes of a leadership mindset.

Mindfulness Reminders

- The behaviours of mindfulness are self-awareness and seeing.
- Self-awareness is the act of being present with ourselves.
- Seeing means understanding what's going on under the surface.
- The gap is the space between receiving information and acting on it.
- Mindfulness helps us to extend the gap.

Chapter 2

Genuine Curiosity

A Human Tradition

I like to imagine that before the first people left Africa, one of them – let's call her Draledge – looks out across the African savannah one day. It's noon, and the heat beating down is warping the light in front of her so all she can see is the wavy, undulating landscape. For a moment it reminds her of water rippling. But she knows it's not water, it's just the distance, and it goes on and on. She doesn't know for how long. She doesn't know what the hunting will be like beyond her familiar lands. But that doesn't stop her wondering. What's out there? It's the question she's been asking herself for a long time now. There's a reason to explore further: the hunting is getting harder. That's what she'll tell her people. But that isn't why she wants to go. It's the question: what's out there? Not just as far as she can see, but beyond that. It gnaws at her stomach every day. *What is out there?* Is it the same as here? Better? She knows, without even thinking, that it won't be long before she's going to find out.

Genuine Curiosity in a Leadership Mindset

For my money curiosity is at the core of what it means to be human. Maybe it's the human quality that led us to explore previously unknown corners of the world. It's the reason why we build and invent, explore the stars, and try out new recipes. Curiosity is the engine that drives everything we've ever done: good and bad. It's the voice inside our heads that wants to know, that's interested, and that wants to learn.

That's why curiosity is one of the six attributes. It's a way of looking at the world with fresh eyes and a mind that wants to learn, wants to be challenged, and wants to know something new. Curiosity wants to know why something is the way it is. We don't get to be the best versions of ourselves by hanging out in a safe, familiar space. Genuine curiosity is a hand placed firmly on our back that pushes us out of the doors of our comfort zones.

"Yes," Pamela Playitsafe says, "but why *genuine* curiosity?"

Well, because it's easy to be curious if we can *get* something from learning, taking a risk, or exploring an idea. Of course we have that kind of curiosity all the time. We want to know how to make more money, how to get the next promotion, how to get ahead: pursuing tangible gains is the grown-up version of curiosity. That kind of curiosity is about gaining information to help us do something; it's a process to get from here to there.

"Why isn't that genuine?" Pamela asks. "What if I genuinely want to learn how to get a promotion?"

OK, I'll give you that.

She winks, in a way that says, "Don't worry, your mistake's safe with me."

Why I'm throwing in the *genuine* is because it reminds me that learning can be for learning's sake. Genuine curiosity asks, "Why do we do it that way?" or, "How did we get here?" because it really just wants to know. It isn't planning to do things differently because of what it finds – that's what flexibility of mind might do. Rather, the essence of genuine curiosity is that it's fundamentally just interested. Like the child who asks why the sky is blue, genuine curiosity isn't trying to get information or insight in order to do something with it: it seeks to understand. The adult equivalent might be wanting to understand someone else's reasoning, or the complexities of a situation. And, because that's its goal, the by-product is that we get an insight into whatever situation we find ourselves in and whatever we're trying to achieve.

"Hold on," Pamela says. "If being curious means I get insight then I'm being curious to gain something. So what's the difference?"

The difference is mindset. It comes down to how we approach curiosity. If we're trying to gain something – let's say, insight into a challenge – we might research what other companies that have faced the same problem have done. We hire a consultant and ask for advice. In short, we do particular things that'll help us to reach our goal. These approaches aren't spurred on by curiosity; they're tactical things we do to get an answer to a problem.

But if we see the supposed "best way" of doing something, we might wonder to ourselves, "Why do we do it that way?" We might ask, "Have we tried other ways and decided this is the best, or do we think this is the best because it's the only way we know?"

That kind of thinking leads to a different place because it starts in a different place. It isn't trying to solve a challenge; sometimes it's looking at things that work perfectly well and wondering why they do. If there's a challenge, genuine curiosity's first reaction isn't to solve it, it's to wonder why the challenge is there in the first place. And if there is an answer, it wants to know what thinking has informed that solution, and why we stopped when we hit upon that answer.

Genuine Curiosity and Ego

To be able to think in this way means to focus on the reasoning over being right. We need to be able to ask questions knowing that some of them will be dead ends. And that means being willing to put our sense of "I'm the leader and the leader has to be right" to one side.

At its heart, genuine curiosity is about learning in all its forms. We're curious about what we can learn from a mistake, about why we do things the way we do, and about what else is possible.

In business, genuine curiosity is about more than finding the right process. It's about asking why we do what we do at all, about being willing to let go of something that doesn't make sense. And, because genuine curiosity isn't about convincing others that we're right, sometimes it's about trying to follow someone else's argument.

It asks *why*, not because it's trying to ensnare someone in their own lie, like a lawyer cross-examining a witness. Genuine curiosity asks why because – like Draledge – it wants to know what's out there. What ideas, what ways of looking at the world, are there? It wants to know what someone else is seeing that has brought them to their conclusion.

If that sounds slightly Zen to you, it may be because it is.

The Behaviours of Genuine Curiosity

Just like other attributes of a leadership mindset, genuine curiosity is abstract. While it may be hard to precisely define, the behaviours that come out of that way of looking at the world are easy to spot, and some of them are listed in the following table.

Attribute of a leadership mindset	Behaviours
Genuine curiosity	Asking "what if?" Stating the obvious Demonstrating generosity of spirit

Though there may be other behaviours that would fall under genuine curiosity, I'd suggest that practising these three sets us well on our way to living the attribute. As in the other chapters, we'll explore each behaviour and what it means in a business context. And just like in other chapters, I'll offer challenges so you can practise genuine curiosity. So, if you're ready ...

The Behaviours of Genuine Curiosity: Asking "What If?"

I don't think it's overstating it to say that curiosity is at the beginning of every great idea. Inventions and innovations begin with someone being genuinely curious: from wondering how to drive a carriage without a horse, to wondering if we could go to the moon. It's what I call the power of *what if.*

What if is powerful enough to shape civilizations. Maybe farming took off in the way it did because, rather than rely on natural water cycles, someone wondered what would happen if we could channel water to irrigate the fields.

The ability to push the boundaries just by thinking is perhaps the only thing that truly separates humans from other animals. Albert Einstein conceived of general relativity armed with nothing more than a thought experiment. The power of asking what if is that it untethers us from the ordinary and opens up a world of possibility: all that with just two words.

Asking what if leads us to interrogate ourselves, and helps us to see whether we're doing what's best or what's easy. It forces us to re-evaluate. Rather than pat ourselves on the back for a job well done, what if asks, "Can we do it differently?" It's like a child who builds a bridge out of blocks: rather than sitting back and admiring her accomplishment, she pushes the supports further out. She adds a few more blocks to see how wide her bridge can span. And when the bridge falls apart, she laughs and builds another. No sense of "I went too far", or "I should have quit while I was ahead". Instead, it's another feeling that wins out – the delight in trying and learning.

There's a famous team-building activity called the spaghetti challenge that shines a light on that way of thinking and its effects as it plays out. Small groups receive masking tape, sticks of dried spaghetti, string, scissors, and a marshmallow. The challenge is to build the tallest free-standing structure that can support the marshmallow in twenty minutes. What happens over and over again is that most people spend eighteen of those minutes planning and designing their idea, usually discussing various approaches and perfecting one. Then, in the last two minutes, they try out their idea, only to discover when they place the marshmallow on top that the whole structure falls down. The marshmallow, they find, is heavier than it looks.

But kids do well at this challenge. They jump in right away and try ideas; they fail and rebuild. And fail and rebuild. And then succeed. They do so because each time they fail, they ask themselves, "What if we did X instead?"

The question for us is, "Why do people spend all of their time perfecting one idea?" For me, the answer is that they think it will work. Of course, most people understand – on an intellectual level – how finding one idea quickly limits them. But time and again in my work as a consultant, that's exactly how people go about solving their business challenges. They settle on an idea quickly, and then just as quickly start developing implementation plans.

Sometimes people are quick to act because the culture of their business is to do things now. More often, they default to the only way most people know. The thinking goes like this: we have a challenge and we need to come up with a solution and put that solution in motion. There are some differences in how that might play out. Sometimes we'll spend time understanding the problem, sometimes we'll map out the process, and sometimes we'll have meetings to decide the parameters of the problem. And then it goes the way it always goes: we come up with our one solution, usually a variation of something we've done before. That isn't always bad; sometimes it's all that's needed. Other times, we need something else.

That something else might be asking what if. Because, in doing so, we're starting in a different place. Asking what if pulls at the edges of the problem. It takes the time to let our thinking breathe. And in that space the magic happens. All it takes is a willingness to be challenged and an interest in the challenge. These are easy things to say, and I'm guessing they make sense to you, at least in principle. Nobody wants to be closed-minded. No one really wants to do what's easy over what's best. Of course, the hard part is living it. And the ability to think that way lies in a mindset, so let's think for a second about what makes that hard.

World View

The thing that makes asking what if tough is, often, that we don't recognize there's a need to. If we think about the spaghetti challenge again, we can see there's a bit more to the question of, "Why do people spend all their time perfecting one idea?" Since mostly no one does what's in their own worst interests, there must be something else at play. And it's this: most people doing the spaghetti challenge focus on one idea because they think it will work. But that begs the question, "Why do they think it will work?" The simple answer to that is, because it makes sense to them.

Some people settle on one idea quickly because their solution reinforces how they think the world works: it conforms to their world view. In this case – given their experience with balance, structure, and gravity – they're sure they've got the best idea. And that's my point: they base their surety on the way the world works *as they understand it.* What the collapsing spaghetti tower shows them is that there are factors that they didn't consider – factors that hadn't figured in their experience.

To leave the spaghetti challenge example aside for now, what happens in our everyday world is similar. We make decisions quickly because most of the problems we have to solve in our roles aren't foreign to us. We've seen them, or a version of them, before. We have a ready-made solution waiting in the wings because it's what we did last time and it worked last time. So there's no need to be curious because we know what to do.

Another way of saying it is that when we're confronted with a challenge in life, we look back on our repository of experiences and filter our ideas about what to do through the system of our own experiences, ideas, beliefs, values, and hopes: our world view. It's that world view that helps us settle on an idea quickly. Often that will work, but other times it won't.

Starting with genuine curiosity helps us to see if we can rely on our world view for a quick decision or if the situation needs a different approach. The hard part is realizing that the decision is filtered through our world view in the first place. That's why this book is about mindset; because being aware of how we think allows us to understand whether, in any given situation, our way of looking at the world is working for us or not.

Understanding Our World View Filter

As we go through life, everything we encounter passes through our world view before we judge its worth. Just like water running down a mountain to the ocean, at each stage that piece of information or experience picks up the sediment of our ideas, beliefs, values, and hopes. By the time it passes through all that and into our conscious awareness, we've already formed an opinion. And what will that opinion be? That's an easier question to answer than you might think. Regardless of what the information or experience is, our assessment will be this: if it echoes our world view, we agree; if it doesn't, we don't.

Our world view is a great way to filter the world around us if it's an accurate reflection of the world. And of course, most of us feel that our world view isn't just right but is the truth. So why wouldn't we make judgements based on it? And there's the rub. What if our world view isn't an accurate filter? What if our world view is made up of a coalition of our biases, preferences, prejudices, and hopes for how things could or should be?

And while you're mulling that over, I'll drop a spoiler: it is.

Our world view isn't always a bad thing. When Martin Luther King, Jr. shared his dream with the world it was based, in part, on the belief that justice is for everyone regardless of their ethnic background – a view which was at odds with the world as it was. A statement published in *The Birmingham News* following King's protest and arrest in April 1963 saw eight moderate white clergymen criticize the march and other demonstrations, including the Easter boycott of white-owned stores. One of their questions was why King was even there. In his now famous "Letter from Birmingham Jail", King gave this reason: "I am in Birmingham because injustice is here."[1]

You could say King saw what was happening in the South through his world view of what could and should be happening. Reality didn't fit with how he felt things should be, so he dedicated his life to ending injustice for African-Americans in the segregated South. Most people applaud him because his willingness to fight for his world view immeasurably bettered the lives of many people. But there are people whose world view might be hate-filled, angry, and violent. And most people deplore those with an outlook like that because their actions leave the lives of many worse off. Then there's the vast majority of us whose world views lead us neither to toxic acts nor to liberate the world.

World View in the Middle Ground

The middle ground is where most of us live. That space is so familiar it's easy to forget that our decisions aren't unbiased. Our world view is moderate, widely accepted, and comfortable, so we don't tend to challenge it. We make decisions based on that world view, and although it may annoy some people – and although some may disagree – we accept that because, after all, we're the leader and the choices leaders make aren't always popular. Naysayers don't have our experience – they can't see the full

---

1   *The Atlantic*, "Martin Luther King Jr.'s 'Letter from Birmingham Jail'" (2008 [1963]). Available at https://www.theatlantic.com/magazine/archive/2018/02/letter-from-birmingham-jail/552461/.

picture – so they couldn't possibly understand why our decision was the right one to make, or so we tell ourselves.

Because we think that's true, we don't stop to question our world view for the simple reason that our decision fits perfectly well with it – which is another way of saying that it feels right. And who's going to argue with right?

But here's the thing – that logic only follows if our world view *is* right. The whole point of asking what if is to acknowledge that there is no way to know if our world view is right.

"But then how do we know which world view is the right one?" Pamela Playitsafe asks. And that's the point of all of this: we can't. There's that Zen thing I was talking about before.

Maybe there is no one right way. Maybe we can only try to make the best decisions possible with the information we have at the time. If that's true, wouldn't we want to be genuinely curious so that we can ask the tough questions, or listen to uncomfortable ideas, in order to make the best decision we can?

The information we have as leaders will always be incomplete. That's both the joy and the challenge of being a leader. Anyone can lead when they have a complete picture. Our job is to lead in the grey and hazy world of incomplete and contradictory information. Which is why genuine curiosity is so important: it keeps us learning and open to all information, even the information that challenges how we see the world and what we think is possible.

The World View Barometer

So the question becomes, "How do we know if we're limiting what's possible by living within the comfort of our world view?" The answer is, "If it's comfortable, we probably are."

Imagine this scenario for a second: you're sitting in a senior team meeting when the CEO, Chuck Chairman, says he's looking for the team's input on your company's strategic direction. He leans back in his brown leather chair, the same as everyone else's around the table. As he does so, the chair tilts backwards and he places his elbows on the armrests and sets his chin on his fingers. To the world he looks like a man about to listen. And he does, for a while. He listens as you and your colleagues offer ideas about what you've seen in the business. What you've noticed in your markets. He listens as you all make suggestions about what the business could focus on, what's in the distance that needs thinking about, and what changes you need to make now to steer the business toward that future. Chuck shuffles in his chair. Sometimes he reaches forward, grabs the pen in front of him, and makes a note. Sometimes he sinks into his chair a little deeper.

As the conversation continues, you feel good – like a world of possibilities is opening up. And although you notice that Chuck looks a little uncomfortable, he's still listening and that can't be a bad thing. You notice a feeling of excitement. And then you see Chuck lean forward. He's smiling as he begins to talk, so it takes you a second to spot what's happening. But you do spot it. How although he invited the team's input, he's now telling you all why your ideas aren't possible. He tells you what he sees instead, and he tells you how he's identified the right direction for the business. Some of your colleagues fall in line. They take Chuck's ideas and add to them. That feeling of excitement dissipates slowly. And then the meeting goes the way it always goes.

What I'd suggest is happening in that scene is this: Chuck started to hear ideas that challenged his world view. He wouldn't say that, of course; he'd say he gave people the chance to offer ideas, but they were off-base, too focused on their departments, not informed by the current business climate, not true to the values of the business, and so on. What Chuck is really saying is something like: "The ideas that I heard made me uncomfortable and, as a result, I steered the conversation back to what I think is possible."

What Chuck's done here is understandable. In our own ways we do the same thing: we listen to what others are saying and sometimes feel uncomfortable because what they're saying doesn't fit with how we see the world. And when that happens, just like Chuck, we argue for our world view. Sometimes we do it passionately as if we're under attack. Sometimes we just ignore opposing views because they can't be right if they don't square with how we see the world.

That uncomfortable feeling when the external world collides with our world view is what makes Chuck push back. It's what makes us do the same thing in our own way. But that feeling doesn't have to be a signal to push back; it could be a signal to listen, to observe the conversation without judging it against what we think is right and, instead, notice that these ideas are challenging us.

In fact, that feeling is to be welcomed because we're experiencing what I call the world view barometer. When we feel the pressure rising, we have a choice. We can push back. Or we can be genuinely curious about the other person's reasoning.

But what do we do when we feel the discomfort of our world view barometer rising? First off, congratulate ourselves for noticing. Too often when that feeling rears its head the next thing we do is defend our point of view. Of course that's an option, but if we want to live a leadership mindset there are other options too. And that is the focus of the first challenge in this chapter.

Challenge: What If and World View

This challenge provides a safe way to start stepping out of your world view. To do this, first find a quiet place where you're likely to be uninterrupted for ten minutes or so. You'll need a pen and paper and something to lean on so you can write. Loosen your clothes if that helps you feel relaxed. When you're ready, begin to recall.

Recall a time when you were at odds with someone – perhaps the last time you felt that you were right, and someone else felt just as strongly that they were. Maybe you're the boss and you dismissed their view on the grounds that they didn't have enough experience, or for any number of other reasons.

I'm not asking you to go back and tell that person they were right, so don't worry about that. All I'm asking you to do for now is just to recall that feeling. Where did it begin? Was it a heat in your chest? A pain in your head? A momentary confusion? A frustration because what you were hearing was silly or ill-informed?

Whatever it was, that feeling is your world view barometer. If you like, stay with that feeling for some time. The more familiar you are with it, the more likely you are to spot it the next time it comes along. That's helpful because spotting it early means we have more time to choose how to respond.

When you're ready, it's time to go beyond that feeling. Draw a line down the paper. At the top, on the left-hand side, write *my world view*.

My World View	

See if you can recall all the reasons why you were right. This should be easy because, after all, you're right. Don't be humble. No one's going to see this: it is just for you. If you need more paper, that's fine; grab another piece, divide it in half, and keep going. When you've listed all the reasons why you were right, put your pen down.

Go back to the top of the list. On the right-hand side of the page – the side you've left blank – write a new heading. This one says *their world view*, just like below.

My World View	Their World View

Now let's think about another question: "What if they were right?" Notice the reaction you just had. The reflex that says, "But they're wrong". Here's the thing: everyone thinks they're right when they're making their point. Even if they're lying, they tell themselves there's a good reason why they have to lie. Maybe later when they reflect, or if they get new information, they think differently. But at the time, when they say whatever they say, they think that what they're saying is right.

You know what happens next in this challenge – why I'm calling it a challenge. The next step is to write down all the reasons why they were right. If you're starting this with ideas like, "Because they're trying to undermine me", for example, then you're not doing this from their world view. You might feel undermined, but they're not acting that way just to undermine you. Instead, they might say, "X has shown that Y isn't fully aware of the issues, and so I have to highlight those issues in meetings so that the team can make informed decisions." Can you see the difference? The end result to you may feel the same – being undermined – but their motivation has nothing to do with attacking you, and more to do with them wanting to do the best for the business or team.

So, just like you did with yourself, list all the reasons why they were right. Keep noticing if you slide into your world view, and try to keep yourself focused on the reasonableness of the points you're making. The more reasonable, the more likely you're on the right track.

When you've completed that list, take a moment to consider. I'm not asking you to go back to this person and reveal your soul and the error of your ways to them. I'm not even asking you to go and speak to them. This is just for you. In the safety of your own mind, consider how the insights from their world view changes the way you see the situation.

Is there anything in their world view that gives you a deeper appreciation of the situation? Does that deeper appreciation highlight how you can modify your idea or change it completely? If you've already read Chapter 3, can you use flexibility of mind to combine the best aspects of both of your thinking and create a bigger idea?

Allowing your world view to be challenged might help you to see things differently. It might point you in a different direction. Or it might not. Either way, what it does do is allow you to entertain the idea that your world view isn't the only way of looking at the world.

Time and Genuine Curiosity

You turn a corner on the main street in your town. You hear the screech of tyres and you know that in less than a second there's going to be the sound of metal against metal. It happens in slow motion: you look up and see the red car swerve in a futile attempt to go around the motorbike. The biker's eyes are covered by his visor, but you know they contain all the shock and fear of a soldier watching a gun being fired directly at him. The two haven't collided yet but you react. Slowly at first. And then you break into a run. In your mind's eye, you see the biker flying from his bike, but when the car hits it doesn't go like that. The biker folds around the front of the car like a Cirque du Soleil acrobat and then, when the car stops, he falls back into the road, his bike landing on his legs. The driver sits in the car, hands gripping the wheel so tightly you know every muscle in his arms are shaking.

When you arrive you look at the biker. He's flailing his arms, trying to get up, but you know he isn't going anywhere. You set a hand on his shoulder, "You'll be alright," you say. You know that's not true but it seems like the right thing to say. His torso is contorted, his legs crushed under the bike. You know the risk of moving him. Although you've never lifted a bike before, you know it has to get off his legs.

His moans turn to cries. "Hold on," you say as you move to grab the handle bars.

At first it doesn't move at all. It rocks and the biker screams. You take a deep breath and with all the strength you have you pull the bike upwards. It's heavier than you imagined. It doesn't matter, you keep pulling on the handle bars – with a strength you didn't know you had – and it begins to lift. The biker groans, more out of relief than pain, and you keep lifting.

You hear the sirens in the distance. The bike gets lighter as you feel the weight being taken by someone else. You let go. You drop down on your knees and hold the biker's hand. "Hang in there," you say. "Help is on the way."

Except when you're in a situation like that one – when someone's life is hanging in the balance – there isn't a single thing in the world that requires you to make a decision now. Not the choice between plan A and plan B, not your boss calling you into her office, not the stock number plummeting. Nothing.

Let that sink in for a moment. In our world of social media and constant connectivity it's easy to think that the world runs at breakneck speed because that's just the way it is. And in that world, pausing to think things through – our reaction, our options – feels like a luxury. Genuine curiosity takes time: not necessarily days or even hours, but certainly minutes rather than seconds. And, yes, in a fast-paced world, not taking action (or reacting) even for a minute feels like wasting time.

But what if, by taking the time to be curious about why our business does something – or to question our reaction, or if we're doing the right thing or the comfortable thing – we give ourselves the space to do something else?

What I'm suggesting is that everything beyond those split-second reactions in a life-or-death scenario benefits from a moment of genuine curiosity. If you accept that our world view informs what we think is right, it follows that it informs how we behave. This means that the reaction we have to a situation, whatever that may be, will be based on our world view.

The value of genuine curiosity lies in questioning. Is there another way to see this situation? Am I doing this because it fits with my world view? Or am I avoiding the best course of action because it is a challenge to my world view?

Even in the situation in which my boss sends me a testy email about how my team has screwed up, and how she wants to see me right away. Am I panicked because my world view says employees are subordinate to their bosses and are in trouble when they get called in? If so, that means I'll behave in a certain way when I go to see her. If that isn't my world view than I'll see the situation differently and, more importantly, behave differently.

Sometimes even a moment of genuine curiosity on why I'm reacting the way I am is all it takes.

Asking what if is about being curious enough to consider other lines of thinking and leaving room to explore ideas that don't immediately fit into our world view. It's about leaving space for perspectives that can only be seen from a different vantage point. There's a humility to asking what if because it's essentially saying, "The way I see the world is only one way to see the world: not the best way, just one way."

But there's another component to asking what if. It allows us to listen, and to gather and explore all the points of view and data that's coming at us – even as we realize that we don't have to act on any of that data right away. It prevents us from making rash choices that feel good, and instead allows space in which to make informed decisions that may lead us out of the ordinary land-scape we often all inhabit.

And then, when we've given ourselves that space, and when we've collected enough information, we can draw on flexibility of mind to connect that information into a bigger idea – more on that in the next chapter.

The Behaviours of Genuine Curiosity: Stating the Obvious

You know that saying "out of the mouths of babes"? Kids can sometimes be funny or profound because they don't edit what they say. Instead, they call the world as they see it: that's the behaviour of stating the obvious. If we're doing something that isn't working in our business, the first question to ask isn't, "How do we fix it?" The most obvious question to ask is, "Why are we doing it?"

Stating the obvious liberates us because it allows us to name the elephants in the room. Just the act of doing that means a differ-ent conversation is possible: one that's based on openness. Stating the obvious isn't a dark art, a technique, nor a tool. All it takes is a willingness to name what we see.

The Expert Mind

For many people who I encounter in my consulting, the hard part isn't the willingness; it's the seeing. That's because, when we're part of a business culture – or in an industry – for a long time, it informs our world view (that again). In this context, our biases and prejudices aren't about discriminating against different groups of people, but against ideas that we think our experience has taught us don't or won't work.

The concept I'm talking about is what's often referred to as the expert mind: a mind that is so knowledgeable about its field that it cuts off the possibility of new ideas or discoveries. It does that for the simple reason that the more we know, the more we think we know. And the more we think we know, the more we think we understand what's possible, attainable, and doable.

Think that's overstating it?

Albert Abraham Michelson was one of the greats of physics. Awarded the Nobel Prize in 1907, his work on measuring the speed of light and his famous collaboration with Edward Morley in 1887 helped end the idea of light travelling through ether. His work influenced Einstein in the development of the special and general theories of relativity. Yet a man so well versed in the scientific method – a man whose own work had displaced theories that had gone before – still managed to put his foot in his mouth when, in 1894, he gave his now infamous speech at the University of Chicago. Here's the infamous bit:

The more important fundamental laws and facts of physical science have all been discovered, and these are now so firmly established that the possibility of their ever being supplanted in consequence of new discoveries is exceedingly remote.[2]

This was just a few years before Einstein turned the idea of gravity on its head, and before string theory's multi-dimensions ever reared its head. If we think Einstein was immune from the expert's mind it's worth remembering that he spent his later years trying, unsuccessfully, to disprove quantum theory. And that's good because it's our understanding of quantum theory that makes everything – from your smartphone to lasers – possible.

My point here is this: be careful when you start thinking that you know your field.

An Empty Mind

Shoshin is a Japanese word that's hard to translate into English. Pop it into a good online translator and it spits out something like "original intention", but that's only half the story. In the West, the word is most often translated as "beginner's mind" – the ability to approach a problem from the perspective of inexperience. But there's a more literal translation of *shoshin*: "a beginner's heart". That's not just a more endearing translation, I think it also better captures the emotional state that is *shoshin* – the willingness to be humble.

There's a Zen story that I feel captures the humility of *shoshin* beautifully.

A Western Zen scholar travels to a remote monastery in rural Japan. He's there to meet the abbot, a famed Zen master. When the scholar arrives, it's late at night. The abbot's attendant greets

---

2   A. A. Michelson, *Light Waves and Their Uses* (Chicago, IL: University of Chicago, 1903), pp. 23–24. Available at: https://archive.org/details/lightwavestheiru00mich_0/page/n9.

the visitor warmly. Though he's been travelling for a long time and he's tired, he wants to see the abbot. "Can I see him now?" the scholar asks.

"The abbot is sleeping," the attendant says kindly. "Let me take your bag and coat and show you to your room. Sleep this evening," he says, "and first thing in the morning I'll take you to the abbot."

But the scholar is insistent, "Do you know how long it's taken me to get here?" he asks. "I've travelled for days, and the abbot said he'd be here to greet me."

The attendant is a tall and muscular man. He could easily be intimidating, but he gently puts a hand on the scholar's shoulder. "The abbot isn't going anywhere," he insists. "I'll take you to him myself first thing in the morning."

"But you don't understand," the scholar pleads.

The conversation, if you can call it that, goes on in this way: the visitor demanding, the attendant trying his best to respectfully lead him to his room. It goes on for so long that the sounds of their voices echo down the hallways of the monastery, waking monk after monk. It isn't long until the abbot is awoken too. But, rather than be annoyed, the abbot calls for the scholar to be taken to his study. "Tell him I'll meet with him," the abbot says.

When the abbot walks into his study it's after 2am. He's a little tired but it doesn't show. He smiles warmly at the scholar, who rushes toward him then stops and bows respectfully. The abbot pats the scholar's head then turns to his attendant. "Please can you make some tea?"

The Westerner has been waiting for this moment for years. From the time when he began his studies in Zen, he's wanted to meet a Zen master. The abbot stands in front of him smiling but otherwise statue-like. "Thank you for seeing me," the scholar says. "I've been studying Zen for fifteen years. I've read all the writings of Dōgen Zenji. It speaks to me …" And then it becomes a monologue. A recap of the past fifteen years of his life: all the studying, the degrees, the late nights, the speeches on Zen, how he's taken on the role of ambassador for Zen, why the West needs Zen. On and on he goes.

So enthralled in his story, he pays no attention to the attendant bringing the pot of tea and two cups. So excited to be where he is, he doesn't reply when the abbot asks if he'd like a cup of tea. So taken by being with the abbot, he doesn't register when the abbot starts pouring the tea. So focused on telling the abbot what he knows, he only barely notices when the tea reaches the brim of the teacup. So sure is he that the abbot will be impressed by his knowledge of Zen, he ignores the tea flowing over the brim of his cup.

The abbot looks at him kindly and keeps pouring the tea, allowing it to flow onto the table and then to the floor. It's only when the stream of tea reaches his foot that the scholar cuts off his monologue. "Abbot," he says, "my cup is full!"

The abbot stops pouring. "Then how can I put anything else into it?"

To approach something with *shoshin* is to approach it with a humility that allows us to be empty of preconceptions. Not as poetic as a beginner's heart, but I like the word empty. It isn't full of knowledge or full of itself. It's waiting. There's potential.

That's the spirit of genuine curiosity. Add to that the emptiness of approaching a subject or problem without thinking we know everything, and now we have space to ask the obvious questions.

Stating the obvious is the ability to think with a beginner's heart. It's about asking the fundamental questions. Questions like why are we doing this? What problem are we trying to solve? Is this achieving our goal? Are we clear about what our goal is? We've tried this three times now, what are we learning from our setbacks? Are we being too timid in our approach? Are we creating strategy for now or for five years from now? These are the kinds of questions that create a foundation for genuine curiosity because they broaden the thinking in a discussion. And although it's easy to list these questions, it can be hard to ask them in the moment.

Obvious Doesn't Mean Evident

The thing about obvious questions is that although they may be obvious, they may not always be evident. If that sounds like a riddle it isn't meant to. Let me give you an example. Without turning around, name ten things that are behind you in the room or space you're in. If that's a struggle, it isn't because those things were hidden from you when you entered the space; it's just because you didn't notice or focus on them.

That's what I mean when I say that obvious doesn't mean evident. Something can be obvious but – because of our world view, or thinking we know a lot about a subject – not evident. It becomes hard to see because of our mental filters.

The cure for that is cultivating a beginner's heart. And we do that by allowing ourselves to ask what if. What if I hadn't spent years in this field, what might I think then? What if our messaging to our customers isn't as clear as we thought? What if we didn't keep diversifying our product lines?

A Beginner's Heart and Experience

"So, what it's beginning to sound like," Victor Veteran might say, "is that you have something against people with experience."

"Does it sound that way, Vic?" I ask. He's a brawny man who's been through more than one boardroom war, so in hindsight calling him Vic may not have been a good idea.

He snorts a little and I get the feeling I may be right on that count. "Yeah," he says, "it does."

And if it is beginning to sound that way, then I'm doing Vic – and everyone else with years of experience – a disservice. A beginner's heart and an inexperienced mind aren't the same thing. In no way am I suggesting that experience is a bad thing. It's all about how we choose to use that experience. Do we use it to bowl others over with our ideas? Leaving the impression that we've been there, done that, and know all there is to know? Or do we use our experience to be genuinely curious about what else might be possible?

When I first worked in one business, I heard the refrain, "We're a learning company, not a know-it-all company." That's great, of course, but what I saw – more often than not – was that when a junior colleague asked a question, or suggested something they learnt at university, the response they got was a list of reasons why that idea wouldn't work. They might hear, "Yes, that's what they teach in university, but here's why that won't work in the real world …" Want to guess how long those junior members of staff kept offering their ideas? I'll give you a clue: it wasn't long at all.

That's an example of using experience to shoot down ideas rather than engaging with genuine curiosity. When we engage, it means we get to use our experience in a different way.

In this way of working, experience isn't used to tell people how they should be thinking, or what works; instead, it's about using that experience to hone other people's ideas. We do that by asking questions that provoke thought (something we'll explore more in Chapter 5). We might lay out the problem as we see it, offer the benefit of our experience, and ask the person how their idea could overcome those problems.

The hard-won experience we've gained becomes a path that others can use to navigate new ideas. And just like any path, new paths can branch off of the route we lay out and lead into new, uncharted territory. And that's possible because of the insight our experience provided.

What I'm saying is that, in a world of genuine curiosity, experience can be the ingredient that makes new ideas work. Maybe the idea the junior member of staff offered can't work in the real world, but what can we bring from our years of experience to add to it? How can we help that person make their idea work? If we ask questions that provoke thought, we're doing more than just making that person feel valued: we're modelling genuine curiosity. And if we – as leaders – model it, then guess what happens? It sets off an avalanche of genuine curiosity. So rather than just saying, "We're a learning company, not a know-it-all company," we prove that's the case.

When our staff see us do that often enough, they get the message that *this is how we operate*. And so, when they talk among themselves, they ask what if, they state the obvious, and allow that line of questioning to broaden the scope of their discussions.

Challenge: Living a Beginner's Heart

So far in this chapter, I've been talking about a beginner's heart in terms of approaching something we know well with an emptiness of mind. That can be hard when we've been an expert for a long time.

This challenge is about being a beginner. The point here isn't to become very good at something new; it's simply to reacquaint yourself with the feeling of inexperience. We'll see what the effect of that might be at the end of the challenge.

To begin, find an activity that you're interested in but have never tried. It could be anything: hiking, chess, baking, indoor climbing, or anything else that appeals. When you settle on that activity, set yourself the goal of doing it on a specific day and at a specific time.

Then, in the run up to the activity, list everything you need to do to prepare. Maybe you need to get equipment; maybe you need to do some research; maybe you need to call on a friend for help. Whatever you need to do, note it down. While it's still fresh, write down how doing these things is leaving you feeling. Are you excited, nervous, feeling over-whelmed, or interested? Is it a mixture of feelings?

Then, on the day you planned, do that new thing. As you do it, pay attention to how it feels to be out of your element. Notice the kind of questions you ask of the instructor, if there is one, or the people around you. Notice the responses you get to your questions from both the experienced people and your fellow novices. If you're doing something alone, notice the kind of questions you're asking of yourself. How many times do you go to YouTube for help? What are you trying to find out when you do that? Notice the feelings the activity evokes in you. Are you frustrated if it's not going well? Thrilled if it is? Are you having fun, or are you annoyed that you can't master the new skill as quickly as you'd hoped?

When the activity is over, find a nearby spot and reflect on the experience. Think about it in the context of a beginner's heart. What did you notice about yourself when you were a real beginner? How did you try to find out about the activity? Did any themes emerge in the questions you asked? What did you do to better understand the parameters of the challenge?

Did your questions cut to the heart of the activity? If so, did you notice that you were asking obvious questions? Did you notice why you chose the activity in the first place? Was it a comfortable or an uncomfortable choice?

Whatever your answers to these questions, this is what it feels like to be a beginner. If you choose to, you can use this experience as a doorway into the mindset of a beginner's heart. If you noticed a theme in the questions you asked, could you ask these kinds of questions about parts of your work you feel accomplished in? What would you need to do to recreate the sense of trepidation you felt as you embarked on this activity? How could you transfer that into your workplace?

That is the real challenge.

The Behaviours of Genuine Curiosity: Demonstrating Generosity of Spirit

Before we leave genuine curiosity, there's one more behaviour we need to think about. Without it, genuine curiosity becomes a lot harder to cultivate. Generosity of spirit is the behaviour of genuine curiosity that is inclusive both of ideas and of people. It understands that others can be right too, and that – even in the most difficult of situations – there's more than one valid opinion. Most importantly, it leaves room for those opinions to be heard.

Generosity of spirit is magnanimous. It doesn't privilege its point of view because it's senior or experienced. It knows that everyone is equal in the marketplace of ideas. Generosity of spirit knows that shooting ideas down stifles genuine curiosity, so it entertains and encourages them instead. If those ideas aren't fully formed, or even helpful, it helps people to see the flaws in their thinking for themselves, so they don't have to be "set right". In that sense, generosity of spirit follows the logic of an idea and either helps it come to fruition or helps it become a learning point for all involved.

Assuming Positive Intent

Generosity of spirit holds one philosophy close to its heart: it assumes the positive intent of the people it works with. What I mean by that is, it's easy to not be generous to our peers and those we directly manage if we think that they have an ulterior motive – if we think they're trying to do what's best for themselves or their business area, for example. Worse still, if it looks to us like they may be sabotaging a good idea for their own ends, then, yes, holding generosity of spirit isn't just tough, we'd be foolish to let them get away with that.

But here's the thing, if we start with the view that people are out for their own ends, or being saboteurs, then guess how we treat them? If our world view is that they always behave this way, that they're always out for themselves, and always throwing a wrench in the works, then, just like everything else informed by our world view, we don't look for evidence to contradict it; we look for evidence to confirm it. In this context that means looking for evidence to support the idea that they're blocking our efforts.

But – and it's a big but – if we're willing to assume that these people aren't acting in their own best interests, or whatever it is we think, then maybe we can give them the benefit of the doubt and assume that they're doing what they think will be the best thing to move an idea on. So when they ask questions, we hear that they're trying to understand. When they offer a solution, they really think it will work in the interests of all. If we can see them that way, then we hear their ideas differently. And that all rests on our willingness to see what they're doing as an honest attempt to help.

Before I arrived at one particular company, I heard about this woman among their staff – let's call her Sue. Sue, I was told, would take every opportunity to divert a discussion and make it about her business area. Given the chance, I was told, she'd always work in the best interest of herself and her team. People were quick to tell me that Sue wasn't a bad person, she just had a myopic view. It was better I knew, they said, because it would help put whatever Sue said in context. If you do challenge her, they went on to say, she'll become defensive and even hostile. So, in the best interests of all, people would let her say what she wanted and then ignore her when it came to implementation.

It will come as no surprise to you that I didn't find Sue to be that way at all. Instead, what I saw was a woman asking tough questions of her colleagues, and trying to see how their ideas could work for her team. She'd voice concerns about how plans that worked on the enterprise level may not be taking account of factors in different business areas – not just hers but company-wide. And she'd become more and more frustrated as it became clear that her concerns weren't being addressed.

By seeing her attempts to understand as something to be indulged but ultimately ignored, her colleagues backed her into the corner of knowing that she wasn't being heard. Even the good ideas she had were seen through the negative world view of her colleagues – that she was a self-interested troublemaker – and so they were also dismissed.

Sue did the only thing open to her. As senior team meetings dragged on, Sue, despondent, would eventually give up and agree with her colleagues. And then, because she was the director of her business area, she'd go back to her department and do what made sense to her, which, of course, only confirmed everyone else's view that she was uncooperative. What the senior team had done by seeing her as a blocker was make her one.

That's the danger of not assuming positive intent. We look for things about people to confirm our world view and make block-ers of colleagues who, in some cases, are simply trying both to understand and to help us understand.

We all have different ways of processing information. If some-one asks lots of questions, we might see them as argumentative. If someone tries to understand by exploring the downsides of an idea, we might see them as negative. And all of those things are compounded if we see them as argumentative or negative in the first place. In other words, if we assume negative intent of them. Since genuine curiosity is about learning, assuming positive intent allows us to hear other's people's ideas as insights we can bounce off.

"OK," Rona Realist says, "in Sue's case her colleagues messed up. They saw her as a hindrance when she was trying to help. But are you telling me there's no such thing as a person who acts as a blocker simply because they really are negative?"

That's fair. Of course we'll encounter negative people. I worked in one company with a team whose main job was to create extravagant remote broadcasts. You know the ones I mean: shows where hosts ski down a mountainside while broadcasting, or they hold a cannonballing contest in an inflatable pool in a public car park – the crazier the better. The point, of course, is to create a buzz so people show up.

It was all in good fun. The thing about organizing events such as these is that they're technically challenging, and they need to be: a boring or simple activity doesn't attract anyone. What I noticed about this team was that when they came up with an idea, the leader – let's call him Jake – would listen and bounce all the ideas around. He'd act like bellows on a fire, fanning the flames of his team's ideas and encouraging them all to stretch themselves.

Then, when they came up with an idea that everyone thought was great, Jake would say, "Run that by Gary." Now Gary was the prototypical negative person. He's the kind of guy who, if you were looking out on a beautiful clear day without a cloud in the sky, he would say, "Don't get used to it, it'll be raining this weekend." Gary was also a technical genius. He had a mind like a quantum computer: capable of thinking through multiple ideas at the same time and smart enough to synthesize those ideas into clear judgements about the direction of a project.

Jake knew that telling Gary meant inviting criticism of the harshest kind. I'd heard Gary talking to a colleague once and he began his response with, "Let me tell you why that's stupid." As I walked away, I heard the person Gary was talking to say, "Maybe I'm not explaining it right."

To which Gary replied, "No, you are, and it's stupid."

What Jake was asking his team to do was tell Gary the idea and then listen to his feedback without becoming defensive. It's hard, but that's what Jake was asking. The point wasn't to convince Gary, it was to get Gary to point out the blind spots in the team's thinking – to ask what if, as well as the obvious questions.

Then, when Jake presented the idea at a departmental meeting, someone would inevitably ask a question about the technical details. Jake would reply by saying something like, "Yeah, we didn't even think of that until we ran the idea past Gary. He really helped us by pointing out X, and that helped us to see that we had a problem we needed to fix."

Gary would be in the room and he'd smile.

The direct answer to Rona's question, therefore, is yes – there are negative people, and it can be hard to see their positive intent. But that doesn't mean they have nothing to offer. What matters is how we approach them and their ideas. Do we ignore them because they're annoying energy-killers? Or do we assume positive intent? In the example, Jake was giving Gary a chance to contribute in the way he did best – by blowing up an idea. Rather than see that as a negative, Jake saw it as a chance to assume that Gary was trying to help, even if he wasn't.

In this case, Jake asked his team to take an idea they all loved to someone he knew would poke holes in it – attack it, if you like.

By attacking it, Gary would reveal the weak parts of the idea that Jake and his team needed to reinforce.

That's the point here: assuming positive intent isn't about the person being positive. It's about looking – admittedly sometimes very hard – for the pearl of insight in what someone is saying or doing. By assuming their intentions are positive, we can take what they say and use it to build a bigger, better idea. Crucially, in the example, Jake let everyone know the value of Gary's contribution. Jake didn't criticize Gary for picking the plan apart; he let everyone know how Gary had helped. Think about the effect that had on Gary.

And more than that, think about this. Everyone in that business knew Gary. Everyone knew what he was like. And everyone, in some way or another, had been witness to the metaphorical grenades Gary regularly threw in meetings. Some people might still be annoyed at Gary for blowing up their idea. Some might be dismissive of him, writing off his comments as unhelpful. So what effect do you think Jake had on how others perceived Gary in that particular meeting? If the leader assumes positive intent they're encouraging everyone to look for the best in whatever someone else has to offer.

To be clear, it's easy to assume positive intent in people who are on your side. But when you assume positive intent of someone who isn't obviously trying to help, that's when you get the points. The easiest thing in the world is to greet negativity with negativity. It's easy to be "polite" and ignore a person, and their ideas, completely.

Assuming positive intent helps us to start in a different place. It forces us to look for the value that people bring – even when that value is hard to see, or when they do intend to be obstructive. Assuming positive intent isn't about other people; it's about how we approach them.

We assume positive intent because we understand that when people push back on an idea, or highlight its flaws, they're giving us a chance to step out of our world view and into theirs. In doing so, we get to see the idea from a different vantage point. We might see the holes in our thinking. If we're listening, we might hear them state the obvious that we were blind to because of our attachment to the idea.

And, if we're doing those things, we're being genuinely curious about what else might be possible.

Challenge: Follow the Reasoning

I said before that generosity of spirit means following the reasoning of an idea. What I meant was, rather than react to the emotion – the kind of emotion that Gary might stir in us, for example – we can follow the thinking that led to the other person's perspective. That will help to keep our emotions in check when we feel we want to defend the idea – and that means we're more likely to be genuinely curious. It also means we can engage in the discussion assuming positive intent, because we're trying to understand the reasoning behind their point of view knowing that from their position there's a good reason for it.

This is a real-time challenge in four parts. We could do the first part as a list, similar to the first challenge in this chapter, but if you've read this far I'm guessing you're up for a harder challenge.

Think about a potentially difficult meeting you're going to be having in the next week or so. You might consider it difficult because there's likely to be a personality clash. It might be hard because the problem you're addressing is complex, there are lots of points of view to consider, and someone will inevitably have an idea that is different to yours.

In preparation for this challenge, spend a few days ahead of time looking for evidence to suggest that the person who holds a different view to you *is* working in the best interests of the project or business. To be clear, that means you're assuming positive intent about them. Look for examples of when and how their challenges have moved a project forward. It may be anecdotal evidence you pick up from others, or evidence you recall just by thinking about them. Either way, the challenge is to find information that challenges your world view of them.

That's the first part of the challenge, so let's think about this for a second.

Now let's consider an extreme example. Let's say you spend all day racking your brain and talking to anyone you can think of, but in all that time you come up with no evidence. What does that mean? Does it mean that there is no evidence and proves you were right all along? That's one interpretation. Another is that you could be looking in the wrong places. If everyone I'm talking to agrees with me, it could suggest I'm talking to people who share my world view. To break out of that means talking to people who don't share that world view – and who might that be? A colleague who respects your difficult person, or someone who can be impartial. To state the obvious, only when we disrupt our current view is a new outlook possible. Though it may be difficult, take the time to find that evidence before moving on to the next part of the challenge. When you have that evidence, you're ready for step two.

Now make a commitment to yourself that when you go into the meeting, you'll look for the positive intention behind whatever your questioner says or does. Remind yourself that although it might not be obvious, it's there. Be clear that, regardless of how it looks, they aren't trying to knock the project off-kilter. They're doing exactly what your evidence suggests: they're trying to move the project on in the best interests of all. Believe that, because no one is messing with you for the fun of it. And because the positive intention is there, they have good reason to say what they're saying. If you can keep all this in mind, you're ready for the third part of the challenge.

Even if it's only for this meeting, decide that you'll assume positive intent when you talk with them. Decide that whatever they say, you won't roll your eyes inwardly or sigh in exasperation. Instead, your objective is to understand where they're coming from and why they feel their idea will work. If it's not immediately apparent, ask a question to understand how they got to their conclusion. That might be a question like, "Could you help me to understand why you see it that way?" or, "It may be that I'm not following your logic – could you explain?" Whatever question you choose, deliver it knowing that there is a rationale behind their perspective and that they feel their idea is in everyone's best interest. If you can't see how their idea delivers the project objectives, ask them how they see their idea fitting into the wider goal. The point isn't to argue, it's to strive to understand what they're seeing. To follow their reasoning, not yours. And to do it all believing that they do have a sound reason.

It's a truism that we can't change other people, we can only change ourselves. That's why the success of this challenge doesn't depend on the person you have in mind morphing into a more benevolent version of themselves. Sometimes it takes more than one attempt to create a new way of working. The success of this challenge depends on you. And that takes us to step four.

When the meeting is over, find a spot where you can be on your own and go over what you noticed about yourself. What effect did assuming positive intent have on how you related to the other person? What did you notice about the tone of your voice when you asked a question while assuming positive intent? Did you sound annoyed, frustrated, or curious? Remember how they responded to you. What did you notice about the effect they were having on you as you followed the reasoning of their perspective? What did you notice about the conversation? Was it easier? Harder? More productive? More challenging? And what effect did that have on the dynamic of the meeting?

Whatever answers you arrive at, that's your measure of success. If you mentally go back over the meeting and can't notice any of those things, consider what made it hard to be mindful during the meeting. If you do have answers but aren't happy with how you carried yourself, that's no problem. Ask yourself, "Is it true that I didn't handle myself well the whole meeting?" Was there anything in how you held yourself that did work? If so, that's a great place to build from. And if you feel you rose to this challenge and shifted the dynamic of the meeting for the better, then well done. For you the challenge is to keep it going in your next meeting.

The thing about the six attributes is that it's not about arriving; it's about the journey. That's true because each time we master an attribute it opens the door to another one. So let's see what's behind the next door.

Genuine Curiosity Reminders

♦ The behaviours of genuine curiosity are asking "what if?", stating the obvious, and demonstrating generosity of spirit.

♦ Asking what if leads us to interrogate ourselves, and helps us to see whether we're doing what's best or what's easy.

♦ Our world view makes it difficult to step outside of our frame of reference.

♦ Stating the obvious liberates us because it allows us to name the elephants in the room.

♦ An expert's mind inhibits our ability to have a beginner's heart.

♦ Assuming positive intent isn't about other people; it's about how we approach them.

Chapter 3
Flexibility of Mind

Challenge: An Experience of Flexibility of Mind

Try this. Think about a time in your life when you were sure that you were right and then it turned out that you weren't. It doesn't matter what it was. Maybe it was an argument with another person. Maybe you were putting together flat-pack furniture and were certain that the instructions must be wrong. Maybe you were working on a project and became fixated on the way you envisaged that it should be completed, only to find out there was a better way.

Have something in mind? Great.

Now see if you can recall why you felt so strongly that you must be right. Were there any signs along the way that pointed toward the answer? What made it hard for you to see them? Did anyone try to show you another way? Why couldn't you hear them?

I'm going to guess that you thought you were right because at no point did any measure you had indicate that you were wrong. So without any contraindications, you continued to believe that you were right. Until holding onto that belief became impossible. That's the thing about being wrong: we keep thinking we're right – argue for our view, in fact – until, all too late, we figure out we're not.

Now think about this: did holding onto the belief in being right make it difficult to allow room for being wrong?

Flexibility of Mind and Leadership

What does any of this mean in leadership? Holding onto an idea like it is the best one possible isn't just unhelpful, it could be the single most harmful thing we do to our team or business. That isn't hyperbole, and it's why flexibility of mind is an attribute of a leadership mindset.

If we're putting flat-pack furniture together, being certain that the instructions are wrong, cursing the diagrams, and telling ourselves – and anyone who will listen – how the instructions are the worst we've ever seen is no big deal. It doesn't matter that we ignore them and use the 10102 screws instead of the 10014 screws that the instructions say to, because our plan makes sense to us and we think it'll work better. And it doesn't matter that when we're nearly done, we realize the 10014 screws are smaller and shiny and would have made the outside of the piece look much sleeker than the dull 10102 screws we used. And so we live with it because we can't be bothered to unscrew the whole thing and start again.

But what if we're talking about our business instead of a piece of furniture? What if the problem isn't whether the outside of the unit has shiny screws, but that our production process isn't as effective as it could be? We think we've got it as streamlined as possible, but what if we're wrong? What would we do differently if we were willing to (metaphorically) unscrew the whole thing and see how else it could fit together?

I've said before that the six attributes meld into one another. Sometimes several work in combination – mindfulness, for example, can give us the presence to be genuinely curious, which might help us to question our processes on an enterprise level. Sometimes, two attributes might dance with each other. That's the case with flexibility of mind and genuine curiosity. Though it's not the goal of genuine curiosity, asking what if or stating the obvious often provides us with insights. And it's flexibility of mind that allows us to do something with the insights that genuine curiosity affords. Genuine curiosity asks, "What if I streamline the operational process?" And flexibility of mind takes the multiple options that question throws up and combines them into a bigger idea: an out of the box idea, if you like.

Flexibility of mind matters because it's about having the mental dexterity to pivot our thinking quickly to find that bigger idea. The crucial word here is *our*. Flexibility of mind is about adapting ourselves. If we're trying to convince someone else, ram an idea into fruition, or remain unmovable as we try to force a change in the world, then we're not living with flexibility of mind. The essence of flexibility of mind is a willingness to change our approach as we adapt to the information the world is sending us; it's not about attempting to make the world adapt to us. Of course, that doesn't mean we have to accept poor processes, bad ideas, or injustice. It does, however, mean we need to adapt our approach to tackling these problems.

Just as is the case with the other attributes, there are tangible behaviours we would exhibit if we were living the attribute of flexibility of mind. So, before we go any further, let's take a look at what those behaviours might be.

The Behaviours of Flexibility of Mind

Attribute of a leadership mindset	Behaviours
Flexibility of mind	Entertaining the possibility of being wrong Recognizing that there's more than one valid idea Creatively combining ideas

Unlike other behaviours that demonstrate the six attributes, the behaviours of flexibility of mind work in a sequence of stages. The first is entertaining the possibility that we could be wrong. We see that our ideas are based on the information we have now, so we allow our understanding, and favoured approaches, to be revised and adapted as new information comes in. Because we know we could be wrong, we don't defend our position, and we more readily drop our view in the pursuit of a bigger idea.

The second is seeing that multiple ideas can be valid at the same time. Notice I don't say "right", because when we think an idea is right, we stop looking beyond it. I know that in the polarized world we live in, the idea of more than one idea being valid is heresy. But just because people tend to group themselves into two camps doesn't mean there are only two ways of looking at something. So, if there is more than one valid idea, that takes us to the third part of flexibility of mind: creatively combining ideas.

We'll explore the three behaviours of flexibility of mind separately, just like we did with the other attributes. And, as in the other chapters, I'll offer you challenges to help you practise the behaviours.

The Behaviours of Flexibility of Mind: Entertaining the Possibility of Being Wrong

In her book *Being Wrong*, Kathryn Schultz likens the experience of being wrong to Wile E. Coyote running off a cliff: he's fine until he looks down.[1] When he does, it's the realization that he's not on solid ground that sends him plummeting to earth, not the act of running off the edge. Her observation is as profound as it is simple: we can be wrong at any moment without even knowing it. Realizing that we could be walking on thin air whenever we profess to be right leaves us with two options: either we ignore the realization and pretend there's no reason to doubt the rightness of what we think and do, or we can realize that, at any moment, whatever we're thinking or doing stands as much chance of being right as wrong. And here's the punch line: just as Wile E. Coyote always finds out, there's no way to know which it is until we look down.

Before we get to the benefit of that, let's think about the feeling that may have just risen in you – perhaps fear and/or anger. Of course, I don't know if that assumption is right, it's just based on the feelings that reared up in me the first time I realized the uncertainty of being "right". The sheer fear and anger that everything I'd known could just as easily be wrong. I had that experience when I was thirteen.

---

1   Kathryn Schultz, *Being Wrong: Adventures in the Margin of Error* (London: Portobello Books, 2010), p. 180.

The first thing I saw when I awoke was the book: Richard Bach's *Illusions: The Adventures of a Reluctant Messiah.*[2] It was sitting flat on the night stand, the spine facing away from me. Without being able to see the title, there was nothing to signal that it was *Illusions.* But I knew. Of course I did. I'd been begging my brother to read it for weeks. And, true to form, he didn't rush reading it for me to have my turn. He didn't even pretend to. He'd sit on his bed, read maybe a page, and then set it down for the night. But now here it was.

I picked it up, held it in my thirteen-year-old hands. On the black cover there was a picture of a blue feather, the title of the book, and the author's name. Today I'd say that it's the kind of book that if read young enough has the power to change a life. It's hopeful, full of possibilities and ideas, and confident in the way it presents them. As a teen, I wouldn't have put it that way, but somewhere in my little head that was trying to make sense of life, it was the answer to everything.

I already knew when I turned the first page that I wouldn't be getting out of bed until I had read the whole thing. It's a small book and I lapped it up. I drank in the story like a lost traveller who stumbles on a water fountain on a desert highway. I knew it wasn't a story but a treatise on life: a way to live. And with each page I turned, I bought into the ideas a little more. Halfway through the book, I was ready to join the cult – and if there wasn't one, I'd start it. We'd camp outside Richard's house and wait for his words of wisdom to wash over us, covering us like a wool blanket on a cold night.

I was maybe five hours into reading, and three minutes away from packing a bag for wherever the cult's headquarters was going to be, when I turned to the last page. And this is what it said: "Everything in this book may be wrong." And then, just in

---

2   Richard Bach, *Illusions: The Adventures of a Reluctant Messiah* (London: William
     Heinemann Ltd, 1977).

case that hadn't sunk in, there was a two-line break and one final word. "End."[3]

At first I felt numb. That lasted a little while. Then it turned to anger. I berated myself for being so taken in by the book. For being idealistic. That lasted for days. That turned to hate. Whenever someone asked me about the book, I'd tell them how stupid it was. That lasted for months. And then it passed.

Now when I think about that day, I laugh. Not at how silly I'd been, but at how something so obvious got me so annoyed. The truth is, that line – "Everything in this book may be wrong" – could just as easily go at the end of every non-fiction book, because it isn't designed as a *look how silly you are for falling for this*, it's just a statement of fact. Everything in every non-fiction book may be wrong. And to make it even funnier, *Illusions* isn't even a non-fiction book; it's fiction, pure and simple.

What I learnt later in life is that the statement isn't just true for books, it's true for life. How can we be 100% sure that we're right? Not about if our foot hurts, or if the light is red or green, but about the bigger things. How do we know for sure that this is the best process to use for operations? How do we know that the sales script we just wrote is the best one for all our telemarketers to use? How do we know that this is the best way to market a product? Of course we'll have our facts; they may be conflicting but we'll take the time to rationalize which are wrong. So that means, for the most part, we'll find facts that support our world view. And we feel good about making a decision based on those facts because, most of the time, we come up with an idea and then look for the facts to back it up: to back up the decision

---

3   Bach, *Illusions*, p. 137.

we were going to make anyway. But how do we really know that we're right?

The honest answer is that we can't know. Not 100%. We can be fairly sure, we can have a gut feeling, but we can't fully know. So why do we act like we're certain? Even get angry when people don't see it our way? Defend our way of thinking tooth and nail? Why are national leaders so convinced they're right to send their soldiers to fight those of another country?

Yes, it's unnerving to think that we may be wrong. Mostly because it leads to a more unnerving idea: there is no way to know if we're ever right. That's the root of the fear. It's petrifying to think the ideas we've based our lives on – all the decisions we've ever made – could all be wrong. As scary as that is, it doesn't make it any less true. The metaphorical ground of truth may feel solid beneath our feet, but as soon as we put a flag in it our tendency is to defend that truth, and doing so leaves us blind to the water bubbling up around the flag pole.

What I'm trying to say is this: to say that we may be wrong isn't a grand gesture of humility, it's an obvious statement of fact. Yes, it's scary to think that any information coming across our desks could be wrong, or that the decisions we're about to make could be wrong. It's understandable if thoughts like that leave us paralysed with fear because, in a world like that, how can we know anything? And I know it doesn't help to say so, but the honest answer is that we can't.

Cecil Certain clears his throat. If it's possible to be condescending without saying a word, Cecil's throat-clearing does it. He's standing behind me. It's tough to see his reflection in the computer screen in front of me, but I'm pretty sure his resting face is smug.

"You want to tell me how we could actually live in a world like that?" He doesn't end the sentence with "young man", but that's only because he didn't think of it. "For that matter," he continues, "even if you did tell me, how would I know you're right?" He laughs lightly to himself. "Maybe we should all curl up in the foetal position and hide from the world? Maybe we just shouldn't make any decisions at all?" He taps the back of my chair. "I'm guessing it's better to make no decision than a wrong one?" He waits for an answer.

Well, that's an option, but there are others.

Reflected in the screen, I watch him disappear. His face is the last thing to fade and as it does I look back down at my keyboard.

Living with Being Wrong

In science, a hypothesis is a guess. It's a way of saying, "This is what I think is going on here." In science, we test that guess with experiments. Take gravity, for example. When Newton sat under that tree and the apple fell on his head, he had an idea. He saw that the apple fell *toward* earth. Common sense told him that the earth didn't rush up to meet the apple. So that meant the earth was exerting a force on the apple: that was his idea. This is a hypothesis because, at that point, Newton had nothing but his observations to back it up. He was saying, "This is what I think is going on here."

The next step in the scientific method is to test a hypothesis by carrying out experiments. Either those experiments don't give the results that were expected, in which case the hypothesis is wrong, or they do give the results that were expected, in which case the hypothesis is on the right track. We'll get to what happens then in a minute. More often than not, in the early stages of an idea, the answer isn't so cut and dry. And the experiment shows us we're sort of right – or at least not entirely wrong. Sometimes a wrong hypothesis points toward a better one.

In the case of Newton, his realization that the earth was exerting a force on the apple saw him test the idea in a series of pendulum experiments. He based his ideas on experiments and observations. He confirmed the principle of gravity that way and showed that gravity was independent of all other forces. What his experiments and calculations showed him was that he was heading in the right direction. He used Johannes Kepler's measurements of the movement of planets to apply his idea on a universal level. When those calculations and the physical experiments that followed could be replicated by others, then, and only then, did his hypothesis on gravity seem to be right. It graduated from a hypothesis on gravity to a theory of gravity.

In the real world, a theory is what we call an idea that we're not sure about. In science, a theory is as close as we get to being right: it's saying, "This is our best current explanation of what's happening and the experiments and calculations that led us to believe this can be repeated by anyone who has the equipment and wants to try."

Even with all those observations and experimental results, science doesn't say that this is the absolute truth. It leaves room for doubt because scientists know that other ideas can come along and either add to or supplant a theory as new information emerges, or as our mathematical understanding deepens. It was that room for doubt that allowed Einstein to give us a new way to think about gravity. He showed us that the earth doesn't exert a force, it creates a distortion in space-time that allows objects to fall toward it. The bigger the object, the bigger the distortion, and the greater the effect of gravity. As we can see, even with the best data, experiments, and maths, science leaves room for doubt.

To recap: a hypothesis is a guess that we test by observation, either experimental or mathematical. A theory is our best explanation based on repeated observations or calculations. That is the scientific method in a nutshell. It's how science has grown its evolving body of knowledge while allowing that body of knowledge to change. I'm not saying that shift is easy. There are lots of examples of hypotheses which turned out to be right that were shot down by the establishment of the day. That happens more commonly than you might think. Take Ignaz Semmelweis, a Hungarian physician who hypothesized that by washing their hands in between seeing patients, surgeons could reduce mortality rates in hospitals. Strange as it seems now, that theory took a while to catch on. Then there's Gregor Mendel, who developed the hypothesis of dominant and recessive genes but whose work didn't make any impact in his lifetime because it was poorly understood by the scientific elites of his day.

So yes, the scientific method doesn't work perfectly, but that doesn't mean we can't borrow from it in our lives.

A Loose Hypothesis

Of course, life isn't science. When we have an idea, we can't feasibly run experiments to test it before we take action. But I'd suggest we can apply the scientific method in two ways: first, by remembering that our ideas are hypotheses and, second, by bearing in mind that even when we think our hypothesis is sound, it becomes a working theory, not a fact.

To help us remember the status of our ideas, I find the term "loose hypothesis" helpful. That's because – in the real world – it's too easy to have an idea, think it's great, treat it as a hypothesis, and then act like it's a fact. In the businesses I've worked with I've seen an idea go through those stages in the space of about sixty seconds – what you might call paying lipservice to the scientific method. That's what I think of as a fixed hypothesis. We know we have a fixed hypothesis because we find ourselves arguing for it. If we share an idea at a meeting, let's say, and think we've offered it as a hypothesis, then during the discussion we find ourselves explaining to everyone why it's right, we've got a fixed hypothesis. The same thing is true if we offer a hypothesis and then find ourselves pulling people back to it time and again. What we're doing is subtly making the point that they're missing the wisdom of our idea. If you notice these behaviours, you're in the grip of a fixed hypothesis.

A loose hypothesis is different. It's presenting itself as one way to see the issue. Not the best way, just one way. It's tentative and it leaves room for other ideas. It's not seeking to remain intact; instead, it invites others to add to and revise it. It's a starting point. And because of that, it welcomes other points of view; it invites others to offer their own loose hypothesis.

We'll revisit loose hypotheses in Chapter 5, but for now my point is that a loose hypothesis can help us to navigate the fear of uncertainty, because it isn't saying it's right to start with. In that way, a loose hypothesis offers a key to escape the prison of needing to be right. And a path to trace through a brave new world of not knowing. It can show us the upside of accepting that we could be wrong.

A Possible Upside to Being Wrong

We've talked about the fear that can arise from realizing that we're wrong. But fear isn't the only possible emotion. More common, when I see people accept that they may be wrong in my consulting work, is a feeling of liberation.

Think about that for a second. If we can take it for granted that we're probably wrong, it means that we don't have to defend what we say anymore. If someone disagrees with us, we can show genuine curiosity and follow their reasoning to understand why they feel that way. If we can take it for granted that we're probably wrong, it means that we can course-correct without feeling like we're making a U-turn. If we can take it for granted that we're probably wrong, it means that we can make decisions faster because our entire sense of self isn't riding on being proved right.

What would it be like for you to operate with the feeling that you don't have to be right? How would it change your meetings? How would it affect your conversations with your peers and those you line-manage? And how would it affect your ability to stop doing things that don't work? I'm guessing that this way of looking at the world appeals to many. So the next question is, what do we have to do to live that way?

Cherished Ideas

Sir Arthur Quiller-Couch was an English author, poet, anthologist, literary critic, and professor of English at Cambridge University. He wrote under the nom de plume "Q" years before the letter found fame in Ian Fleming's James Bond series. Prolific in his day, Quiller-Couch offered perhaps the best piece of advice for any budding writer. It was this: "Murder your darlings."[4] Of course, he wasn't advocating the murder of our loved ones. His idea was more radical than that.

If you've ever laboured over a piece of writing – a report, an advertising campaign, a paper – you may already sense what Quiller-Couch is getting at. There are moments when you stumble on the perfect combination of words to express an idea. It's so perfect, you read it over and over. You can't believe you wrote

---

4 Arthur Quiller-Couch, *On the Art of Writing: Lectures Delivered in the University of Cambridge, 1913–1914* (Cambridge: Cambridge University Press, 1916). Available at: https://www.bartleby.com/190/12.html.

it because it's just so good. You read the paragraph that it sits in and, although it doesn't dawn on you at first, you slowly realize that the paragraph doesn't quite make sense. It feels awkward. You make adjustments to the surrounding text, but not to the sentence. Because the sentence is perfect, after all. You keep reworking the paragraph. You rearrange it; you change the paragraphs before and after. But no matter what you do, it doesn't work. You can't see a way out and although it bugs you, you let it go and move on. But when other people read the draft, they tell you the same thing: the paragraph doesn't quite work. So you labour some more, always rearranging the words around your perfect sentence.

The solution is obvious to any observer. I'm sure you see it too. Quiller-Couch is telling us the solution. The sentence is your darling. And it needs to be killed. It won't surprise you to hear that this idea isn't just useful for writers.

In the real world, murdering our darlings is the most graphic demonstration of our acceptance that we can be wrong. We call them darlings for a reason. We hold onto ideas or ways of doing things because they're precious to us. Maybe because we think they're great. Maybe because it took us hours to come up with them. Maybe because we think they work well. Living the behaviours that demonstrate flexibility of mind means being able to see the cherished ideas that we have. It asks us to see that those ideas may be good, but they may not be the best.

A fixed hypothesis is that cherished idea. That's why it's fixed in the first place. Ideas that we just throw out don't run the risk of becoming fixed hypotheses, because we're not attached to them. And because we're not attached to them, we can adapt or abandon them quickly.

I know that's a big ask. More often than not, if other people don't jump on board with our cherished idea, we think it must be because they don't understand it. And that's when we get trapped in a fixed hypothesis loop: we keep explaining our cherished idea and, as we do, we become more and entrenched in it, and more and more frustrated when other people still can't – or won't – understand.

That's the value of putting an idea out as a loose hypothesis. It helps us remind ourselves that the idea isn't the truth. It may not be right. It's just an idea. And ideas aren't monuments. They're jigsaw puzzle pieces that can be rearranged.

To think like that we need to live the second behaviour of flexibility of mind.

The Behaviours of Flexibility of Mind: Recognizing That There's More Than One Valid Idea

You've heard the saying that "there's more than one way to skin a cat". Animal cruelty aside, what that adage is getting at is that there's always more than one way to do something. Take painting a house, for example. Let's think of the different ways we could do that:

♦ Do it yourself with a brush, using a ladder to reach the higher parts.

♦ Do it yourself with a brush for the edges and a roller for the bigger areas, using a ladder to reach the higher parts.

♦ Do it yourself using scaffolding you set up and a brush.

♦ Do it yourself using scaffolding you set up and a brush for the edges and a roller for the bigger areas.

♦ Pay someone else to set up the scaffolding then do the painting yourself.

♦ Pay someone else to set up the scaffolding then pay someone different to do the painting.

♦ Pay the same person to set up the scaffolding and do the painting.

There are more ways than I've listed here, I'm sure, but let's stick with these. Each of these methods will get the job done. Some will be harder than others; some more expensive. But each one will achieve our goal. In that sense, each is a valid idea. Of course, we'll have a preference about the route we want to take. The point is that our preference is just that, since all the options will produce the same result.

How does that help us to operate as leaders, knowing we might be wrong? Because it means that we don't have to be paralyzed by indecision; we can make any decision knowing that it may not be the best way, but it will move us in the right direction. That's what the graphic below is showing:

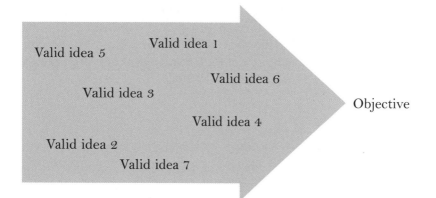

But we can take the idea further. Erwin Schrödinger was a physicist who designed the famous thought experiment about a cat in a box. Often called Schrödinger's cat, it plays out like this: Schrödinger places a cat in a box and seals it. In the box there's a vial of poison, a Geiger counter, and a radioactive sample. When the sample decays, the poison will be released.

Since we can't look into the box, Schrödinger's question is, how can we know whether the cat is dead or alive?

His answer: until we open the box and observe the cat, there's an equal probability that it could be dead or alive. For our purposes, what if it wasn't a cat in the box, but a variety of solutions to a problem? Each idea is workable and all are possible. So what we have are multiple valid ideas. And it's from this pool of valid ideas that we choose one to put into motion. Being able to hold that way of thinking is the essence of flexibility of mind.

Let's move away from painting and putting cats in boxes. Let's say we're looking to plan the strategic direction for our business for the next five years. If we understand that there's more than one valid idea for how the business can develop, then we know that each idea will provide us with the growth, the market share, and the capital investment we desire, and grow the culture we need. In that sense, each idea is valid. Some will achieve our desired results quickly, some slowly.

Too often we go into a strategy meeting without focusing on the multiple ways of doing something – the probability waves, you might say. Instead, we try to quickly decide the best or right way of doing something; in this case, developing a strategic focus. Like I said, that can mean our meetings become a battleground in the marketplace of ideas, with everyone fighting for their idea and pointing out the flaws in each other's. Then, the CEO makes their point and, more often than not, the rest of the team fall in line around it. That way of working doesn't produce the best ideas; it just means that the person with the loudest voice or most seniority wins.

Seeing the potential success of multiple valid ideas changes that dynamic. It does so because if there's a probability that several ideas will lead to success, it means that our idea is just one of many. And because we already know that we can be wrong at any time without even knowing it, we offer our idea accepting that it may not be the best one – it's just one way of doing it. We already know that we'll naturally think our idea is best because it fits with our world view, not because it's objectively true. So, although we love it, we offer it as a loose hypothesis. And that's true whether we're the CEO or the most junior member of staff.

And here's another thing. If we're clear about what we need our strategic focus to achieve and we know that multiple ideas could be successful, then it means that rather than argue, we can begin the meeting by figuring out which ideas are the valid ones.

That's easier than it seems. Because, don't forget, a valid idea is one that achieves our stated goal. And we can figure that out by being genuinely curious about how someone sees their idea doing that. We ask questions, not to interrogate, but to understand how an idea helps create the growth to get us to where we want to be five years from now. We can only do that if we acknowledge that there's more than one way to achieve our goal. What that means is we're weeding out the ideas that have a low probability of working – the non-valid ideas, you might say – from the ideas that can: the valid ideas.

"OK," Sam Strategy says. "So let's say I've done that. My team and I have sat down and figured out the range of valid ideas at our disposal. How does that help me make sure I've got the best idea if I could be wrong at any minute? All I've got is a bunch of valid ideas and no way to know which is most likely to succeed. If that's supposed to make me feel less scared about making decisions, then it hasn't."

He folds his arms, in a manner that, if not childlike, is certainly petulant.

He pauses and I think he's done. But he isn't.

"I don't have the resources to implement all of the ideas, so what do I do? You're causing more fear about making the wrong decision, not less. Now I have multiple ideas that I know will work, so how do I decide which to pursue?"

He frowns, but that doesn't make his point any less valid.

My goal isn't to create more fear about being wrong. So let's be clear about Sam's point. What he's saying is, "We don't want to do something the hardest way possible, we want to work smart and choose the best idea. How do we do that knowing we might be wrong?"

To answer that we need to move on to the next behaviour of flexibility of mind.

The Behaviours of Flexibility of Mind: Creatively Combining Ideas

Back in the early days of Buddhism there was a problem. After the Buddha's death there were so many interpretations of his teaching that different groups or lineages sprouted up, each claiming to adhere to the true teachings of Buddha. There were so many lineages that the fledgling movement risked diluting itself out of existence. To prevent this, it was decided that the heads – or lamas – of different lineages would debate each other in what you could think of as a debate to the death. Whichever lama showed that his philosophy explained and encapsulated the other's would win the debate.

"But how is that a debate to the death?" you may ask. Well, because when that lama won, the other lama and all his followers became followers of the winning lama. "The death" was of the lineage. And that is the myth of how the many lineages of Buddhism were consolidated.

I don't know if that story's true or not. I've heard it countless times in Buddhist circles, but have never seen it referenced. But that doesn't matter. What really matters is the concept that one idea can explain and encompass another. Here's another way to think about valid ideas:

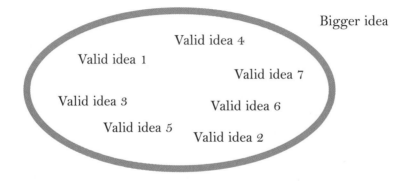

Notice what the circle represents: a bigger idea. In the graphic on page 106, all the valid ideas are real and open to us: probable, you might say. Just like Schrödinger couldn't know the fate of his cat until he opened the box, there's no way to know which idea is best until we try one. If it goes badly, we know it wasn't the best idea. If it goes well, we know it worked, but we don't know whether it was the best possible option. That's Sam's point.

But what the above graphic is showing us is that many valid ideas exist within a bigger idea. It's like a three-bird roast of ideas. Except in this case we're not stuffing two birds into a third to create a questionable concoction. We're combining ideas to find a bigger idea, a hybrid idea, so to speak.

The advantage is that we can take the best parts of multiple ideas to create an idea that we can be sure – but not certain – is the best option available to us at the time. That doesn't mean we can't change course down the road. What it means is (to address Sam's point) that we can feel confident about what we're doing and avoid the existential angst of not knowing.

In truth, it does more than offer a salve for our insecurities. It gives us the chance to build bridges between ideas. To see that the ideas of our colleagues are not as far apart from ours as they may seem. In fact, looking for the bridges between valid ideas connects not just the ideas, but the team, because we're intentionally looking for the wisdom in each other's ideas.

Challenge: Building Bridges

The success of finding the bigger idea depends on two things: one is our willingness to admit the advantages of another idea. It also means acknowledging that there are holes in our idea that can be plugged by another idea.

For some, that in itself is a struggle. If we're living the six attributes, practising the behaviour of generosity of spirit I talked about in Chapter 2 is a good place to begin overcoming that struggle. Building bridges depends on our ability to see the bridge between ideas in the first place. And that's something we can approach either by problem solving or with a leap of creativity.

This challenge is all about the problem-solving approach. You can do this by yourself or with your team. You'll need a wall or a whiteboard, some sticky notes, some marker pens, and multiple valid ideas about a problem you're trying to solve. I'm taking it as read that you've got those multiple valid ideas. If not, it's as simple as holding a brainstorm meeting or inviting your team to email ideas. From there, whittle these down to the ones that meet the requirements of your goal. Voila: multiple valid ideas.

Now write those ideas on sticky notes. If they are complex or long, write the stages of the ideas in a column on individual sticky notes – that'll make it easier for you to move them around.

Measure each idea against your desired outcome. See where ideas come up short, and where ideas excel. Maybe rewrite the favoured ideas on a different-coloured sticky note – let's say green – so all your best ideas are on the same colour sticky notes. Leave them in their original columns. Now you should have columns of sticky notes with the occasional green one. The green sticky notes are the elements of your bigger idea.

Now the challenge begins (yes, that was all pre-work).

Can you build bridges between all the green sticky notes – the best parts of your valid ideas – to create one bigger idea?

If it helps, leave the green ones where they are and copy them out again. This time set them on a separate wall.

Look at each green sticky note closely. What makes that idea excel? What would need to be in place for that element to work? Are there other green sticky notes that would support that element? How can it be combined with other green sticky notes? It may be that you need to come up with additional ideas to connect the green sticky notes That's OK; you don't have to connect all the green items, just enough so that you and your team feel you have a strong idea made up of components of your valid ideas.

Keep measuring the bigger idea against your objective as you go. We're not building bridges as an intellectual exercise, we're looking for a bigger idea that fulfils our objective.

When you're done, find a quiet place where you can reflect on the challenge. What was the experience like for you? Did you find yourself scratching your head and looking at the green sticky notes blankly? Did the bridges feel forced? Did you find yourself adding to the idea as you built those bridges? Did it flow easily?

If you found it tough, don't be too hard on yourself. This is a muscle we're strengthening. When we're used to seeing ideas as either good or bad, quickly dismissing options and moving on to the next, or rushing toward a final idea, spending time to hone an idea can feel awkward – even uncomfortable. And that's OK. The difference between building a skill and building a mindset is that a skill is a technique we can apply; a mindset is a different way of seeing things. The reason we work on mindset is because if we apply a new skill with a process mindset, let's say, we turn that skill into a process. If we apply a new way of looking at something to a problem, it doesn't become a process; it allows us to see the components of the problem differently. That's why this takes time. And that's why it doesn't help to be hard on ourselves.

Creativity and the Bigger Idea

If it helps, think about the last challenge like a game: a creativity game. In the land of creativity we can take two creative approaches to solving a challenge. The first we're perhaps all familiar with. We get a piece of paper, sit down, and start working on solving the problem. Maybe we write out ideas, think through the merits and negatives of each, and work toward a useable idea we think will work. Maybe we use trial and error, or build a model of what we think we can do and see how it holds up. Whatever we do, the thing these approaches have in common is that we're working in a linear way toward solving a problem. That's a form of creativity but it isn't the only one.

Back in the first century, the Roman architect Vitruvius relayed a story of how Archimedes of Syracuse tested a golden wreath. The wreath was a dedication to the gods, and though the king of Syracuse had paid for it on the understanding it was made of pure gold, he suspected the craftsman had used an alloy of gold and silver. As the story goes, Archimedes – mathematician, philosopher, and inventor – puzzled on that one for days.[5] Then, stumped and near exhaustion, he climbed into a bath that had been prepared for him. As he did the water overflowed and he shouted "heurēka", meaning "I've found it" – the origin of our word "eureka".

What Archimedes had discovered was the principle of hydrostatics. According to Vitruvius, he reasoned that he could measure the gold content by filling a bowl with water and measuring the amount of water displaced when he put the amount of gold that the wreath should contain in the water. Then he could put the wreath in the water and see if it displaced the same amount of water. If it did, it was pure gold; if not, it wasn't.

---

5   Joseph Gwilt (tr.), *The Architecture of Marcus Vitruvius Pollio in Ten Books* (London: Priestley and Weale, 1826), pp. 264–265. Available at: https://archive.org/details/architectureofma00vitr/page/n7.

Just as with all good stories, there's doubt about whether that really happened. What's important about the story is how Archimedes connected several ideas: he understood that water is displaced by weight; he knew he could measure weight through volume; he knew that different metals have different masses. And he connected these pieces of knowledge, not by problem solving but in a moment of insight.

That's called insight creativity. These two creative approaches – problem solving and insight – were studied by a husband and wife team of psychologists. Sarnoff A. Mednick and Martha T. Mednick developed the random associates test (RAT), which asked the participant to connect three words with a fourth that can make a compound noun with the other three.[6] Here's one example:

railroad, class, girl

The challenge is to find the word that fits with all three.

The question is: how do you go about solving the challenge? Do you think of a word and try it against each of the three? Say "friend". Girlfriend makes sense; class friend could be a thing. Railroad friend is not a thing. So friend is out. We could do that with a bunch of words, trying different options against the three until we find one that works.

The second approach is what happened to Archimedes: we could have a moment of insight. When that happens, we often can't explain our thinking or we simply say, "It just came to me." What happens is we look at a challenge and see the answer. It might happen when we take a break after looking at something for a long time, or it might happen right away. Either way, it feels like the solution just pops into our heads. That's insight creativity. Maybe that happened to you with the RAT example, and you

---

6   Sarnoff A. Mednick and Martha T. Mednick, *Examiner's Manual: Remote Associates Test: College and Adult Forms 1 and 2* (Boston, MA: Houghton Mifflin, 1967).

connected those three words with working: working railroad, working class, working girl (this was devised in 1967, after all).

Mednick and Mednick used their RATs and developed their work to describe creative thought. They felt RATs predicted a person's creative ability. But we've learnt a lot since 1967. Dr Simone Ritter of Radboud University Nijmegen has shown us through her experiments that just by disrupting our everyday activities – the route we take home, the way we make our food, the order in which we clean our house – we can grow our creativity.[7] That matters because flexibility of mind depends on making creative connections.

In my consulting work, almost everyone I meet agrees creativity is needed. And yet most people also tell me that they don't feel creative or don't have time to be. For many, creativity is something that happens over there or has little to do with the often process-driven world we inhabit. "Sure, Google and Amazon thrive on creativity," they might say, "but we're selling insurance here."

What I've found in business – time and again – is that there's not only room to be creative, there's a need to be. Why? Because if we want to liberate ourselves from the fear of living in a world where nothing is certain, then pursuit of the bigger idea is a pretty good way to do that. Although the idea of creativity at work may sound like an even bigger leap into uncertainty, what Ritter is telling us is that we can learn to be more creative. All it takes is a willingness to disrupt the way in which we usually do things. We can practise that at first by disrupting the routine in our everyday lives. The more we do that, the more open we become to seeing new ways of doing things. And that means we've developed a new mindset.

---

7   Simone M. Ritter, et al. "The Creative Brain: Corepresenting Schema Violations Enhances TPJ Activity and Boosts Cognitive Flexibility", *Creativity Research Journal*, 26(2) (2014): 144–150.

The Revolutionary Idea

But why stop there? Remember the graphic on page 110 about the bigger idea? What if there's an even bigger idea: a revolutionary idea?

What if, once we combine our valid ideas, the bigger idea we come up with is just one bigger idea in a river network of bigger ideas – all moving toward the sea of a revolutionary idea? Kind of like this:

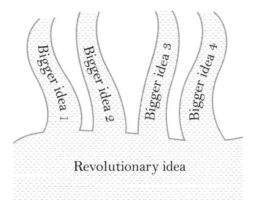

Revolutionary idea

"Now just wait one minute," Penny Process might say. "What are you talking about now?" She furrows her brow. She's not angry, I'd say just frustrated. "It's one thing to come up with a bigger idea, I can kind of see the point in that – I mean who doesn't want to make sure that they have a solid idea before they begin? But a revolutionary idea!" She throws her hands in the air as she says it, "When is enough enough?!"

But it's not really a question. Not the way she says it.

I get it. For someone like Penny, who's worked with processes their whole life, processes are comfortable and familiar; they usually work for them. Maybe they work most of the time.

She opens her mouth, because she's seen her opening and she's going to take it, "So if they work, why change it?! Especially for the endless process you're offering."

Again, it's not intended as a question. This time it's pure frustration.

And Penny is right. If our process works for us most of the time, why bother doing something else? Well, because if we truly know that we can be wrong, and if we truly want to make the best decisions possible despite that, then we owe it to ourselves to find a way to make those decisions.

"But haven't we just done that?" Penny Process asks. "We've combined our valid ideas and we've come up with a bigger idea. What's the problem with that?"

The problem is that world view thing, because the bigger idea – the one we've arrived at having combined all our ideas, the one we really like now – is still going through the filter of our world view. And because it has passed through that filter, my guess is that we're comfortable with it. That comfort is our clue that the idea isn't revolutionary. It can't be because revolutions are many things, but comfortable isn't one of them.

The bigger idea will be different to our current idea, but it may only represent an incremental change. Let's say I manage a factory that makes gizmos. We currently make 1,000 gizmos a day. The bigger idea could lead me to streamline production processes; it might mean buying another gizmo machine, or shopping around for cheaper suppliers. If that's our bigger idea, we're doing the same thing, but quicker and more efficiently. Nothing wrong with that. With those improvements we could make 2,000 gizmos a day. No one's baulking at that: it's a 100% improvement in performance.

A revolutionary idea is different in that we set our sights much higher. Let's say 50,000 gizmos a day. We could streamline our processes as much as we like, but we're never going to meet that objective. To achieve that goal, we need something else: a completely different way of working. And we can find that different way of working by first developing a different way of thinking, which is where the six attributes come in. We can be genuinely curious about what's possible. We can be flexible in our thinking to acknowledge that our bigger idea is just one of many bigger ideas. That leaves the door open to discover the revolutionary idea. But before we go too much further, let's define the term.

What is a Revolutionary Idea?

Put simply, a revolutionary idea is one that stretches us beyond our comfort zone. It isn't incremental change – or evolutionary change, if you prefer – instead, it's a conceptual change in the way we operate. And because it requires us to operate differently, it will have the hallmarks of a revolutionary idea. It will leave us feeling nervous and excited in equal measure: nervous at the thought of doing it, and excited by the promise it holds.

The revolutionary idea could be something that crosses our minds as we work toward the bigger idea. We'll know if that's true because it'll be the idea that we shy away from. And we do that for the reason I just mentioned: it makes us feel nervous. But that nervous and excited feeling is a signpost: it's directing us to something important.

Let's think about that for second. Why does a revolutionary idea leave us nervous? It may be because it's difficult to do, but we all know that just because something is difficult doesn't mean we shouldn't do it. It may be that there are obstacles – both cultural and systemic – in our business that makes us think we can't do it, or that it won't be well-received if we do. That's the mentality that sees us doing pretty much the same thing over and over again.

What a revolutionary idea is doing is challenging our world view. The reason we shy away is because, in our current outlook, the revolutionary idea is impossible. If we don't question our world view when it tells us that our business can't be systemically changed – that the culture can't be shifted – then what we're doing is the opposite of living the six attributes. We're arguing for a point of view. To be clear, the reason why that point of view seems worth arguing for is because we think it's right. And we think it's right because it fits our world view.

The willingness to pursue the revolutionary idea, then, is a statement to the world. What we're saying is that we're willing not just to see our challenges differently, but to be uncomfortable as we do things differently. Implementing a revolutionary idea means being willing to change our behaviour. And we're willing to do that because we can see that whatever behaviours got us here won't allow us to make that revolutionary idea happen. In short, we can only find a revolutionary idea by being willing to think differently, and we can only make it a reality by doing things differently.

"OK," Penny Process says, "I'll accept that seeing things differently and being willing to do things differently is a core quality of leadership, so no argument there. But down here in the real world, it's a small jump from doing things differently to failing completely." She pauses – not frustrated now, just thoughtful. "So, not to be rude, but I'm not sure that's a risk I'm willing to take."

Revolutionary Ideas and Failure

Penny's point is one we can't argue with. We don't get paid to fail. We get paid to make things happen. It's not a tough point to understand. I'd be lying if I said there's no chance of failing when we pursue a revolutionary idea. Trying out new ways of thinking, new ideas, or new behaviours all come with an inherent risk. I could say that this doesn't mean we shouldn't do it; or that failing isn't failure, it's a learning opportunity; or any number of other platitudes, but none of them would remove the real fear or the consequences of messing up in our professional (or personal) lives.

But what if we could pursue a revolutionary idea and not fail? What would happen then? That's possible because a revolutionary idea pushes us to exceed what we think is possible. Let's go back to the gizmo factory example. Remember that the revolutionary idea was to make 50,000 gizmos a day? Any self-respecting leader would say that this is beyond an aspirational target; it's setting ourselves up to fail.

But what would we have to do to make that happen? Well, maybe after a lot of brainstorming, combining valid ideas, and combining bigger ideas we come up with the revolutionary one. Let's say that idea is to refocus our factory as an assembly facility. In this model, we'd outsource the manufacturing of parts to multiple companies on mid-term contracts, with each signing a non-disclosure agreement. That allows us to protect our product by not having one company producing all the components, and allows us to maintain competition among manufacturers to ensure the best price point. That's scalable because we can add as many companies as we want to the roster of manufacturers, and scale back if there's a reduction in demand. With a revolutionary idea like that, risk is managed because we can adjust at any time. Even if things don't go as well as planned, and after three months we've only hit 50% of our goal, we're still making 25,000 gizmos a day: 23,000 more a day than we would with our bigger idea.

Even if we fail, it turns out, we succeed.

Revolutionary Implementation

But a revolutionary idea isn't just about doing more; it's about living the attributes and behaviours we're talking about in these pages. As a consultant, my job isn't just to help businesses increase the number of gizmos they make, it's also about helping the people in them to grow and to embed the practical application of the six attributes. That's because, once employees are armed with the six attributes, the businesses I work with are equipped not just to solve the challenges of today, but the challenges coming down the road we don't even know about yet. Once we embody the six attributes, they're ours to keep.

For that mindset to filter through a business, how we choose to implement a revolutionary idea matters. If we implement it using a process we've used hundreds of times in the past, we run the risk of the wider business not seeing the idea as revolutionary. And that means though they'll implement it – it's their job after all – they won't feel that things have changed. And that means no shift in mindset because the attributes aren't being cascaded through our business.

Revolutionary ideas need revolutionary implementation, because that sends a message. What message? That things are different around here. That we don't just have a new strategy, we have a new way of working. By developing a revolutionary implementation plan, we're demonstrating the new behaviours that we, as a leadership team, are living, and that we prize in the business.

What Does Revolutionary Implementation Look Like?

The answer to that is simply, it's different to what you currently do.

If you normally send out a communication over the intranet, reveal a new strategy in a general meeting, or consult with employees in workstreams, then rolling out a revolutionary idea that way won't work. I'm not saying it can't ever work, but if that's the way you currently do things, then it's not the way to roll out a revolutionary idea.

You need something else. Something revolutionary, in fact.

But this is a revolutionary implementation plan, don't forget, so what we need isn't just a fun or different way to get the message out: we need a different way to actually implement that idea. And that means finding different ways to operationalize the idea.

It could mean creating action teams, or creating network teams to connect departments – so they work as one unit. It could mean having managers work within their departments to do a process analysis and determine the best way of implementing the idea. It could be any of these options, or something completely different. The point is that the way your idea is implemented needs to be different from what you normally do. That's the only requirement.

Of course, finding that different way takes flexibility of mind.

Revolutionary Implementation to Create Behaviour Change

If you're up for it, part of that implementation could encourage not just a different way of working – for example, following a new process – but a different way of behaving. Let's say your revolutionary implementation involves creating network teams – non-hierarchical structures that allow for small teams to have the flexibility and agility to adapt and implement your revolutionary idea. While that might be scary for Penny Process – what with people working outside of established systems – it also creates the need for teams to operate differently, which leads to a change in the way they have to behave, which leads to a change in how they think about their role, their company, and what's possible. In short, it creates a shift in mindset. So not only do you have a revolutionary idea, you have the beginnings of a shift in your business culture.

When the revolutionary idea is implemented and the dust has settled on it, the shift in the way your business operates will still be there – all because you pursued flexibility of mind.

That's the thing about the six attributes: if we shift our own mindset, it shifts the mindset of those around us.

Challenge: Everyday Creativity

I said before that flexibility of mind is a close cousin of creativity. So let's round this chapter off with a creativity challenge.

I mentioned Dr Simone Ritter and her work on variety and creativity a few pages ago. This challenge is based on an experiment she developed to grow creativity by disrupting everyday tasks. Think of it less as a one-off challenge and more as ongoing flexing of your creativity muscle.

The ability to adapt is essentially a creative leap. It means jumping into the unknown. The hard way of doing that is to wait for a high-risk situation, which forces us to adapt – the strategic direction of our business, let's say. The likelihood of demonstrating creativity under those circumstances is slim. That's because when our back's up against the wall, and there's lots at stake, it doesn't feel like a good time to experiment, take a risk, or try something new. In this case, "something new" is a creative approach. But under those circumstances we do what most people do: we default to tried-and-tested ideas, and we draw on familiar behaviours because familiar equals safe.

If creativity is something that we rarely engage with, it will be unfamiliar. That makes it uncomfortable and means we shy away from it. The irony is that, in business, new and innovative approaches are not just helpful but necessary. That has always been true, but in today's world that moves at the speed of the internet, innovation helps us to keep our business relevant. So the more we practise creativity, the more familiar we feel with it, and the more likely we'll be to think creatively in higher-stake situations.

That's one reason behind this challenge, but it isn't the only one. The other difficulty we face in adopting a creative approach is when we're expected to be creative right now. Putting people on the spot is the best way to create inflexibility of mind and inhibit their creativity. Doubt that? Then pick up a pen right now and sketch any picture you like. Anything at all.

If that request left you staring blankly at the page – or you drew a house, a car, or something similarly conventional – that's a good example of what can happen when you put people on the spot: they resort to what they already know.

So this challenge is about making the creative leap easier by inviting creativity into our everyday lives. The more we do it, the easier it feels; and the easier it feels, the more we can draw on our creativity. The more we familiarize ourselves with drawing on it in small ways, the more likely we are to use flexibility of mind when the stakes are higher.

And we do that by making creativity ordinary. So when we're called on to be adaptable we come up with ideas easily because, first, we have begun to have fun with ideas and learnt not to judge them (or ourselves); and, second, we're used to coming up with different ways of doing things.

That's what this challenge is all about: everyday creativity.

Find something that you do with ease. So much ease, in fact, that you don't even think about how you do it. It could be anything at all. Something in your personal or professional life: driving home, baking a cake, washing the car, making a sandwich, or formatting a document. Start this challenge with one of those activities.

The challenge is to do that thing differently. We want the same outcome, but by different means. Let's say it's making a cup of tea. Maybe you normally boil the kettle, set a cup out, put a teabag in the cup, add some sugar, pour the water, let the teabag steep, squeeze out the bag, throw the bag in the bin, and then add milk to the cup. Now think of another way to do it.

How about if you boil the water in a pot? Turn off the stove then add the teabag to the pot. Mix the tea around while it steeps and then add the sugar. Then set out a cup. Add some milk to the cup, and then pour the tea from the pot into the cup without squeezing the bag.

Just a different way to do an ordinary task, that's all.

Because this is a challenge, I'm not asking you to *think* of different ways, I'm asking you to *do* your task in as many different ways as you can. In this case, each time you make a cup of tea see if you can find yet another way of doing it. When you've explored all your possible ways of making a cup of tea, move onto another task on your list. And keep going.

As a way to monitor the progress of your creativity (and therefore your flexibility of mind), note down a number from one to ten before you start this challenge. One is not very creative and ten means you're an inventive genius. Keep giving yourself a number every week and see if your mindset toward creativity shifts.

Flexibility of Mine, Flexibility of Others

The joy of growing our flexibility of mind isn't just that we get to think differently. Yes, we get to see the possibilities, to combine ideas to come up with bigger, even revolutionary ideas. And, yes, that's fun. But the real joy of flexibility of mind isn't what it does to our thinking. When we demonstrate flexibility in our thinking, we ignite possibility for those around us.

Our teams, our business, our world isn't just about choosing between staid answers and standard options. We're working with others to find solutions that may never have been tried before. And the beautiful thing about that is it encourages courageous thinking from everyone we come into contact with.

Think about that: a company full of people looking for a revolutionary idea.

Flexibility of Mind Reminders

◆ The behaviours of flexibility of mind are entertaining the possibility of being wrong, recognizing that there's more than one valid idea, and creatively combining ideas.

◆ A loose hypothesis reminds us that our view is one of many.

◆ A cherished idea makes flexibility of mind difficult.

◆ Many valid ideas can be combined into a bigger idea.

◆ A revolutionary idea stretches us beyond our comfort zone.

◆ If we're nervous and excited by an idea, it's likely to be a revolutionary one.

◆ Revolutionary ideas need revolutionary implementation.

Chapter 4
Resilience

Never Again

She's twelve years old and sitting in front of Mr Happel. He's holding a wooden block in each hand. Both have a large number 1 painted on each of their six different-coloured sides. She looks down at the desk. There are three other blocks: one bears the minus symbol, another the equals symbol, and a third the 0 symbol. A moment ago the two 1 blocks were also on the desk – arranged as a problem waiting to be solved. But Mr Happel raised them. Maybe to help her. Maybe to make her feel even sillier. She knows where this is going before the teacher opens his mouth. "Pay attention now, Nicola," Mr Happel says. "It's important."

But that's a lie. This isn't important. What's important to Nicola is narcolepsy – falling asleep as soon as the exam began, and then being treated like she was only smart enough to write her own name. What's important is feeling weak, like staring out on a lifetime knowing it will always be like this. She rubs her temples, fingers at the ready to rub out any tears the instant they emerge.

What's most important is finding a way out of the hole she's in: being the pupil that everyone thinks is so backward she needs blocks to help her understand that 1 - 1 = 0.

She looks into her teacher's eyes. She wants to scream at him. Scream something that will make him see. But see what? She stares at the minus block. To make him see her. But that can't happen. Not while she's the falling-asleep girl, or the can't-finish-a-test girl.

And that's when it happens. In that moment looking at the minus block she makes a decision. It doesn't form as a plan in her twelve-year-old head. It's just a realization. But more than that: a feeling. It begins in her stomach, then radiates out to her whole body.

The girl in front of Mr Happel smiles and it throws him for a second. "Did she find the answer?" he wonders. He looks at her closely, nodding to encourage her to say it. He repeats the word zero in his head as if somehow he can beam it into hers.

But she's not thinking about the sum in front of her. It's the idea that's filling her body that she's thinking about. "I am never going to feel this weak again." She raises her eyes and locks them onto Mr Happel's. Never again.

It begins by reading. She learns that narcolepsy can be helped with exercise and diet. So she trains. She trains in taekwondo. She gets better, she gets stronger. She's fighting. It keeps the narcolepsy at bay. But she doesn't stop. She studies hard at school. So hard that when she's not training she's studying. And she keeps fighting. She wins medals. She represents England internationally. She wins the world title in taekwondo. She's injured. And she keeps fighting. She makes it to the final fifteen to represent Great Britain in taekwondo at the 2016 Olympics. She loses out on that chance because of her injury. And she keeps fighting. She moves into K1 kickboxing. She wins the UK southern area title. She becomes the British amateur K1 champion. And she keeps fighting. She turns professional. She wins her first professional British K1 title on her fifth fight by unanimous decision. She's not weak anymore. She's stronger than she's ever been. She isn't that weak child. She's so much more.

Resilience Road

The fighter in that story is real. Her name is Nicola Barke, and I'm proud to say that she's my niece. "There's something about some people," so the story goes, "that gives them an edge in life." Determination we might call it, and that's certainly part of it. Then there's the rising in the face of relentless knock-backs. That's more than determination. That's being willing to fall down, get up, dust ourselves off, and get at it again. That quality is resilience, and it's what Nicola has in spades. Great as Nicola is (and, of course, I think she's the greatest), she wasn't born that way. I tell her story because for everyone who ever walked down Resilience Road there's a story just like that: a moment when they made the decision that changed their world. They set their sights on a target and march toward it. One foot in front of the other, day after day.

As I said in the introduction, growing the six attributes is hard. If you've tried some of the challenges in this book so far, you might have had experience of that already. So here's the question: if it's so hard, why bother? Why practise flexibility of mind, or enterprise thinking – heck, why practise any of it – if it might take years to master?

Whatever your answer to that question, it's why resilience is an attribute of a leadership mindset. Because, as we'll see, what resilience amounts to is finding that answer for ourselves and using it as a reason to keep going, even when it's hard. Especially when it's hard. Like steel, our leadership mindset is forged in fire: except our furnace is one of setbacks, disappointments, failure, out and out rejection, and, yes, moments of joy. For us to keep going through all of that means we have to have a pretty good answer to the question I just posed. You don't need to find your answer now. Read the rest of the chapter, and I promise that we'll come back to it.

What is Resilience?

Before we try to answer that question, let's have a go at a slightly easier one: what is resilience?

In a 2007 paper, a team led by psychologist Angela Duckworth exchanged the word "resilience" with the more evocative "grit", which they define as "perseverance and passion for long-term goals. Grit," they continue, "entails working strenuously toward challenges, maintaining effort and interest over years despite failure, adversity, and plateaus in progress. The gritty individual approaches achievement as a marathon; his or her advantage is stamina. Whereas disappointment or boredom signals to others that it is time to change trajectory and cut losses, the gritty individual stays the course."[1]

Their paper goes on to tell us that resilience – more than other physical or mental ability – is the best indicator of success. Think about that. Remember Thomas Edison's famous "Genius is 1% inspiration and 99% perspiration"?[2] What Edison is telling us is to stick with it. And the most important ingredient that allows us to stick at something is the mindset to recover when we're down: it's resilience. Without it, the best of intentions are

---

1   Angela Duckworth, Christopher D. Peterson, Michael Matthews, and Dennis R. Kelly, "Grit: Perseverance and Passion for Long-Term Goals", *Journal of Personality and Social Psychology*, 92(6) (2007): 1087–1101 at 1087–1088.
2   See https://quoteinvestigator.com/2012/12/14/genius-ratio/#return-note-5018-8 for a discussion of the sources.

just that – intentions. With it, our ability to realize who we truly are and what we're capable of improves dramatically.

Without putting too fine a point on it, anyone can keep marching forward when everything's going their way. That doesn't take resilience or the other five attributes. To keep going when the outcome is in doubt, when we keep getting turned down, when our last chance has passed us by again; that's the definition of resilience and it's what makes the difference.

Before we begin to feel that maybe we don't have that kind of grit, let's remind ourselves that – just like a leadership mindset – resilience isn't a God-given gift. It can be gained with effort and practice over time. Before we get to how, let's dispel a myth.

Myth: Confidence is the Key to Resilience

It isn't. Although confidence is a great thing to have, trying to gain it as a precursor to action isn't just close to impossible, it's a red herring. That's because confidence isn't the driver of resilience, it's the by-product.

If we're trying to get something done but we keep getting knocked back in the pursuit, perhaps it seems obvious that the thing that will keep us going is confidence in our idea and in our own ability to make it happen. To be clear, I'm not saying that these things aren't helpful. What I am querying is how likely is it that when we have our first idea, we're fully confident in it and in our ability to carry it out?

Isn't it more likely that as we take a few steps toward our goal – and meet with a little initial success – our confidence deepens? We may look at someone who works relentlessly toward their goal and admire their level of confidence. Perhaps they are a confident person. But how did they develop that level of confidence? By being touched by God or by building it with each small success?

You can guess where I stand on that question. Too often we lose confidence in an idea or strategic direction at the first obstacle. We attribute that feeling to a flaw in the idea, or in ourselves, when perhaps neither is true. What if obstacles actually help us to sharpen the idea? What if these barriers are telling us that we're jumping too far, that taking a smaller step may be more likely to succeed and help us gain momentum?

If you've read Chapters 1 and 2, you'll already know that obstacles and opposition aren't the end point. They're the chance to improve and the beginning of the next round. And it's the willingness to remain flexible which helps grow our confidence in ourselves and the idea. That's why confidence is a red herring: it doesn't get us to where we want to go, it grows out of our attempts to get there. But before we pull ourselves up by the bootstraps and march toward our goal, let's think about why so many people who do just that don't create leaders of others, and may not even be effective leaders themselves.

A Cautionary Tale

The streetlamps came on hours ago and the yellow light is pouring into her office. Outside, the hallways are clear – they have been since 3pm. A few faces poked around the door, wished her a good evening, then high-tailed it out of there. Not one foot crossed the threshold. Why would they? Then they'd have to stay and talk. And what would they say? That they saw this coming? That they warned her a year ago? Jessica looks at the screen. It's all she's been doing for the last five hours. Hoping that the numbers would change so that the graph for the last three quarters doesn't descend at a perfect forty-five-degree angle. So perfect that it could be a page out of a textbook from her MBA programme. How could she have missed this?

She pushed for the expansion. She had the data to prove that it would allow them to double production. With an expanding market they could be selling twice as much with a 26% bump in fixed costs. It's basic maths, how can she have got it so wrong? She was sure she was right. Everyone told her she wasn't getting the right data, but she was sure they were just making excuses and couldn't stomach the risk. So she pushed. And when nothing moved, she went to board meetings and pushed harder. When that didn't work, she went straight to the major investors.

The major stakeholders said they loved her tenacity. That the company needed more doers, more risk-takers. She won them over alright. By dint of sheer willpower. And when the expansion began she knew that she was leading the company into a new future. A better future for everyone. She gets up, walks to the doorway and looks back into her office. The desk lamp is still on when she turns to leave. Of course they'll fire her. They'll ask her to clear out her desk, but there's no need. There's not a single thing in there she needs.

There's a difference between resilience and pig-headedness. Pig-headedness is about pushing an idea through come hell or high water. It's related to the behaviour of resilience, but only distantly. In fact, you could say that pig-headedness is resilience without a leadership mindset. Without the other attributes, resilience runs the risk of making a person closed to learning; inflexible in their thinking; unaware of the impact of their actions on colleagues and the business; and determined to push ahead on their own without empowering others to act and share the initiative. If we're ploughing forward like that, that's the definition of being pig-headed.

So although resilience is a great quality to have, it works best alongside the other attributes.

Guarding Against Pig-Headedness

Percy Pighead raises a finger, "OK," he says, "I admit it. I have been known to charge in bull-in-china-shop-like when I have the bit between my teeth. I'm not saying that's always bad." He smirks, "You've got to break a few dishes if you want to make omelettes."

His metaphor makes no sense, but maybe there's a good idea on the horizon so I let it pass.

He raises both hands skyward, as if I have a gun pointing at him. "I get it, that's not leadership." He sighs, "It's just that when everything's pointing me in one direction, I'd be a fool not to fight for it."

Here's a thought. Is everything really directing you down a certain path, or just the things you're choosing to look at? That's the difference between resilience and pig-headedness. Resilience adapts to roadblocks and setbacks because it sees the options and is willing to learn along the way. Pig-headedness just ploughs ahead.

"OK, OK," Percy says, "I'm trying to understand. So, tell me, how do I see the options?"

Turtle Earth

Here's a question: is it possible to say that we're seeing all the options if we hold onto a world view that's objectively not true – that the earth sits on the back of a giant turtle, for example?

If that's our position, can we really say that we're open to seeing all the options? Let's say our Turtle Earth proponent spends hours on the internet, poring over NASA pictures of earth from space; they join chat groups where they share their view of Turtle Earth with others; they hold Turtle Earth seminars; they post their Turtle Earth "research" on Facebook and get into tirades on Twitter. Can we say that they are open to seeing all the options?

Let's say we encounter this Turtle Earth proponent on a street corner. They ask us to stop and, because they seem earnest and harmless (and because we have a few minutes to kill), we do. What might we say to help them see the error in their thinking? We might point to a lack of evidence for the position. But they'd counter that with the grainy picture that supposedly comes from an undoctored NASA image which shows the faintest outline of a turtle beak. So we try a different approach, and ask what the turtle eats. To which the believer smiles (they've heard this idea too many times to count), and replies that although it looks like a normal turtle, it's actually a cosmic turtle which doesn't ingest food but instead gets its energy from the sun.

And on and on it goes. Whatever we say, the Turtle Earth believer has a counter. My question is: what is the mechanism that allows them to think they're being reasonable? Because, don't forget, they really believe that Turtle Earth is true. The easy answer is to say that the believer must be a fool. But all the research they've done and all the information they've memorized seems to suggest they're not. So what is the mechanism that allows them to go through life with that perspective?

Confirmation Bias and Sheep Farming

Sheep farmers have to divide their flock for many reasons. It might be to medicate them, to separate ewes from lambs before shearing, or simply to sort them by fleece type to make packing fleeces easier after shearing. Whatever the reason, many sheep farmers use a gate system to separate the sheep. In its simplest form, it could look like this:

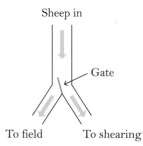

The farmer can swing the gate to either side depending on the sheep approaching.

"Great, thanks for the sheep farming lesson," Percy Pighead says. "I asked about how to see the options, remember?"

The point is that there's a similar system playing out in our world. Except for us, it's not sheep we're separating; it's the ideas we want to believe in from those we don't. This is how it might look for our Turtle Earth believer:

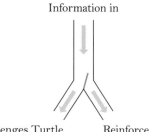

It's a way to think about a phenomenon called confirmation bias. For our Turtle Earth believer it works like this: for all the information coming down the alley – newspapers, conversations, books, you name it – the gate swings to one side or the other depending on whether that information reinforces the belief in Turtle Earth or not. If the information coming in supports the Turtle Earth belief, then the gate allows the information in. But if that information contradicts Turtle Earth, the gate blocks it, and the believer can ignore or dismiss it. The result? Our Turtle Earth believer maintains their world view, despite evidence to the contrary being available.

Percy Pighead nods silently. He won't be quiet for long, so I take my chance.

What we're seeing is the mechanism that allows us to disregard information. And that mechanism also allows us to believe that marching toward our goal is us being resilient, rather than pigheaded. It might be an unconscious mechanism, or it might be fully conscious. In real life, we don't just passively receive information; instead, we seek it out. What confirmation bias is showing us is that in our own ways we accept and seek out information that supports our way of thinking.

That's why if you meet a Turtle Earth believer they could counter any point you put forward. They've gone to the trouble of seeking out sources – regardless of how obscure – to support their point of view. And while doing so, they've also gone to the trouble of actively ignoring or not exposing themselves to anything that might contradict that view. You might be surprised at just how easy it is to do that.

For a real-world example, take the news. In the United States there are different news channels to support left- and right-wing political beliefs: MSNBC on the left, and Fox News on the right. They'll tell viewers the stories they want to hear, spun in the way viewers want to hear it, while at the same time under-reporting unfavourable news that isn't what their viewers want to hear.

I hear a throat clear and I know what's coming next. Percy Pighead leans forward, "So you're saying I'm lying to myself?" he asks, a frown crossing his brow. "You've already admitted that confirmation bias can happen unconsciously, so if the gate swings one way or the other on its own, how is that my fault?"

And that's where my sheep pen illustration breaks down. Because the problem of thinking of unconscious bias as an automatic gate is that it separates the bias from the mechanism that allows it to continue.

Percy Pighead strokes the side of his nose with his index finger. He's waiting for me to say something else.

The truth is that the gate doesn't swing on its own. It's our hand doing the swinging when views and opinions disrupt our belief. We all have our gate and, on some level, I think we all know when we swing it shut.

Our belief, whatever it is, has become a cherished idea. Most of us are willing to do anything to keep that belief intact. And that includes looking for things to confirm our own biases. Telling ourselves that we're fighting the good fight, that we're Cassandra seeing things that others can't. We believe our justifications, so we don't seek out an alternative point of view, or keep looking for more facts to counter any dissenting ideas.

Our swinging gates make it possible to be earnest in our arguments – we really believe what we're saying, even while pushing ideas that won't feasibly work. And just like with every cherished idea, we can't see the holes in the thinking because we want it to be true so badly that we've lost our ability to be objective.

If we draw on genuine curiosity for a moment, closing the gate on counterarguments closes our ability to learn. And because of that we can keep listening to whatever we'd like to hear.

Confirmation Bias and Leadership

"All very interesting," Percy Pighead says, "but this is a business book, not a manifesto for fairness in reporting."

OK, that's true. Let's think about what that means for us. What if one of the things we let through the gate and into our acceptance is the belief that leaders shouldn't be challenged? The belief that we have all the facts about the strategic improvements to our operational processes? Or the belief that the market supports expansion?

How can we make sound decisions if we're biased against information that might prove us wrong, or that might suggest another course of action? And how will we know if there's a better way if we're so pig-headed that we don't realize we're biased toward a certain way of doing things in the first place?

The biggest problem of unconscious bias is the belief that we don't have it. Realizing that we, like everyone else, are biased means that we have the choice to challenge our biases and develop a more rounded perspective. Then we can make decisions based not on what we would like to have happen, but on the facts – regardless of how unsettling those facts may be. Awareness is our guard against pig-headedness. If someone is telling us to give up, resilience is about bouncing back. If someone is giving us information that offers a better picture of what's going on, resilience is about course-correcting to achieve our goal. If someone shows us that our goal can't be achieved using our current means, then resilience is about finding another way to achieve the end.

Let's take Jessica's story as an example. Her objective was to grow the business and she felt that the best way to do that was by expanding to double the output. She was wrong but pushed ahead regardless. If she had used the other attributes, she may have discovered another way to grow the business without expansion: by outsourcing to show proof of concept before making the capital investment, for example.

She still gets where she wants to go, she's just found a different way of getting there.

That's the difference between pig-headedness and resilience. And I'd suggest it's a difference worth keeping in mind as we continue to explore the behaviours of resilience. After all, leadership isn't about stubbornly forging ahead on our own. It's about creating leaders of others as we bring them along with us.

The Behaviours of Resilience

Perhaps more than any other attribute of a leadership mindset, an industry of "Yes, you can!" has built up around resilience. Books that talk about visioning, living your passion, or making plans to reach a goal may offer some people the antidote to giving up. But, for me, they miss the point. Even if we do follow our passion, we will inevitably get knocked back at some point. Even if we're trying to change the world for the better, there will be people who couldn't care less – and some of those people will be the ones we have to convince to act. If knock-backs and indifference lead to us telling ourselves to move on to something else, then being told to keep following our passion isn't going to help.

Resilience is often demonstrated in our darkest moments. Late at night, all alone, with a problem in our lap and energies failing, resilience is choosing to get up the next day and persevere. Resilience isn't a magical quality. We choose to press on not because we've got a special gift, but because we've been living the behaviours of resilience. Understanding and living those behaviours has affected the way we think about ourselves and our ability to arrive at the goal we're aiming for. That's what we're about to do: become familiar with the behaviours of resilience.

So let's begin by outlining what those behaviours are:

Attribute of a leadership mindset	Behaviours
Resilience	Bouncebackability Discipline Keeping your eyes on the prize

The Behaviours of Resilience: Bouncebackability

Bouncebackability is the behaviour of being able to recover from a setback. The faster we can do that, the more effective our ability to bounce back. That sounds easy enough, but if you've ever lived through a turn of events that required a big change to what you're doing, you'll know that easy isn't the word that comes to mind. Understanding how we can regroup and recover in those times helps us to take a big step in understanding how we can improve how quickly we bounce back.

The Change Curve

In her 1969 book *On Death and Dying*, Elisabeth Kübler-Ross offered a way to think about how we deal with change.[3] If you can agree that change comes in many shapes and sizes – from easy changes, like changing toothpastes, all the way to imposed changes, where we have no say in what the change is – I think we

---

3   Elisabeth Kübler-Ross, *On Death and Dying: What the Dying Have to Teach Doctors, Nurses, Clergy and Their Own Families*, 40th anniversary edition (Abingdon: Routledge, 2009 [1969]).

can honestly say the change she explored is the most imposed change of all: becoming terminally ill. Through her conversations with terminally ill people she began to see a pattern, which she represented as five stages of grief. Quickly developed into the recognized change curve, Kübler-Ross' work offered a way to think about how we deal with change and has been widely accepted in many fields ever since. In case you're not familiar with it, the change curve looks like this:

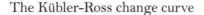

The Kübler-Ross change curve

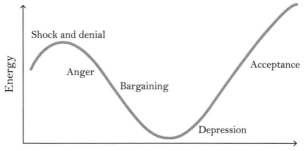

It represents the emotional journey we go through in response to change. Kübler-Ross' five basic stages were: denial, anger, bargaining, depression, and finally acceptance, as terminally ill patients came to terms with their own mortality. The curve has been adapted for use in businesses as a chart to manage the change process and support employees, leaders, and stakeholders as they go through the stages of change. As a business tool it's been very helpful.

It's helpful in our quest to understand resilience too. Although Kübler-Ross didn't talk about resilience, her curve illustrates a key factor in our ability to bounce back. So although most people talk about the stages the curve represents, I'd like to shine a light on the very bottom of the curve. The point at which the curve begins to go back up. And this is my question: why? A possible answer might be that when we begin to accept our situation, we slip out of our depression and begin to feel better. That may be true, but it doesn't answer the question, it just kicks the can down the road – we're not getting to the core of why we began to accept.

Let me illustrate what I mean. Think about a recent historical change you've lived through. By historical I mean complete – as in one you've lived through and come out the other side of – not something that happened in the 1800s. Think about that for a second. If you can recall an imposed change – one that wasn't your choice – that's even better. Recall the emotional journey you went through, the denial, the anger, the sleepless nights when you were cooking up plans to make a deal with whoever seemed to be running the show: God, your boss, whoever. And then the sinking feeling when you knew there was no deal to be made. Since this is a change you've now dealt with, try to identify the point at which the curve began to go back up.

And now answer the question: Why did it go up? Think hard. What happened? Trace the contours of your shift from the darkest moments of that change to the point when it started to feel light again. Was it a change in your perspective? If so, what helped you to think differently? Was it help from someone? If so, what did you do to get that help, and what did you do with their suggestions or input? Take your time, because if you haven't thought about this before it might not be readily obvious.

Oh, and don't read the next paragraph until you can answer the question.

Because now I'm going to take a stab at guessing what happened. Not the details, I'm not psychic, I'm just going to have a go at guessing your state of mind. My guess is that somewhere in the bottom of the change curve you saw something. And what you saw was a point of control.

It could have been something practical that you were able to do, like apply for a bank loan from a bank you hadn't thought of before. It might have been a mental shift – like you just decided you had to make the best of a bad situation. It might have been that a word of advice from a friend made enough sense to you, and you felt you could action it. Whatever it was, I'm guessing that a point of control is what allowed you to turn the corner and set you on the path to the next stage: acceptance.

As I'm sure you've guessed, finding a point of control is key to bouncing back. So key in fact, that I'll now offer another way to think about it.

Subjects and Agents

In the days before constitutional democracies, people were considered subjects rather than citizens of the state. To be precise they were subject *to* the King. And that also meant subject to the whims of the King. The King wants you to stand on one leg while playing the lute? That's what you did. My point is, subjects have things done to them or for them. And they live that way because they see no option to affect their lives in a meaningful way.

As you can imagine, agents do the opposite. There's a reason why James Bond is a secret *agent*. Have you seen the film in which James Bond sits around waiting for things to happen? No, neither have I. That's because they never made it. Agents feel that they can control a situation: they can act to create a different outcome.

Psychologists use the term external or internal locus of control to think about subjects and agents.[4] It's a technical way of saying what I just said: that we feel events in our lives are determined by forces outside of us (an external locus of control) or by us (an internal locus of control). How we see ourselves – as subjects or agents – determines our bouncebackability.

So how does any of this help us bounce back?

Finding a Point of Control

As I'm sure you can see, it comes down to finding a point of control that allows us to act. In the face of adversity, that point can be small. Small matters here because if we've been knocked down for the thirtieth time it can feel like we'll never get to our goal, that the whole enterprise has become too big and too difficult – impossible even. That's the kind of setback that saps our ability to bounce back. Finding a point of control that asks us to make a big leap – to host a board meeting and unveil a new direction for the business, for example – is setting ourselves up to fail, and that decreases our chances of achieving the goal. So, small is what we want here.

In short, working on a point of control that's too big is the best way I know to hinder our bouncebackability. That doesn't mean we can't host a board meeting, but it does mean breaking big ideas down into smaller ones. Each chunk gives us a smaller point of control, and a greater likelihood of success, which then leads us to another point of control. Here's an example of how that might play out.

---

4   Julian B. Rotter, "Generalized Expectancies for Internal Versus External Control of Reinforcement", *Psychological Monographs: General and Applied*, Vol. 80(1) (Washington, DC: American Psychological Association, 1966): 1–28.

Ellie External is sitting on her couch. The TV flickers in front of her. The sound is muted but that doesn't matter because she's not really watching. She licks the ice cream off the spoon pressed against her lips and sighs into the empty room. She's at the bottom of the curve.

She's in this state because she thinks she's overdue for a promotion. And it's true. She's been doing a great job and peers that started at her level have already moved on. One is now her manager's manager. So this afternoon, in her annual review, she asked about the possibility of a promotion. That took a lot of courage because usually, when you have an external locus of control, you don't ask for a promotion, you think you'll get it when it's time. But this time, Ellie did ask, and she got a vague answer about being ready, her visibility in the organization, and potential company-wide cutbacks.

For Ellie this was the worst news possible. Not only was a promotion not on the horizon, but there was the chance that she could lose her job in the cutbacks. You see, that's why she's sitting in front of the TV, with a half-empty tub of ice cream and a licked-clean spoon.

Of course, she could do nothing. But nothing is what has seen her peers storm past her. She could go and ask her boss again, but wouldn't she just get the same answer? There was that point about visibility and being ready. She could prove she's ready, but the visibility? She's not going to march into people's offices and start introducing herself to everyone, or hang out with colleagues after work hoping that the right people show up. She sticks her spoon deep into the tub. It comes off like a stabbing gesture.

"Why do some people get promotions so quickly and others languish in their role for years?" That's the question she's mulling over. And that's when she has the idea. "What if I talked to the managers on the major projects I've been working on and ask them how they think I'm doing?" She jumps ever so slightly on the couch then settles again. She can feel anxiety bubbling up and knows she'll never do that.

She raises the spoon to her lips and licks the mountain of ice cream sitting on it. "But what if I started with Lucy? She's kind and maybe she'll give me a few pointers. Maybe even tell me if this is a good idea at all?"

She reaches for the remote, finds it wedged between the cushions, and turns the volume back up. The TV spits out the sounds of *The Princess Bride*, the best ice cream and depression movie ever. Only now she doesn't feel quite so defeated.

The thing about a point of control is that it gives us a way back into the fight. It doesn't matter if it's a big or small inroad. It just matters that we're back. And as we take the steps that give us control, we uncover a version of ourselves we may very well be proud of. But that depends, of course, on taking the steps. As you can imagine, there's no point finding a point of control if we don't exert that control. And that brings us to another element of bouncing back.

Self-Motivation

Years ago, when I was a one-to-one coach, I could have made a living from people who wanted help to improve their motivation. They would begin by saying something like, "I really want to write a book/start a business/build a house, but I just can't keep myself motivated." What I learnt from those clients was this: the word "motivation" isn't a great way to understand our drive to get something done.

Motivation is an abstract noun. Unlike concrete nouns – like book, chair, and apple – abstract nouns refer to concepts – love and hope, for example. In other words, when someone asks for help with motivation, they're asking for help with the idea of it, not the act. That's important because although motivation is abstract, it's always referring to an action – the motivation to do *something*.

"OK," Polly Procrastinator says, "thanks for the grammar lesson. Now, how do I get motivated enough to bounce back?"

Well, that all depends on whether we want to act. Not on the idea of doing something, but actually doing it. We need to have a reason. What I've found is that the *reason to* do something is a more helpful way to think about the abstract concept that we call motivation. Self-motivation is *my* particular reason to do something. So once we find a point of control, all we have to do is find our reason to act. But of course, it's not that simple. If you go to the gym, answer this question: how easy is it to get on a machine in early January? How about by the middle of March?

If you answered hard and then easy to those two questions, you demonstrated that you know all there is to know about self-motivation. If you answered that they're both hard, you need to find a gym with more equipment. My point is that the person who goes to the gym in January does so because they have a strong reason to: they want to lose weight, start the year fresh, turn their life around, get fit. So does it mean that if they've stopped going by March they want to gain weight, undo what they've done, or become out of shape? Of course not. What's happened is that they have overriding reasons not to go to the gym: that's it's too hard, that they prefer hanging out at the bar, that their workload is overtaking them, for example. Another way to say that is now they have reasons to do something else and, ultimately, their reasons not to go outweigh their reasons to go.

Put simply if our reason *not to* outweighs our reason *to* do something, we won't do it.

So if we're after a short bounce-back time, then when we find our point of control, we need to have more reasons to act than to not. Find those and our bouncebackability improves dramatically. The question is: how do we do that?

Challenge: Your Reasons To

Have you ever wanted to do something, got started, and then given up? Or maybe never got started? This challenge isn't about giving you a hard time. It's about understanding why you stopped pursuing the goal. When we understand that, we'll be able to see how our motivation works. Then we'll be able to use it to help us act when we're at the bottom of our change curves.

All you'll need is a real-life instance, current or not, when you started something but didn't finish it, or you never started something that you wanted to. Like I said, our goal isn't to get you doing that thing, it's about understanding. To make that easier, look for a small example – something with low emotional attachment – because that means you can be more objective. But something meaningful is also good, because it means it'll matter to you.

When you have that thing in mind, grab a piece of paper. Divide the sheet in half and write two headings at the top: on the left-hand side, "reasons to"; on the right-hand side, "reasons not to".

Now fill out your sheet of paper. On the left-hand side write down all your reasons for doing the thing in question. When you've exhausted your ideas, move onto the other side and write down all the reasons not to.

Don't hold anything back. No one is going to see this. If one of your reasons not to is because you can't be bothered, write it down. If your reason to do something is because it'll open the door for you to meet Ellie Goulding, write that down. Don't edit, just write.

When you have your list, take a closer look. It may be that your sheet looks something like this:

Get a promotion	
Reasons to	**Reasons not to**
More money.	Longer work hours.
More influence.	Less time at home.
Better office.	Less time to pursue personal goals.
More challenging projects.	Potentially uncomfortable – would be more senior than current colleagues, who are friends.
More respect.	
Opportunities to mentor.	
Feel it's due to me.	
Will be more invested in company.	
Better job satisfaction.	
Positions me for better jobs with other companies.	

If your list does look like this, there's one trap we need to avoid falling into: thinking that all reasons are born equal. Just because I have more on one side – in this case the reasons to – doesn't mean I will do the thing in question. If it were just a numbers game, we could manufacture any number of reasons for either column. If you haven't done the thing, despite the number of reasons to, it must be more subtle than the raw numbers. And that's true because more important than the number of reasons in each column, is the weight each reason carries. In our example, let's say the biggest reason not to is because of the concern about becoming more senior than my friends. If that's true, then it explains why I haven't taken a promotion yet: despite the numbers, I have more important reasons not to.

If we really do want our goal, finding a way to balance both sides of the table is the focus of this challenge. You can do this by reducing the weight of your biggest reason not to. As I'm sure you've guessed, that's the real focus of this challenge.

So let's have a go at tackling it.

First of all, take a look at your reasons to. Do you agree with them? You haven't acted yet, so it may be that you don't really want to. So if your reasons to are things like "the business should be growing faster", "I should be moving faster in my career", or any other variations of shoulds, it may be that although you feel you're supposed to want the goal, you actually don't. If that's the case, then you can demonstrate leadership by deciding not to. But if that isn't the case, look at your reasons not to and identify the one that carries the biggest weight. You'll know it because it'll be the one that you're drawn to. Maybe it seems insurmountable. Maybe it's emotional. When you've found the reason not to that carries the most weight for you, write it on a separate piece of paper.

Now examine it.

Ask yourself whether this is a valid reason not to do the thing you want. What would you tell a friend who offered this as a reason to not move forward? Is there a way to minimize the weight of this reason? If this reason involves others, would sharing the concern with them change anything? Is this reason based on an assumption? If so, how can you check whether your assumption is right? Is this reason a cherished idea? Does it need to be murdered? How would you argue against this reason? Do those arguments shine a different light on it? Why do you want to do this thing even though you have this strong reason not to?

Write down the answers to these questions on your sheet of paper. Once again, don't edit your answers, just write them down. What I'm asking you to do is to interrogate yourself – so if other questions come to you, ask them of yourself. Use as many sheets of paper as you like. When you're done, set your pen down.

At the start of this challenge, I said our goal wasn't to get you doing that thing, it's to understand. So take a break if you want because we're about to look at your answers to see what we can understand.

When you're ready, take a look at your answers. Our goal is to accept the reason not as intractable, but rather as a hurdle to overcome.

Ready? Then let's have a go. Look at your answers to the questions I've offered above, or any that you added. What does that do to your reason not to? Do they cast it in a different light? Does it change at all?

The attributes weave together in a tapestry, which grows as we develop. To do this part of the challenge requires genuine curiosity to be willing to ask ourselves the questions that will help us learn. It needs flexibility of mind so that we can connect the answers we uncover in new and interesting ways. My hope is that by exploring your answers you begin to see the parameters of your reason not to – the edges, if you like. You'll begin to see that it has dimensions, and that there's a way around it: an action, however small, to be done to get around it. Like I said, I'm not asking you to do that small thing. I'm just wondering whether you can see it. Being able to see a way around our biggest reason not to is the first chink in the armour of all our reasons not to. Identifying it is the first step in bouncing back.

As I'm sure you can see, bouncing back doesn't involve a coach screaming "You can do it!" at us – there's much more to it than that. It's not an attitude, it's a behaviour that we hone (and here's those words again) with effort and practice over time.

Bouncebackability is just one of the behaviours that will allow us to keep that effort going over time. So maybe it's time to think about a few others.

The Behaviours of Resilience: Discipline

If the ability to bounce back is acquired over time, another behaviour that will help us to keep going is the discipline to keep trying. And before you say it, I know, discipline isn't fun. In fact, even the word sounds austere. It conjures images of Auntie Tight-Bun, ever ready to send a child to bed without dinner. I get that – in a culture in which instant gratification is king, and in which waiting two seconds before looking at a message on our phones is considered patient – discipline is synonymous with sacrifice, even punishment. It can feel like an antiquated concept practised by self-flagellators (both literally and metaphorically).

But here's the thing: discipline happens in all walks of life. My niece, Nicola, trains every day, as all athletes do. Investment bankers study market trends every day. Business owners review the metrics of their business every day. Those professionals, and many others, have discipline because they can see a tangible cause-and-effect relationship between what they do and the results they get. A virtuous circle, you might say, that provides instant feedback about whether they're doing the right thing. We'll talk more about that in a moment, but for now we're talking about the early stages of developing discipline in a new area, when it will take a while before the cause-and-effect relationship becomes clear. Here, the virtuous circle is replaced with doubt about whether we're on the right track, and a constant nagging feeling that this is never going to work.

Take the six attributes, for example. Let's say we're working on flexibility of mind. At the very start of the journey we're being asked to flex our thinking by not relying on the ideas we normally have and the patterns of thinking we usually employ. The point, we're told, is so that we can develop our ability to pivot our thinking quickly. Once we have flexibility of mind, the benefits are obvious: we possess an ease at incorporating new and even contradictory ideas and data into our plans or decisions. But getting there, that's tough. And the first few days or weeks of effort don't immediately highlight those benefits. Instead we might feel slow, or even dumb. Especially when we compare ourselves with others who flex their minds as easily as breathing. As I said, in that sense, the virtuous circle is gone and instead we have a sinking feeling that we're wasting our time. Enter giving up stage left.

We could look at making plans. We could go over setting objectives and planning the days and times when we'll practise the thing we're trying to do. But my guess is that you already know how to make plans. You already know how to set a target and march toward it. And although a section on planning might be helpful for some people, and although it does, to some extent, involve the kinds of behaviours I'm talking about – because planning, and especially following through on those plans, would affect the way we think (our mindset) – I'm afraid that if you have a pen in hand, poised to take notes on the wisdom of planning, I'm going to disappoint. You know how to set up an action plan.

What I'd like to do is think about discipline in a slightly different way. Then, at the end of the section, if you still want to write an action plan, I'm all for it.

Discipline as Practice

"Hold on," Rodney Rebel says. He must be in his early fifties but that doesn't stop him wearing ripped jeans, and a tee-shirt that says, "Death to the establishment." He's wandered into my office, and is standing two feet away from a Louis XIV reproduction chair. It's not worth a lot but it is a family heirloom. "There is no other way to think about discipline," he says. He pauses and scans my face, but I get the feeling he'll interrupt whatever I say so I don't bother. "It's all about giving things up and doing things I don't want to."

I mull over the thought of guiding him out of the room. It's a mistake because he takes my silence for agreement.

"You said it before, bro. Discipline's all about rigidity, inflexibility, and sticking to rules." I didn't say that, but that doesn't stop him. "For that matter, what's it even doing as a behaviour of an attribute at all? Isn't a leadership mindset all about not conforming, pushing boundaries, and being flexible?" With that he lifts his leg and sets his boot down on the plush seat of the chair. He looks at me, daring me to ask him to move it.

I don't. You put discipline in that frame and of course the Rodney Rebel part of all of us wants to push back. But what if discipline wasn't about being told what to do, following a code, or shadowed by the spectre of impending judgement? In fact, what if discipline wasn't about what we can't do and instead was about practising being the kind of leader we always knew we could be?

See it that way and discipline isn't a rod to beat ourselves with; it's a chance to develop the habits of leadership.

"Hang on," Rodney Rebel says. He takes his foot off the chair. Maybe because without my objection, the act of rebellion seemed pointless. "I saw what you did there. That's just playing with words."

But it isn't. Because – just like Rodney Rebel – we only feel the need to push back if someone is pushing us in the first place. So why not remove the force altogether? What if discipline that comes from an external source feels like we're being asked to make a sacrifice or being rebuked? And what if internal discipline, the sort we ask of ourselves, is a chance to practise a different way of doing things?

In the context of the behaviour of resilience that means practising keeping going, trying on what we could be. In the context of the six attributes it means committing to a path.

Tea Ceremony

The Japanese tea ceremony – *sado*, or the way of tea – is a practice that dates back over a thousand years. It flows through distinct stages, each unfolding in a prescribed order. Everything from where to place the teapot to where the practitioner and guests should sit follows formal rules. Each utensil has a purpose and a place. Each stage has a beginning, middle, and end. Rodney Rebel would hate it because to truly take part in the tea ceremony means knowing and following all of those movements, all of those positions, and all of the stages.

It's mesmerizing to watch mostly because, even to someone with limited understanding of the symbolism, process, and ritual, it's clear that there's a depth to what they're watching. With that depth is a beauty so evident that even the uninitiated observer will realize that they're missing the levels of meaning. But what the uninitiated observer will notice is the discipline that goes into the ceremony: both to learn the stages and, more importantly, to embody the art of *sado*.

Intentionality

What we can learn from the tea ceremony is focus: there's intention behind each movement and position. The ceremony isn't simply about making tea. On one level it is art, but there's more to the ceremony than aesthetics. It expresses the heart of the practitioner and allows that heart to flow into the tea being made. It's about stilling the practitioner's mind through intense concentration on each and every moment. Ultimately, it's about honouring those around the practitioner, and growing as a person in the process. The tea ceremony is an active meditation: its intention is to seek harmony and balance.

That's what discipline is: an intention. It's that intention which informs any plans we make or any steps we take. And growing discipline means being clear about what we're intending to achieve and why. If we know why we're doing something then we have a reason to keep going when we're not immediately successful. Some gas to put in the tank, if you like, before the virtuous circle kicks in.

A reason *why* differs from a reason *to* because it plays out on a bigger scale. A reason to lose weight may be to play football with my toddler daughter; a reason why might be to live long enough to see her graduate from university. Or, another example: a reason to map our production processes may be to grow efficiency; a reason why might be to systemize the business so we can be less involved. And one more: a reason to grow flexibility of mind could be to be less restricted by the way we've always done things at work; a reason why could be to help us to see the world differently in order to change how we see ourselves and how we live our lives. In short, a reason to is the short-term goal; the reason why is the long-term objective.

Our why could be anything. Any why will do, we just need to have one because it gives us the focus for our practice. And keeping practising is the point of discipline.

Types of Why

Before we have a go at settling on what our why might be, let's think about the two main types: attainable and unattainable whys. An attainable why is one we can achieve. For example, getting data for our business so we can create a system for shifting production quickly is an attainable why. We might have to work hard to develop the mechanism of data collection, but with lots of work, money, and time that can happen. That's the kind of why that virtuous circles work so well for: as we begin to see returns in the form of better data, we begin to make adjustments to our processes, and that, in turn, generates more efficiency and more revenue. Notice the full stop at the end of that sentence. It's not just because it's grammatically correct, it's also there because it's the end of the cycle. After we generate more income we may want to refine our processes, but eventually that cycle will run its course. When the approach has delivered our goal, the desire for bigger, better data will fade and so too will the disciplined drive to reinvent our form of gathering data. In other words, because attainable whys can be achieved, they have a shelf life in terms of driving our discipline.

Unattainable whys are just as they sound: they're not achievable. Let's consider practising the behaviours of the six attributes to be the best leader we can be. Or practising being the best boss we can be by establishing new work practices to help staff see themselves as partners in the business rather than employees. Both of these have a cause we're working toward, and imply that we will be going on a journey. They both lack a defined end point: when will we be the best boss we can be? As a result, ambitions like this have the potential to serve as whys for years to come. As you might have guessed, whys are connected to our purpose in life. At this level it's not about our reason for doing something, it's about why we're here at all: what we want our life to mean and what we want to leave behind.

That's what makes whys powerful. That's why we want to keep working at it. And that's what gives us the discipline to keep going. So every day we practise, knowing that we'll never fully achieve the focus of our why, but finding a reason to take the next small step. It's those steps in the journey we can make plans for. And we can furnish those steps with reasons to take them. And if you want to make plans for those steps, like I said, all power to you.

Whys are much harder to make plans for because breaking whys into small steps makes them lose their most powerful quality: it makes them feel attainable. And we want to keep the sense of unattainability. So we don't make plans for our unattainable whys, we're guided by them instead. It's our personal North Star that keeps us moving toward the best version of ourselves.

Challenge: Your Why

I said earlier that we'd have a go at defining our why. If you feel that you already have a handle on your purpose, feel free to skip or skim this challenge. But if you'd like to take part, we'll have a go at uncovering your why – your purpose in life. If that sounds enormous and like something we're unlikely to achieve in the next few hundred words, then I've got good news for you: you already know what it is.

In fact, although there are hundreds of books written on finding your purpose in life, I believe in you enough to trust that you'll say what it is in three paragraphs' time. Ready to have a go?

Take a moment to find a space where you're not likely to be interrupted. Go for a walk if that helps, perhaps somewhere beautiful, go to an art gallery, or sit on a bench overlooking your favourite view. Or just sit in your favourite chair at home. As you take that moment, ask yourself what you want to leave behind when you finish your current job. Try not to intellectualize this too much. You don't have to put your thoughts into full sentences, some people don't even try to put them into words. Do whatever makes sense to you. If you've read about mindfulness in Chapter 1, this is a bit like that practice. Just notice the thoughts or words that come to mind when you ask yourself what you want to leave behind when you leave your current job. Keeping asking yourself that question and let the answer bubble up in you the way air bubbles to the top of a clear lake. As you keep asking that question, notice how you keep coming back to one phrase or thought.

When you have that thought, hold onto it for a second. Then look into it the way you might look into a wine glass.

Notice that as you look at your thought – the answer to the last question – you look right through it. And as you look through it you see another, slightly different question. Let your thought go and ask yourself that question: what do you want to leave behind when you finish your career? Again, don't try to figure this out, just let the answer rise like a cloud of smoke from a campfire – with no effort. As before, it could be a phrase or a thought. It meanders its way to you with no effort and no sense of self-consciousness. As that phrase or thought begins to impress itself on you, notice that it isn't new. It's familiar. Stay with that phrase or thought for a while. Reacquaint yourself with it. And then, just like before, look into that thought, connect with it. Look into it and through it just as you did before. You already know there's another question coming. So when it comes it's no surprise.

Now ask yourself: what do you want to leave behind when you finish your life? Though you saw it coming, the question may jar, but see if you can go with it. This time it's like a leaf falling from a tree in an autumnal forest. The question floats gently through the air, swaying from side to side. You watch it fall and then you see it come to rest gently on a patch of grass. Notice how a phrase or thought is forming. Like before, maybe it's a phrase or a thought you've come back to time and again in life. But unlike before, this one may have seemed too grand, too difficult, or too simple. Maybe, for that reason, you set it aside and focused on other things. But when you did that you still felt the tug of the phrase or thought you're experiencing now. This time, avoid the reaction to pull away from the answer to that question. There's no one else around. No one here to judge you, laugh, or think you're getting too big for your boots. Hold onto that phrase or thought. You can let it go in a second, but for now, just hold onto it. Imagine it's that leaf sitting on the grass. And then imagine that the leaf turns into a coat. You reach out and pick it up. You can't help but try it on. When you do, notice how perfectly it fits. How it feels like it's been tailored for you. Notice how it keeps out the cold and damp. Notice how it suits your style. How it makes you feel not just great, but the greatest you've ever felt. Notice what it feels like to be so snug, so comfortable in your skin. And then answer that question out loud: *what do you want to leave behind when you finish your life?*

The answer to that question is your why. Discipline is about being brave enough to practise living that answer every day. You don't have to tell your why to anyone. You just need to commit to yourself that every day you'll look to that why and allow it to guide you through life. To allow it to inform your decisions and be present in your plans.

Discipline isn't about living your why perfectly: it's a great target to aim for and an impossible one to hit. It's just about constantly trying to.

The Behaviours of Resilience: Keeping Your Eyes on the Prize

Grouse Mountain sits on the North Shore in Vancouver, Canada. One route to the top is a trail made up of 2,830 steps that starts at the base of the mountain and goes straight up. Locals call it the Grind. Because it is a grind. 1.8 miles long with a 2,800 foot elevation gain. The fastest it's ever been scaled is 23 minutes and 48 seconds. Most people manage it in about an hour and a half.

Jane's puffing when she sees him and although she was aiming for a personal best, she slows down as soon as she sees him. He's a way off but she can't take her eyes off him: an older man, hunched over as he walks, wearing a waterproof baseball cap even though it's a sunny day. They're half way up the Grind and he's wearing regular street clothes: a shirt and smart trousers. But that's not what has her mesmerized. It's the way he's handling the trail. Slowly, but with purpose. He climbs for a few minutes, then stops and takes a break. Ten seconds later he tackles another few minutes' walking. Stops. Rests. Then off again. When she reaches him, he's just about to take a break.

"Mind if I join you?" she asks.

He shrugs.

She takes that for a yes and waits with him.

He's sweating hard, but there's a smile on his face.

She doesn't know what to say, so she says what she's thinking, "I have to say I'm impressed."

He smiles and sets off on his next leg.

She walks alongside him, knowing she'll need to pick up the pace in a moment to keep the goal of a personal best alive.

"I'll get there," he says more to himself than to her.

"I've got no doubts," she says.

He pauses after a few minutes, and turns to take in how far he's come.

"What's the secret?" she asks.

"No secret," he says simply.

"But what makes you keep going?"

He takes off again. "Have you seen the view from the top?" he asks.

She shuffles beside him. "Many times."

He raises his hand and holds out a crumbled photograph that he must have been holding all along. It's an old photograph of a man and a woman, maybe in their mid-thirties, posing on a mountain top. Their arms are wrapped around each other and she's looking past the camera at the view around her. "This'll be my second time," he says. He looks up the mountainside. "The first was thirty-five years ago today."

She's not thinking of personal bests anymore. Right at this minute she just wants to walk the distance with this man.

Bouncebackability and discipline are both important behaviours on the road to resilience. Just as important is putting one foot in front of the other. The man in the story had his reason to. He had his why. Those are great things to have but what we do with both of them is what the man in the story was doing: using them to help keep our eyes on the prize.

The phrase was popularized during the civil rights movement in the 1950s. The adaptation from the traditional hymn "Keep Your Hand on the Plow" is widely attributed to Alice Wine, and it's been sung as a protest song countless times at marches, churches, and gatherings. If it isn't the most powerful song that arose from the period, it is the song most imbued with the feeling of struggle, patience, and nobility. If resilience made a sound, that song is the sound it would make.

Implicit in the phrase "keep your eyes on the prize" is the expectation of setbacks. After all, why would we need to keep our eyes on the prize if we were sure that we were going to get what we want? Instead, we keep our eyes on the prize in the darkest times when it's unclear if things will work out. And, because it's unclear, remembering what's at the end of the road is what makes each step possible.

That's why keeping our eyes on the prize is a behaviour of resilience. It's beginning something knowing that we'll fail along the way, trusting that we'll find a way through, and knowing that all the obstacles will be worth it. To say that's anything but tough is to sell anyone who's ever achieved against the odds short.

In our discussion on discipline, I talked about how virtuous circles kick in when there's a tangible cause-and-effect relationship between what we do and the results we get. The instant feedback loop shows us we're on the right track, and in many cases that provides all we need to keep going. But what if we don't have that feedback loop? What if the prize is so far away that we can only make small incremental steps toward it? And what if those gains have the potential to be erased by one setback?

Keeping our eyes on the prize is about having the cognitive ability to see those setbacks for what they are. As a behaviour it is patient, unfazed by adversity because adversity is expected. With our eyes on the prize, we have made the commitment to struggle through those setbacks before we even begin.

Thinking About Thinking

But how do we get to see something for what it really is? Psychology has been working on the connection between what we think and how we feel since Aaron Beck began his work on depression in the 1960s.[5] A psychoanalyst by training, he set out to test psychoanalytic concepts of depression. Maybe he felt he'd confirm the theories he was familiar with, but that isn't what happened. Instead, he found that depressed patients had what he

---

5   Aaron T. Beck, *Depression: Clinical, Experimental, and Theoretical Aspects* (New York: Harper & Row, 1967).

called negative automatic thoughts that reinforced their depression. Although we're not all depressed, many of us experience a version of negative automatic thoughts. Maybe it happens when we drop a plate accidentally and think something along the lines of, "Oh, well done! How do you get anything done when you're always so clumsy?" Or maybe it's impostor syndrome and we can't shake the feeling that we don't really deserve our role. In that case, when something goes wrong – and it will, since nothing ever goes right all the time – we hear that voice reminding us we're going to get found out.

It's Beck's observation of automatic thoughts that lead to the birth of cognitive therapy, referred to these days as cognitive behavioural therapy (CBT). Of course, while one or two moments of negative self-talk isn't the biggest deal in the world, think about what happens if we're repeatedly harsh with ourselves. Think about the hopelessness it can engender. If you can imagine that, you've got a good sense of what depression feels like. Today we might call these automatic thoughts self-limiting thoughts or self-limiting beliefs. I'm sure you can see that self-limiting thoughts about what we can achieve, what the future holds, or what's possible can make it difficult for us to keep our eyes on the prize.

But before we think about how we can overcome self-limiting beliefs, let's cover one more idea from cognitive behavioural psychology. Although we can think of Beck as the father of modern CBT, it won't surprise you to know that the basic idea has been around for a long time. In fact, way back in the first century AD, the Stoic Epictetus coined the phrase that stakes his claim as the grandfather of cognitive behavioural psychology. In section five of the *Enchiridion* – the book of doctrines summarized by his pupil Arrian – Epictetus makes the case that we aren't disturbed by things, but by the view we take of things.[6] Events in and of

---

6   Elizabeth Carter (tr.), *The Moral Discourses of Epictetus* (London and Toronto: J. M. Dent & Sons, 1910), p. 257.

themselves, Epictetus argues, are neither good nor bad. Instead, his thinking goes, it's the judgements we make about events that determine how we feel them. Unconvinced? Try this. If I said you weren't going to win the lottery at the end of the month, would that bother you? What if I said you weren't going to get paid? My guess is that the former doesn't bother you, while the latter does. Silly though the example is, it highlights what Epictetus is saying. In the first example we're not disturbed because we had no expectation of winning the lottery. In the second, our view is that we've worked hard throughout the month, so we're entitled to be paid. In the former scenario, we don't feel hard done by; the latter represents an injustice.

Self-Talk and Setbacks

Self-talk matters when we're thinking about keeping our eyes on the prize because if we call a setback insurmountable, it influences how we see that setback. That's the value of thinking about the way we think: it makes us agents in our own thought processes. But how do we do that?

Socrates didn't write his philosophy down, but through his student Plato – who in turn taught Aristotle – he helped shape the thinking of Western civilization. He didn't preach or advocate for his point of view. He simply questioned the views of anyone who would talk to him. His goal wasn't to disapprove their point of view. It wasn't even to convince them of his. The conversations, captured by Plato in his *Dialogues*, reveal a man who exposes the contradictions and thinking errors in the views of his conversation partner.[7] If that sounds harmless to you, it wasn't. It was an uncomfortable experience for many. Imagine beginning a conversation convinced of your own rightness and

---

7   Edith Hamilton and Huntington Cairns (eds), *The Collected Dialogues of Plato*, tr.
    Lane Cooper (Princeton, NJ: Princeton University Press, 1961).

finishing it questioning your most fundamental beliefs about life. If you can imagine that you'll have a glimpse into how the people who engaged with Socrates felt. Leave people feeling that way often enough and they begin to dislike you. Keep going and those people will do anything to make you stop. And that includes handing out a death penalty. That's what happened to Socrates. In 399 BC, he was condemned to death for refusing to recognize the religion of the state and for corrupting the youth.

That's the power of questions: they can reveal the flaws in a person's thinking and send that person hurtling on a new trajectory. We don't need someone else to ask the questions. We can turn that kind of questioning onto ourselves. What Socrates gave us, along with a philosophical world view that has survived to this day, is a method with which to evaluate the way we think. To be an agent in our own thought processes.

Socratic questioning is popular in CBT. Its goal is for us to disrupt our own thought patterns by exploring our reactions to the events in our lives. Questions can highlight the assumptions that we make, challenge our reasoning, or drive us toward evidence that supports or dispels our perspective.

How do we use Socratic questions? Well, let's say we're looking to make our workflow more effective. Despite everything we try, we can't get major stakeholders to agree. We sit through endless meetings of people making cases for things to stay the same. "This is the best way to do it," we keep hearing, and we're told that any change will cause untold problems we can't fully understand from our vantage point.

Let's say this really matters, that we really believe in what we're proposing. We have a reason to and it's part of our why. We know it's something that if addressed will not only help the business, but help streamline everyone's workload, which will make them more productive – this is our reason to. And doing that means they'll enjoy being at work and feel that they're not just part of a company, but a group of people looking to leave the world better than they found it – this is our why.

That's why it feels like there's a lot at stake and so much to gain. Our only problem is, no one seems to see a way through. People aren't being obstructionists, they just can't see it. And because they can't see it, the project is beginning to falter. We could call the endeavour pointless and give up. That's always an option. Or we could do something else. To keep our eyes on the prize we need to be able to see the setback for what it is. And more than that, we need to trust that there is a solution even if we can't see it.

Enter Socratic questioning. We might want to start with a logic question. Does it mean that because we can't see a solution, there isn't one? Thinking that way means we might draw on flexibility of mind to start from a different point and maybe arrive at a different idea. What about checking our assumptions? What are we assuming that leads us to our conclusion? What about the available evidence? Do we know of any other company that has solved this problem? Or what about questioning the consequences? What effect will continuing with our existing processes have long-term? In this case, we can use the consequences of non-action as a driver for action. Thinking like that gives us the chance to draw on genuine curiosity and start asking what other companies may have done, or why we've settled on the approaches we have.

Thinking about the way we think gives us the chance to deescalate our reactions to events, and to cultivate the patience and nobility that epitomizes the behaviour of keeping our eyes on the prize. Seeing things differently means we're less likely to focus on the struggle and more likely to see the opportunity and points of control in a setback.

Challenge: Self-Limiting Beliefs

This challenge is about using the Socratic approach we've just talked about to dispute a self-limiting belief of your own. Begin by thinking of a self-limiting belief that's small but real. This is primarily practice after all, so resist the temptation to start with the most pressing and ingrained belief you might have. Maybe, as with Ellie External, the self-talk says you're not progressing fast enough in your career. Maybe it's self-talk that says you don't have time to take a holiday.

Whatever it is, this challenge is a chance to probe your thinking by questioning the assumptions, logic, consequences, or evidence tied up in your thinking.

To probe your belief by testing your assumptions ask yourself, "What am I assuming about the challenge in front of me?" Notice where your thoughts go. Do you move on quickly, certain that you're not assuming anything? As well as drawing on Socratic questioning, see if you can lean on genuine curiosity. In that spirit, ask yourself the question again. No one has to know your answer, it's just for you, so be honest with yourself. If you can spot an assumption, ask yourself another question to test it. Maybe something like, "How could I prove or disprove my assumption?" Or perhaps, "What's the criteria I'm using to decide if my assumption is true?" Notice your answers and notice if your answers change your thinking.

A logic question can take the form of "does it follow?" To illustrate how this line of questioning might work with Ellie's example, we could ask, "Does it follow that if I'm not where I want to be in the company now, I'll never get there?" Or, "If I'm not where I want to be in the company now, does that mean there's no way to get where I want to be?" This might allow Ellie to gain a different perspective. Ask yourself a logic question that makes sense to you and follow the thinking that it throws up.

Now try a consequences question: one that asks, "What's the effect?" Ask yourself if you're willing to live with the consequences of not addressing whatever the issue may be. And if not, what are you willing to do differently?

If we're exploring evidence, the question to ask is, "Is there proof?" Sticking with Ellie as an example, an evidence question might work like this: "Is there proof that a promotion is possible in this company?" Then, "What can I learn from others who did get one?" Ask yourself evidence-based questions and notice what changes in the way you think about the issue.

As you've guessed, you can use all of these types of questions on the same self-limiting belief. Sometimes that helps us embed a different way of thinking, sometimes we don't need them all. The point of asking ourselves these questions isn't just to arrive at an answer, it's also to find the actions that we can take as a result. If your answers affect the direction of your thoughts and send you on a new trajectory, what can you do with that new perspective?

For example, if our belief is that our workload makes it impossible to take a holiday, we could ask ourselves, "Do I know anyone who is busy but still takes regular holidays?" If we're asking the question with genuine curiosity, we're not seeking to gain something, but that doesn't mean we can't then use flexibility of mind to see what we might be able to do with the insight. That's how a shift in thinking can lead to a shift in behaviour. It's how we can overcome the limiting beliefs we place on ourselves.

That Question

So, let's return to the question I asked at the start of this chapter: "Why bother practising to grow a leadership mindset given that it'll be hard?" If you haven't already, here's a chance to reflect on what your reason to might be and how that might connect to your why.

Resilience is hard by definition. If what we're doing is easy, we don't need to be resilient. That's why it's important to take care of ourselves while we're doing whatever we're trying to achieve. I don't say that glibly. If we work ceaselessly in the face of adversity, we will wear out. That's not an amazing insight, it's just true. So yes, while we want to achieve the focus of our why, constantly chipping away without taking breaks, without taking time to recharge, or without feeding our souls may help us get there fast, but it might be worth asking what kind of person we'll be when we arrive.

I guess what I'm trying to say is, yes, work toward what you believe in. But don't forget to be kind to yourself along the way.

Resilience Reminders

♦ The behaviours of resilience are bouncebackability, discipline, and keeping your eyes on the prize.

♦ The key to bouncebackability is finding a point of control.

♦ Internal discipline, the sort we ask of ourselves, is a chance to practise a different way of doing things.

♦ Remembering what's at the end of the road is what makes each step in a difficult journey possible.

♦ Unattainable whys are not achievable and as a result have the potential to serve as whys for years to come.

♦ Socratic questioning can help us to undermine our self-limiting beliefs.

Chapter 5
Creating Leaders

Dependency Cycles and Enlightened Leaders

Jim's first experience of leading was managing a team. When he got that role, he wanted to do the best job he could. He wanted his team to succeed and maybe because of that he hung over their work to make sure it was of the high quality that the company expected and that his team wanted to produce. He didn't do that because he's a micromanager, but because that's how he was managed. In fact, that's how all the leaders he had ever met managed, so this must be the right way. Whatever the reason, his leadership began to take on the look of a manager working flat out to make sure his team was doing what it needed to when it needed to do it. If you'd asked Jim what managing felt like, he'd say it was like running under a high-wire act, bracing himself to catch the wire-walker, who could fall at any minute. Despite that, he kept going because he knew that if the team failed, he failed too. And he did all that while doing his own job as well.

The challenge of leading that way is that it becomes a vicious circle. Jim can never leave the team to do its job because the team can't function without him. Instead of making him seem approachable, his "always open" door policy created an environment in which people feel free to ask questions they should already know the answers to. He's noticed that they don't so much check in as ask for permission to do simple things. And then he noticed that when he asks questions in meetings, they wait for him to answer them too. He can't see how things got this way. All he wanted to do was help his team succeed.

Though Jim can't see it, there are lots of reasons why a leader can find themselves in a situation like that. Like with Jim, it may happen through a combination of what we've seen leaders do, and a real desire to help the team as best we can. Many leaders, intentionally or unintentionally, lead the way they do because their style of leadership was modelled by someone who led them.

If that someone leads in the way Jim's managers did, we can become trapped in a way of leading that breeds dependency in our teams – a dependency cycle. That happens because our team is in a cycle of their own; a cycle of trying to please the leader, and of guessing what the leader wants. Eventually it leads to the team giving up and waiting to be told what to do. They realize that they can't guess what the leader wants, so they will always feel like they're not doing a good job. Their solution? To wait for the leader to tell them what to do.

But that isn't the only way to lead. Some leaders are what I call enlightened leaders – someone who truly empowers their teams and is forever looking for ways to grow the team and themselves. Those enlightened leaders operate that way because their leadership world view is informed by the subject of this chapter: they strive to create leaders of others.

Years ago I came across a poster that I've never seen again. It was one of those inspirational posters and it depicted a tall ship, sails bellowing in the wind as it sailed on the ocean. The only thing was, the ship was sailing toward the edge of the world, its crew blissfully unaware that in mere minutes their captain would be leading them into oblivion. The caption read something like, "If the whole world followed you, would you be proud of where you led it?" I like that idea because the implication is that we have a responsibility to the people we lead. To my mind, the highest place we can lead someone is to the point of becoming a leader in their own right – able to think critically, to challenge, to take responsibility, and to guide and nurture those around them. It may be a cliché, but it's one worth repeating: great leaders don't have the most followers, they create the most leaders. If that makes sense to you then you'll understand why creating leaders is one of the six attributes.

My guess is, if you're reading this book, that does make sense to you. My other guess is that enabling people to grow is what you want to do as a leader. So, before we get into the behaviours of creating leaders of others, let's focus for a moment on two concepts that underpin this chapter.

Talking to People's Highest Self

The beautiful thing about people is that we're each a mix – not always in equal measures – of the best we can be and the fears that hold us back. It's my experience that both sides of that coin are available at any given moment. Let's say that someone you line manage has just made a mistake that's cost the company thousands. Right now they're certain that they're going to lose their job and secretly vowing to never take another risk if, by some miracle, they do get to keep it – that's their fear. It's also true that at the same time they're in a position to learn and grow from the experience – to exhibit the best that they can be. Which road they head down depends on which side of them we choose to talk to: their fear or their highest self.

Here's what those two conversations might look like. In the first, we're talking to their fear.

It's been ten minutes since the stuff hit the fan, and Bill's heading to Jane's office. It's on the corner: glass on two sides. It's like a giant aquarium, in which his colleagues can watch him flounder. They may not be able to hear what's going on, but that just means their imaginations will be running wild.

She's sitting at her desk, and looks up briefly as he walks in.

"Thanks for coming, Bill," she says. She gestures to a chair on the other side of the desk.

"No problem," he says. It comes out quietly and he shakes his head at himself.

"I'll be honest, Bill," Jane says, looking at the printouts on her desk. "This is a real problem." She pushes the papers to one side and looks up at him. "I'm not blaming you," she says, "it's just that we all have a boss, and this doesn't help me or the department."

He shuffles in his chair, "I'm sorry."

She softens momentarily. "Bill," she says, "I'm not blaming you, we just have to sort this mess out."

We could go on, but I'm guessing you get the point. Jane is trying to be as kind as she can; that's not the problem. She's even said twice that she doesn't blame Bill. I think it's fair to say that Jane is trying her best to take care of Bill while struggling through the fallout of his mistake. So here's the thing: how do you think Bill's feeling? Since it doesn't look like Bill's going to be fired, how likely is he to take an initiative, own a project, or encourage those around him to step up now?

This is what I mean about speaking to someone's fears. Notice that Jane is doing that unintentionally. She doesn't mean to play to his fears; she's doing it, on the one hand, because she's dealing with her own, and, on the other, because she's probably trying to figure out a solution. Her focus isn't on developing Bill, it's on crisis management.

Speaking to someone's fears fuels the feeling that their worst fears are true. In this case, that reinforces Bill's world view that playing small and not leading is the best route to take at work and in life. And to reiterate, we don't speak to people's fears on purpose. We do so because our focus rests on getting things done rather than taking every chance, even the difficult ones, to grow the people we lead.

Now here's what talking to someone's highest self might look like.

It's been half an hour since the stuff hit the fan, and Bill's heading to Jane's office. It's on the corner: glass on two sides. It's like a giant aquarium, in which his colleagues can watch him flounder. They may not be able to hear what's going on, but that just means their imaginations will be running wild.

As he turns the corner, he sees Jane get up from her desk and head to her office door. She smiles when her eyes meet his and for a moment he wonders why.

"Thanks for coming, Bill," she says. She leads him over to the couch pressed against the glass wall.

"No problem," he says. It comes out quietly and he shakes his head at himself.

"Well that didn't go the way we planned," she says, sitting down.

"No," he says, sheepishly.

"Bill," she says kindly, "don't lose confidence on me now. That was a bold thing you did. Yes, it's caused a problem, yes, we'll have to sort it out, but we'll have a bigger problem if the only thing you see in this is the mistake. Do you want to have a guess how many mistakes I've made on the way to that seat?" She points at the leather chair behind her desk. She pauses and then says, "Let's just leave it at many."

She relaxes into the couch.

"I'm not sure what went wrong," he says.

"We can do lessons learnt in post-mortem," she says. "For now, what do you think matters most?"

He feels the tension drain from his shoulders. "I have an idea for how we can fix it."

"Good," she says, "Jason and Emily have been working on this for the past half hour. They have a handle on what's happening. Between the three of you we can figure out how to right the ship."

The differences are subtle but important: Jane meeting Bill at the door; sitting with him on the couch; acknowledging the problem, yet encouraging the drive that led to it; admitting that she's made mistakes too; and creating space for Bill to be part of the solution. All of those actions combined speak to Bill's highest self. Jane sees his fears – in this case manifested in his sheepishness – and consciously chooses to not play to them because she knows he's already beating himself up about the mistake. Instead, she demonstrates that he still has plenty to offer and reinforces the world view that mistakes are part of leading.

How likely is it that Bill takes the risk of leading again? And how likely is he to learn from the mistake he's just made? That's the difference between talking to someone's fears and talking to their highest self. Just like all the behaviours we're discussing in this book, getting that right consistently is hard. But getting it right isn't the prize, trying to is.

That conversation wouldn't have gone so well if Jane had spoken to Bill the minute she found out there was a problem. But that doesn't mean Jane has to wait to address the issue. Just like in the first scene, Jane has to report to her own boss, so she has to act. And she does. The thing she does right away is to ask Jason and Emily to start work on righting the ship. Knowing that the problem was being worked on cleared some mind space to allow her to choose how to talk with Bill. Even in a crisis – especially in a crisis – acting right away reduces our ability to talk to someone's higher self.

Though I won't always refer to speaking to someone's higher self, take it as being implicit in everything that follows in this chapter, which is also true for our second concept.

Giving What Others Want to Receive

Let's say Phillip has a ball. It's a great ball and one that any child, in his opinion, would be proud to play football with. One day he sees his nieces and nephews sitting in the garden, clearly at a loose end. He offers them the ball to play with and because their answer is non-committal, he sets out goal posts for them and marks out a centre line. "Who's ready to play for the World Cup?" he says excitedly, his back to them. He sets the ball down in the middle of the makeshift pitch and turns to the kids, expecting them to be mirroring his enthusiasm. Instead, they're sitting just as they were, still looking bored.

It's fair to say that he's more than a little annoyed as he picks up the ball and heads inside.

I'm sure you can see the problem in that scenario. Helpful as he's trying to be, Phillip offered the kids what he thought they should have. How many times have we done that as leaders? We offer the team a project, a solution, an afternoon of training only to be puzzled why they're not as enthused as we think they should be. Though it may look ungrateful, what the team – and the children in our scene – are telling us is that they want or need something else. Our challenge is figuring out what. I'm not saying that it's always going to be easy. Sometimes asking will work, sometimes it won't. But what definitely won't work is assuming that we know what someone else needs.

Just like the concept of speaking to someone's highest self will run through this chapter, so will the idea of offering what some-one needs as opposed to what we want to give. Both are based on the idea of creating leaders as opposed to making sure a task gets done well. It's implicit that as we grow leaders, those leaders become effective in what they do.

A Small Caution

When I consult on this attribute, it often comes up that who we hire is an important factor in the success of this approach. I don't disagree with that. Creating leaders only works if the people we're trying to grow want to lead. That's why hiring matters. If we want a company full of leaders, hiring people who have the potential to work at that level is the first link in the chain.

Of course, unless you're a brand-new business, your staff is already in place. That doesn't mean you can't create leaders. It just means starting small, perhaps with a receptive team, and then moving the work out slowly. Think of it as a culture change.

The Behaviours of Creating Leaders

Now that we have the ground work in place, let's take a look at the behaviours we'll be focusing on in this chapter:

Attribute of a leadership mindset	Behaviours
Creating leaders	Empowering others Positioning others for leadership

I'm sure you can see why the two concepts we've just looked at underpin these behaviours. To empower someone, we have to speak and act to who they can be, not who they currently are. To position someone for leadership we have to first make sure that they have what they need to succeed. And we do all that while making sure we're getting our own work done, and while doing our best to make sure that we're not setting the team – or ourselves – up to fail.

Leadership is daunting. Creating leaders is even more daunting. As with everything else in this book, you will hit setbacks – personality differences, staff making mistakes, people not moving as quickly as you'd want, and so on. And just like everything else in this book, success isn't determined by how quickly you create leaders; it's measured by your willingness to keep trying.

The Behaviours of Creating Leaders: Empowering Others

It's a truism that if we want to grow leaders, we'll need to empower others. The problem with a statement like that is it doesn't really mean much. What does empowering someone look like? Does it mean giving them more responsibility? More control over their schedule? More decisions to make? Of course, as they become more empowered, they may take these on naturally, but if we give them away, are we empowering the person?

To answer that question we'll need to first understand the way in which we currently lead. Or, I should say, how we currently think about leading. My premise is that the way we think about leadership determines how we'll lead. So let's conjure a scene and see if it helps us to answer that question.

Imagine a group of leaders standing on one side of a large field. Scattered in front of them are the remains of a 1990s' office:

upright filing cabinets, monolithic wooden desks, heavy chrome floor lamps, unrolled venetian blinds hanging magically (it's all in our imagination, don't forget), cream PC monitors with their equally cream floppy disk drives, and, of course, overhead projectors balancing on small plastic tables.

As they survey the scene, a flying goblin flutters in front of them and reveals the challenge they're about to face. "Before you," it says in a voice that sounds as sweet as vanilla smells, "is your leadership challenge. You must navigate to the other side of the field with a partner – one leading, and one following – going through, not around, the office debris before you." The goblin begins to fade slowly until there's nothing left of it.

The leaders, unfazed, pair up. They decide who will lead and who will follow and then, just as each follower takes their first step, a blindfold magically appears over their eyes.

The vanilla voice appears from nowhere: "Sorry, forgot to mention that," it says.

The leaders brave on because it takes more than blindfolds and dated office furniture to unsettle them.

As you watch this scene unfold in your imagination, you notice how the pairs of leaders are going about the challenge. Some have the blindfolded person place their hands on their guide's shoulders. The guide marches ahead like it's a competition. They place their hands on their follower's hands and hold them there so they don't fall off as they twist and turn their way through the nineties.

Then there's another approach. In this method the guides each stand beside their blindfolded partner. They offer instructions: turn left, turn right, walk straight. With each instruction, their partner makes a move. They're making good time, but the hands-on-shoulders bunch are way out ahead.

But then you notice a pair that hasn't moved yet. They're the only ones yet to leave the starting line, and because of that, the blindfold hasn't appeared on the follower's eyes. You can see that they're talking, but you can't hear what they're saying. You sigh, but then remember that this in your imagination so you turn up the volume and listen in.

"OK, so I'll go straight and then right and then left." The follower pauses and looks into the distance, possibly at the overhead projector ten feet away. "I'll touch that projector, then turn right and walk straight."

The guide nods sagely. "Listen," he says, "I don't have a tape measure or anything with me but how can you know when you have to turn left or right?"

The question throws the follower. She thinks for a second. "I can feel my way, I can count steps, or I can ask you to tell me."

"Let's explore the steps idea," the guide says. "How many would you take before you need to make your first turn?"

The follower thinks that through, counting out steps in her head. "I'd say ten."

"Small steps or normal steps?"

"Yeah, good point. Smaller steps since I'm blindfolded, so fourteen."

"Let's run through the plan one more time with the steps," the guide says.

The follower runs through the plan out loud. Lists off the number of steps. When she's done she turns to the guide, a smile of anticipation dancing on her lips.

"Ready?" the guide says.

She nods and takes a step. As she does the blindfold appears. She keeps going. Her guide is standing at the starting line, watching her make her way across the graveyard of office furniture.

Task, Teach, Create

Three different focuses when leading: on completing the task, on teaching people, or on creating leaders. All three are valid. All three are needed at different times. If you haven't already, ask yourself which guide in the scene best reflects your focus as a leader? Which do you inhabit most often? I'm not saying all the time, no one approaches everything the same way all the time. Maybe you drift to one when your back's against the wall. Maybe one feels more comfortable than the others. Our focus as a leader can shift for all sorts of reasons. Being aware of what we focus on by default means we can make choices about where we might want to focus instead. So let's explore those three areas of focus.

Task

If our focus is on getting the task done, our behaviour will reflect that. In our scene a focus on the task played out as the follower placing their hands on the guide's shoulder as they headed out. Like all task-focused leaders, our guide just wants to get the task done quickly and correctly. Because the focus is on the task, not on developing the follower, the guide doesn't consult with the follower. The guide has an idea in mind and off they go. That doesn't mean that there aren't good reasons to be task-focused in real life. If the task is critical, if there's a very tight deadline, if – for all sorts of reasons – there's no room for error, then focusing on the task is probably a good idea. To repeat, those aren't bad things. And they're good reasons to focus on the task.

Of course, there are limits to being task-focused. In this method the guide is doing more than guiding. You could say that they're doing the task *for* the follower. Not because they're control freaks, but because they want the job done fast and right. That kind of leading comes from a good place – from caring about the task and having a desire to make sure it gets done, not to mention a willingness to take full responsibility for the well-being of the follower. The thing is, when we translate the metaphor of leading that way into the real world, we find that if we, as leaders, put so much effort into getting a task done right, we'd save time and get the job done even quicker by not having the follower involved at all. What I'm saying is that leading a follower with a task focus can actually make the process take longer. Not only that, it can make leading frustrating since the follower is contributing little or nothing. What's also true is that, although the approach builds trust in the guide – more so with every successful crossing – the follower doesn't have the chance to learn in the process. And there's bad news for the guide too. If we're putting so much focus on the task that we're doing it for our people, we fall behind in our own day jobs.

Teach

When our focus is on teaching, we use our skill, expertise, and vantage point to show others what to do. In our scene, the guide's focus on teaching the follower leaves the guide giving step-by-step instructions about how to get across the field. When might a focus on teaching be a good idea in the real world? Well, how about if there's a specific, company-approved way to write a report, perhaps using a specific branding format? What about existing systems and process, which – until there's a good reason to change – the company adheres to? If that's the case, why wouldn't we teach people what they are? We teach that kind of information because simple tactical and technical details can be easily remembered and learnt. If staff need to, they can write it down and use that for reference. The point is that we're teaching stuff that's learnable by rote – that doesn't need to be thought through. And that's what makes the teach focus a good idea.

Just like being task-focused, there's a time and a place for focusing on teaching. That also means there's a time and a place not to. What happens, for example, if a job isn't repeatable? What if our staff are dealing with fast-moving situations or we need them to solve problems that are different each time? What might be the implications of focusing on teaching in situations like that?

The Limits of Being Task- and Teach-Focused

Let's take a walk back to that imaginary office graveyard. Focus on the task and teach teams. Notice how two guides – one task and one teach – both reach into their pockets at exactly the same time. They each pull out a phone, accept the call, and hold the phone up to their ear. Their followers stop dead. They can't remove their blindfolds, so they wait. The guides look horrified. As if dancing in sync to an inaudible beat, they each clasp their free hand to their mouth. Then in the same synchronized motion they shout, "I've got to go, it's an emergency!" to their follower and high-tail it out of there.

Because this is all in your imagination, do a split screen of the two followers left alone in the office graveyard. Notice the nervous looks, the nervous smiles on their faces. And then the slow-dawning realization that they're on their own.

OK, that might be a bit dramatic but you can see the real-world parallel. If we allow ourselves to only focus on the task or on teaching staff, what happens when we get called away, are in a meeting, or are otherwise unavailable? How likely is it that the team can carry on without us? That's a serious question because although there are pros to both the task and the teach approach, they share a big downside: they breed the dependency cycle that we talked about at the start of this chapter. Here that dependency cycle occurs because we're giving staff a reason to abdicate responsibility for thinking for themselves – there's no need to since their leader will eventually give them the answer to the challenge. And since doing what the leader says is the best way to ensure that staff don't take the flack if things go wrong, it also means we're encouraging our teams to take no responsibility. That's some fallout when we're just trying to get the task done or to help our team.

To be clear, that doesn't mean the task and teach approaches should never be used. It just means there isn't a single approach (including the six attributes) that works in every situation. Sometimes we have to resort to another way.

Create

If you have time, jump back to the scene and read about the third approach again. When you're done, see if you can answer these questions:

1   How does the guide communicate with the follower?

2   How does the guide get the follower to count steps?

3   Why is a "smile of anticipation dancing" on the lips of the follower?

If you said, by asking questions, by introducing the idea of measuring – but not giving a solution – and because she's excited to give it a go, I'd agree. Here's another question: why does the third guide lead that way?

To answer that question we need to think about another one: what does the guide's focus say about their leadership world view? While you puzzle that one out, let's see if we can ask them.

You can't believe your luck when you catch up with the task and teach guides coming out of a conference room: it turns out that the calls they got on the field were summoning them to the same emergency meeting. They're chatting to each other, and the teach guide is smiling so you guess that the emergency's over. "Hi," you say, "I was wondering if I could ask you both a question?"

They nod kindly, and it reminds you that they're both good people who are doing the best they can.

"Thanks," you say, because you're kind too. "If I were to ask you to sum up your view on leadership in one sentence, what would you say?"

They think about that. It's the task guide who speaks first, "For my money, it's making sure things get done right and on time."

The teach guide nods, but offers a different view. "I'd say leadership is all about sharing the knowledge and expertise I've gained to help my people be as effective as they can be."

They're textbook answers and you're not surprised in the least. Then, with the kind of luck that only happens in stories, the create guide comes strolling down the hallway. "Hey," you say, "I've a question for you."

The create guide stops short and waits for the question.

"Leadership in one sentence," you say, realizing too late that it's come out as a statement.

The guide doesn't even pause to think: "A chance to help others become leaders."

As we'd expect, each world view gives rise to a different understanding of what it means to lead. And that understanding leads to focusing on different things, which is why each guide leads in the way they do.

Maybe now is a good time to return to the question I posed when we first considered what it means to empower people. What I wanted to know was whether we're empowering people by giving them things.

Our answer depends on which leadership world view we hold. If we're drawn to a task or a teach world view, we might give more responsibility, more flexibility in scheduling, or any number of things. That might lead to creating leaders but, to be honest, I'd be surprised if it does. That's quite simply because people aren't thinking for themselves. They're not involved in the process. They feel that things are being done to them – that they are subjects rather than agents.

For example, what if we don't need to get the task done fast, it's not confidential, and we're not just following the usual repeatable process or doing things the way we do them around here? Those kinds of situations can become moments in which we have the chance to encourage others to think, and lead, for themselves. If that makes sense to you, then the first question to ask ourselves in any leadership moment is this: what am I focusing on? Am I focused on getting the task done? Teaching a process? Or am I encouraging people to think? If you want to get people to think, does doing something for them, or teaching them how to do it, achieve that? Will it encourage people to problem solve, or to take initiative in the best interests of the company?

The core of the shift toward a create mindset is seeing our leadership roles differently. To see our purpose as encouraging others to think and act for themselves. If creating leaders of others is what we're looking for, the create approach is one way to get started. So let's take a closer look at the create pair and see what the guide was up to.

You probably anticipated that of the three guides in the office graveyard, create took the longest to complete the task. More time in the front end, and more time in the execution. But here's the thing: if you asked the followers of the task and teach guides to go back to the start and walk through on their own, without help from anyone, how likely are they to be able to do it? What about if we asked the same of the create follower? How likely is it that the create follower will be able to continue if her guide gets called away like the other two?

Unlike the others, the create guide realized that they could use the challenge to grow leadership in the follower. To be clear, that means the create approach isn't a model or a process. The magic of create is that it empowers people by involving them.

An Involvement Digression

Sometimes when I talk about involvement with a group of leaders, there's pushback. Not because leaders don't want to involve their staff, but because the intention to involve staff and actually involving staff aren't always the same thing.

"Don't I know it," Ingrid inVolve might say. "We've been offering opportunities for staff to be involved for years. And do you think they take it?" She sighs. "We have open-door leadership meetings, we don't pass major decisions without asking for staff input, we have voluntary staff update sessions where they can voice any of their concerns ..." she pauses, exasperated. "If people want to be involved, there are sooooo many opportunities." She drags out the "so" to convey that she could list more.

And if any of that did make people feel involved, that'd be great.

Ingrid shakes her head, "So now I'm responsible for how people feel too. Is that it?"

OK, so maybe "feel" was the wrong word. What I meant to say was if any of that actually involved people, that'd be great.

She laughs, and it's not the laughing with you kind.

There's a difference between informing, consulting, and involving people. Great as all the things that Ingrid's company is doing are, the effect of all that effort results in either informing or consulting people, not involving them. That isn't just true for Ingrid's company. Every time we invite staff to a meeting to update them on progress, or to share information, we're informing them. If we ask for their view, we're consulting them. What both of these have in common is that neither allow staff agency.

"The agency is giving them a chance to have their input," Ingrid says softly.

Softly, I'm guessing, because of what the leadership of her company does with the staff input. The challenge isn't in asking for input, it's in doing something with what people offer. If we don't then there's a good chance we'll leave our staff worse off than when we started.

"Worse because we asked for their input?" Ingrid says, "How can they be worse off?"

I know, the concept sounds flawed, doesn't it? If we consult staff on a change, a new direction, or even the processes they use every day, how can that leave them and the business worse off? It doesn't sound possible.

If we're asking for input, we have an obligation – as leaders – to do something with the information we receive. Let's look at an example from outside of the business world. Let's say you have a friend who asks your opinion on whether they should buy a brand-new BMW i3 or save the money for a deposit on a house. Your friend has a family: a family that's outgrowing the two-bedroom flat he's living in with his wife and two kids. You know they've been saving for a while. So you're confused by the question because the answer is so obvious, and you remind your friend about his priorities. He nods, and thanks you for the reality check. Job done, right? It would seem so, but when he pulls up in front of your house in the said i3, you're more than stunned. You're annoyed.

Let's not stop there. Let's say this isn't the first time that's happened. Let's say your friend repeatedly asks for advice he never takes – even when the right thing to do is obvious. What would be the long-term effect on your friendship? How long would it be before you get frustrated? How long before you stop offering your opinion? How long before you resent being asked and write him off as a lost cause?

That's about the same amount of time it'd take before your staff give up on offering their input if they see nothing is being done with their ideas. What's more, your relationship with your staff gets damaged each time you ask for input and do nothing with it.

And that's why we end up puzzled if staff don't come to open-door leadership meetings, updates, or anything else we throw at them. They don't come because, just like the friend in the example, they figure out quickly that nothing meaningful comes of it.

Informing and consulting with staff is the best way to provide the illusion of involvement: both for you and for your staff. But that illusion will wear off if no action is taken. In my observations, it always wears off faster for staff than for leaders. That's what the create guide understands. To get that smile on the follower's face, the follower has to feel they've been listened to and that their ideas have been implemented. The result is a follower who's invested in what's happening. And that's the same feeling we want in our staff when projects require buy-in – staff engagement and change management, for example. Because the create approach requires staff to be involved in the process, they can also be involved in developing and then implementing the idea. Thought of like that, engagement is the by-product of involvement.

Since we need to act and think for ourselves to be involved, it also means that involved people are empowered people. So if empowerment rests on a foundation of people thinking for themselves, let's explore how we encourage that as we create leaders of others.

Challenge: Letting Go

The focus of this challenge is to begin the journey of really involving your people. For some, that may be a scary idea. It means letting go and giving some autonomy to your staff. But to start with, this challenge isn't about your team, it's about you. To be clear, I'm not asking you to action anything: it's just about being genuinely curious.

So if you're ready, let's begin.

This challenge involves three questions. That's it. You can answer them in your head or on a piece of paper, if that helps. I'm not asking you to share your answers with anyone; you don't even need to do anything with your answers. For now, I'm just encouraging you to notice your reaction to the questions.

And here they are:

1   Is there an area in your team or business where efficiency or effectiveness is not where you'd like it to be?

    Don't work hard here. Go with the first thing that comes to mind. There's no need to delve deeply into the question, just notice if you identify an area or not.

2   Who in that area has the potential to lead?

    This might take a bit more effort. Think about the team or specific people in the area. Is anyone particularly self-driven? Do they offer ideas? Has anyone indicated that they want more responsibility, even though none has been available?

3   What would it take for you to allow that person, or those people, to develop their own ideas to address that challenge?

Notice your reaction to this question. Do you come up with reasons why that's not possible? Are you at a loss about what it would take? Or do you have an idea? Are you feeling that you already give chances for others to lead?

If we're giving people chances to lead, but the challenge remains, then the approach we're taking might not be working. If we have an idea but haven't implemented it, we're at a loss, or our first reaction is to list reasons why we can't let others lead, could we be feeling that the risk of letting go outweighs the potential reward?

If that's the feeling, it's a real one. So, here's another question: is it possible to start small?

Can you find a low-risk challenge, so if things go wrong it won't have a major impact? You might not find one in the area you started thinking about in this challenge, but that's OK. The point of this challenge is to help you prove to yourself that creating leaders of others may work in your team or business. Building on success might be a useful way to get that ball rolling.

If you're up for it, hold onto the low-risk challenge you've just identified. Go back to questions 2 and 3 and answer them again. You'll know that you've reached your risk tolerance when your answer to question 3 comes easily.

The goal isn't to action that low-risk area — that's your call. The goal is to find your entry point into an area of leadership that can be nerve-racking for even the most seasoned leader.

Provoking Thought

The best way I know to encourage thinking is to actively provoke it. That's what the guide in the create example is doing. The guide is asking the follower to solve the puzzle for herself, and while he doesn't give the answer, he supports, prods, and encourages. And he does all that with questions. In fact, the create guide in our example did nothing but ask questions.

That's important because the shift in thinking for the leader who wants to grow leaders of others is to see clearly that directly sharing our expertise by doing or telling doesn't empower people. That may sound harsh, but I'm not saying that our expertise isn't valuable, or that we shouldn't share it. We just need to do so in a way that provokes thought in the person we're sharing it with. Wondering how to do that? Well, that brings us back to questions.

Rather than telling someone what to do, or doing it for them, the trick is to use our skill and experience to ask questions that help focus the thinking of the person we're trying to grow. It's about asking the right question at the right time to lead someone to a journey of discovery of their own. Maybe that's too poetic, but I do mean it. The gift of a question that's informed by our expertise and insight is that it helps people figure out a problem for themselves while becoming aware of the challenges they may encounter.

Let me try to illustrate what I mean with a real-world example of the office graveyard.

Greg walks into Leigh's office and she smiles warmly, leaning back in her chair. "Hi, Greg," she says. "I have a project you might be interested in."

Greg walks over to her desk, glances at the papers strewn across the surface for a clue then looks up at her. "What have you got?" he asks, no idea what he's getting into.

"The numbers from the employee feedback survey came back, and we're still getting low satisfaction scores for middle managers." Leigh pauses. She's been in senior management for over fifteen years. Of course she's seen numbers like this before, and of course she knows what she'd do, but this time she's not interested in what she'd do.

Greg looks nervous. He's wondering if his name's at the top of the list of unsatisfactory middle managers. It's the only reason he can think of why he'd be here. "OK," he says.

Of course Greg would assume that. Leigh knows it's only the outstanding managers who question their abilities. She doesn't attempt to alleviate his concern. It'll dissipate, she thinks. "I'd like to get your take on what we can do to create some shifts, Greg."

He begins a sigh of relief but catches himself before it gets too long. He takes the empty seat on the other side of the desk. "Where would you like me to start?"

Of course she could tell him, but that's not what she's going for. "We know where we want to end up."

"With a more empowering middle management group?" he asks.

"That's the goal, yes, but how do we get there?"

"We can remind them of their job descriptions, write it into per-formance agreements ..." he trails off.

They're ideas, but not Greg's ideas. It's textbook human resources stuff. "Isn't 'supporting staff' in a middle manager's job description now?" she asks.

He nods, "I guess the question is: how do we get people to do what they're already supposed to be doing?"

She nods, but doesn't offer anything.

"How can we do that?" he muses.

The question isn't aimed at Leigh, she knows that.

"We could find out why it's not being done," Greg says, then pauses for a second. "We could do a survey. That would give us a handle on the challenges people are facing in supporting their teams." He pauses again.

"And you feel we'll get the information we need that way?" Leigh's seen the kind of surveys Greg's thinking about. Standard questions leading to standard answers. It's probably because of those kinds of surveys that they still have the problem.

"Well, what we need is honest feedback," he says.

"That would give us an understanding of the real issues," she agrees. "How could we go about getting honest feedback?"

He sighs and this time he doesn't try to rein it in, "Well, there are surveys, senior manager interviews, peer discussion groups ..." he trails off again.

"What would a peer discussion group look like?" she asks.

"Well, it doesn't have to be framed like that. We could call it a focus group," he nods to himself.

"What if middle managers don't show up?"

"That's true, but if we make it a lunch-time session, maybe lay on pizza, that'll help the numbers. Plus, managers will have a chance to talk about the challenges they're facing." His voice picks up pace a little. "From there we can figure out the themes from their conversations." He's talking faster now, he can feel it. "We can take the themes and compare it with the data from your staff survey. That'll let us figure out where the problem is." He takes a breath before heading for the final assault. "Do that and we'll have a new outlook on how to handle the problem." He stops dead. Smiles. "It's a big step, that last one, but I'm sure we'd be able to take it."

"Makes sense," Leigh says. "Are you willing to make that happen?"

Greg's still smiling when he nods.

What Leigh's doing is using her experience to ask a question in response to what Greg is saying. She doesn't necessarily know where Greg's thinking will take him, but she does know what ideas are unlikely to work. That's why she doesn't add fuel to the survey idea but does encourage the focus group concept. Greg feels involved because the idea was his and empowered because he's charged with actioning it.

And this was done by asking questions.

Types and Qualities of Questions

Before we go too much further, let's take a moment to remind ourselves of the types of questions we have at our disposal with some examples from Leigh and Greg's exchange.

Type of question	Definition	Example from Leigh and Greg
Open	A question that can't be answered with one word.	"How could we go about getting honest feedback?"
Probing	A question designed to get more information (a type of open question).	"That's the goal, but how do we get there?"
Leading	Questions that suggest a direction.	"Isn't 'supporting staff' in a middle manager's job description now?"
Hypothetical	What if questions to expand thinking.	"What if middle managers don't show up?"
Closed	Questions that can be answered with one word.	"Are you willing to make that happen?"

We can use those questions as a sort of funnel to guide the thinking of the leader we're trying to grow.

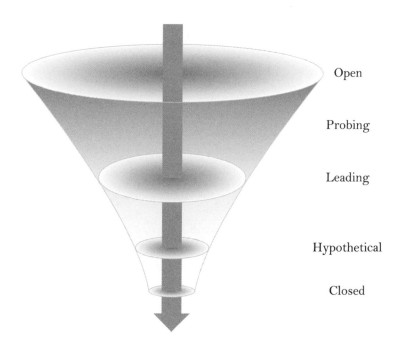

Open

Probing

Leading

Hypothetical

Closed

I'm guessing that nothing you've read so far about questioning is new to you. If that's true, you'll be pleased to know that that was a precursor to this: now that we've been reminded of the types of questions, let's think about what makes good create questions.

When I was training in psychological coaching, one of the things I saw people doing was writing out lists of what they thought were good questions. Questioning is the bedrock of the psychological coaching approach, so the thinking was that collecting good examples is like a carpenter collecting tools. The only thing was that they ended up with nothing more than a list of questions. What makes the create approach work isn't preformed questions, it's the ability to ask questions based on what the other person is saying. So rather than come up with a list of examples, I'd like to offer the ingredients of questions that grow others as leaders. Good create questions:

♦ Are clear.

♦ Are concise.

♦ Are asked one at a time.

♦ Follow on from what was just said.

♦ Provoke thought.

♦ Get to the point.

♦ State the obvious.

If you've read Chapter 2, you'll recognize the importance of stating the obvious, so I won't dwell on it here. All I'll say now is that the ability to ask the obvious question helps us learn in any situation. That's why asking obvious questions helps when we want to take the create approach.

Questions with a Purpose

What makes a question work, though, isn't just that it contains all of those ingredients: it works because it combines the ingredients with purpose. When we're empowering others, we're asking questions for a reason. That reason is based on a friend we first met in Chapter 3: a loose hypothesis. In that chapter I encouraged framing ideas as a loose hypothesis, to remind us that holding onto cherished ideas is a great way to limit our flexibility of mind.

Loose hypotheses can have other uses. And here's how they apply to questions with a purpose. When we empower others, we might have an idea – a hypothesis – about what could be making it tough for the person to take on the mantle of leadership. So we test that hypothesis but we can't carry out experiments as we would if we were applying the scientific method. So how do we test a loose hypothesis? As I'm sure you've already figured out, it's with a question. If the answer we receive suggests we're on the right track, we keep going; if it doesn't, we drop the hypothesis and form another.

In the Leigh and Greg example, although Leigh never states her hypothesis, it's informing her line of questioning. Questions like, "Isn't 'supporting staff' in a middle manager's job description now?" and, "And you feel we'll get the information we need?" are based on the hypothesis that a real or imagined challenge might allow Greg to think beyond standard procedures. That's why the focus of Leigh's questions encourage Greg to come up with a different approach.

Here are two more of Leigh's questions and the loose hypotheses that inform them:

Question	Loose hypothesis
"What if middle managers don't show up?"	Greg hasn't considered the obstacles to getting managers to attend.
"What would a peer discussion group look like?"	Greg doesn't yet have a clear idea about the format of the group.

Here's one more thing: when Greg does offer an innovative idea, or shows that he's considering the obstacles, Leigh drops her hypothesis and gives him the space to develop his thinking. That's what I mean by a *loose* hypothesis. We adjust and let go as it's proved wrong. If we didn't it would be a fixed hypothesis and that would give the conversation a different focus: rather than growing a leader, we'd make them feel like we're trying to catch them out.

Challenge: Forming a Loose Hypothesis

If around now you're feeling a little daunted by the prospect of developing loose hypotheses, don't forget that your ability will grow over time. To help with that the intention of this challenge is to offer some practice.

For the purpose of this example, let's think about a simple, non-business context. Let's say a friend comes to you, out of the blue, and says that they'd like to talk about an idea they've had of quitting their job – in an industry they've been in for the past ten years – to become a travel writer. They've never mentioned this before, and you don't know of any writing ambitions. You've never thought of this person as impulsive, so this isn't something you dismiss as a whim.

Forming a loose hypothesis is essentially asking yourself why you're asking a question, by identifying the possibilities that you think might be at play. So let me ask you: why might your friend be considering becoming a travel writer? Here are a few possibilities:

♦ Bored with current job.

♦ Looking for adventure.

♦ Wants to travel.

Some or none of these might be true. A loose hypothesis isn't about being right, it's about forging the direction of the conversation. So if forming a loose hypothesis is about seeing the factors at play, asking a question based on that involves deciding what you think the root of the person's challenge is. Can you think of a question that might test whether any or all of these possibilities are true? If you like, think on that before you read the next paragraph.

What about asking something like, "What prompted that idea?" It's a question that gives your friend room to mention any number of possibilities, including the three you've speculated about.

But let's say they come back with, "I've been reading travel magazines for years, I even write little articles about places I've been, I just never show them to anyone."

Now you know that your friend has the passion and maybe the talent. So the three loose hypotheses you considered are out and you need a new one. You could think about why they're coming to you with this rather than just doing it, and so a new loose hypothesis might be: they're nervous about taking the next step.

What question might you ask to test that hypothesis? Once again, have a think before you read on.

A possible question might be something like: "Is it feeling like a leap in the dark right now?" or "Are you nervous about taking the next step?"

Let's say your friend comes back with: "Not really, I already have an agency willing to represent me." Now you know your friend isn't acting on a whim, has the talent, and has a plan. So the thought now might come back to why they're coming to talk about it rather than telling you they're doing it. Ready for another loose hypothesis? If you're still playing along, give that a thought before reading the next sentence.

How about this new loose hypothesis: they're looking for reassurance.

What might be a question to test that? How about: "Are you feeling good about making the move?"

If your friend comes back with, "I know I've got it all laid out, but there is that little voice that says quitting my career is crazy," you know you're on the right track. That means you can refine your loose hypothesis. If they need to be reassured that this is right for them, what factors might be at play that have left them feeling nervous? Perhaps loss of security from quitting their job?

And a question to test that? "Can you ramp up to become a full-time travel writer?" It's a leading question and it introduces the idea of starting part-time. Let's say your friend gets a smile in their eye when you ask that. That's the clue they've figured something out.

You can practise with small but real situations you face in your everyday life. It amounts to consciously asking yourself two questions: "What factors are at play?" and "What question can I ask to get to the root of those factors?"

The Behaviours of Creating Leaders: Positioning Others for Leadership

What's implicit in our discussion of empowering people is the idea that when people are aware of the factors in a challenge, they're more capable of determining a course of action. In the Leigh and Greg example, Leigh highlighted those factors for Greg in her questions and that, in turn, helped him to address her concerns. But could Greg have understood why his first ideas – surveys and senior manager interviews – weren't going to work before he walked into the room? In other words, what if he saw the strategic value of the conversation from the beginning?

In our example, Leigh didn't share the strategic direction. She was looking for a tactical answer – the thing to do – and so that's what Greg offered her. But being an effective leader means being able to see and understand the strategy behind the tactics. So positioning others for leadership means helping our teams to think strategically. Their ability to think strategically means that they become trusted advisors to others across the business, and that means people look to them for leadership.

The Dots of Strategic Thinking

Before we explore how to position others as leaders by helping them to grow as strategic thinkers, let's remind ourselves of what we mean by strategy. In its simplest terms, a strategy is a plan to do something. But if it were that straightforward, we wouldn't need our people to be strategic thinkers, we'd just need planners. So, of course, strategy is more than that. Beyond planning, strategy is about recognizing that our plans aren't formed in a vacuum but instead require us to navigate through the landscape we operate in. For example, in the business environment, that could be stakeholder challenges, financial pressures, and maybe even political factors that affect our operation. What all that means is that in order for a plan to work, we need a strategy for how to navigate in unpredictable terrain. Practically, it means we need to be able to see, connect, and interpret the factors — what I call dots — that make up that landscape. Doing that well means we don't wait to come across them; we actively look for those dots. When we find them, we target our actions and discussions on what we need to change now to accommodate the shifting landscape and make our plans a reality. It's what prevents us from being full-time fire-fighters, because the hope is that we're seeing the fires coming and so course-correct before they burn the plan down. That's easier than it sounds, because, as leaders, we need to make those kinds of calculations every day.

For example, when Leigh speaks to Greg, she knows she's not only looking for an improvement in middle management performance to improve the numbers on the next survey. She knows that she needs to lead middle managers who can one day become senior managers (dot 1), and she needs front-line managers who can then move into middle management roles (dot 2). She knows that the best way to approach the issue is to find out why middle managers aren't stepping up and to address those challenges (dot 3). Alongside that, she's also thinking that if her middle managers are struggling, morale could be the next casualty (dot 4). Front-line managers might leave out of frustration, while middle managers might settle into a complacent rhythm (dot 5).

It may turn out that these challenges are systemic. If that's the case, she knows she's got the right people in place but is hamstringing them (in identifying this, she is connecting the dots). If they're not, she knows there may be problems in the middle management hiring processes (again, connecting the dots). If it's both, she knows she needs a two-stage strategy (which also connects the dots). She knows that if these challenges are allowed to continue unchecked and people do start leaving, then when they win the big contract that's coming down the pipeline, her team won't be up to the task of effectively delivering on their part of the contract (and now, she's making meaning from those connections).

She doesn't tell any of that to Greg – which doesn't mean she isn't growing him as a leader, it just means that she isn't encouraging him to think strategically. As a result, Greg walks away to develop ideas about improving manager satisfaction. If he speaks to other leaders about what he's doing he'll be viewed as a tactician – since he'll be talking about things he can do – not as a strategic thinker, which impacts on the wider perception of him as a leader.

Growing Strategic Thinkers

That's why growing strategic thinkers in our team helps position them as leaders. So how can we do that? The answer is by helping them to see, connect, and make meaning of the dots. As I'm sure you can see, doing so does something else besides helping our people think strategically. If you're thinking that helping people think strategically is a stop on the bus route of empowerment, you'd be right. The ability to think strategically allows us to be more involved because our input is more likely to be heard and acted on.

Since there's a connection between empowering someone and helping them to develop the ability to think strategically, it makes sense that we can take a similar approach to growing our strategic thinking muscle. In that quest we meet our old friend again: asking questions.

Let's go back to Leigh and Greg's conversation. It's the same situation, but this time Leigh's focus is on growing Greg's strategic thinking muscle.

Greg walks into Leigh's office and she smiles warmly, leaning back in her chair. "Hi, Greg," she says. "I've got the numbers from the employee feedback survey, and we're still getting low satisfaction scores for middle managers."

Greg looks nervous. He's wondering if his name's at the top of the list of unsatisfactory middle managers. It's the only reason he can think of why he'd be here. "OK," he says.

Leigh sees his reaction. "This isn't a telling off, Greg. I'm wondering if you'd be interested in helping to improve those numbers."

He begins a sigh of relief but catches himself before it gets too long. He pulls out the chair opposite Leigh and takes a seat. "Where would you like me to start?"

Leigh doesn't take the bait. "Well, before we start on a strategy, I'm wondering about the long-term effects of these numbers – what might they be pointing to, how might they impact the leadership of our area?"

He's surprised. He's never thought of an employee feedback survey in that way before, but it makes sense. "Well, any problems with middle management set the tone for the whole team," he says.

"And what's the implication of that?" Leigh asks. She leans forward and sets her hands on the glass desk in front of her.

"It's hard to say," Greg says. He looks to the ceiling as if waiting for an answer.

She gives him a second and when he doesn't offer anything she jumps in, "What's the impact on our ability to perform?" she offers. "Not just now, but in the future too."

Greg nods, "Well, it'll be hard to fill a senior management role with one of us if we're not performing."

"And are we just concerned about succession planning from middle management up?"

He can see where she's going. "Right, there's also the message we're sending to front-line managers, and staff for that matter, about what it means to lead here."

"Anything else?" Leigh asks.

"Well, yeah," Greg says. "There's the question of whether staff will stay competitive in a potentially demoralizing environment," he's on a roll now, "and of course that means we might start developing issues in the business as the quality of work starts to fall. But there's also the chance of losing really good staff. It goes on," Greg says. He smiles at first but consciously lets it fade: he doesn't want to look like he's pleased about all this.

Leigh doesn't mind the smile. "So what problem are we really trying to solve?"

"There's a lot to it," Greg says, "but we're really talking about the leadership culture and ensuring it's cohesive throughout the levels of leadership."

"What do we get if we solve that?"

"A leadership pipeline."

In this example, Leigh is asking questions with the same ingredients as create questions, and she's allowing her questions to be informed by a loose hypothesis – in this case that Greg needs help to think strategically. At the point that we left their conversation, Leigh could jump into create mode and establish how Greg will go about developing that leadership pipeline.

But there's an important difference as well. And it's this: Leigh's questions have a slightly different function here than when they were only seeking Greg's ideas. Now her goal is to consistently ask the question that prompts his strategic thinking. She does that by transparently asking questions that point Greg in the direction of the dots he needs to be thinking about. Each question she asks is geared toward either helping him see, connect, or make meaning of the dots. If you're up for a mid-section challenge, skim over the exchange again and see if you can spot the questions that encourage Greg to see, connect, or make meaning of the dots.

If you played along, you may have noticed that Leigh's questions worked like this:

Question	The question helps Greg to ...
"Well, before we start on a strategy, I'm wondering about the long-term effects of these numbers – what might they be pointing to, how might they impact the leadership of our area?"	See the dots.
"And what's the implication of that?"	See the dots.
"What's the impact on our ability to perform?"	See the dots.

"And are we just concerned about succession planning from middle management up?"	See the dots.
"Anything else?"	See the dots.
"So what problem are we really trying to solve?"	Connect the dots.
"What do we get if we solve that?"	Make meaning of the dots.

Questions to encourage strategic thinking also help to funnel people's thinking in the desired direction: see the dots, connect the dots, and make meaning of those connections. In my experience, people aren't silly. The more dots we help them to see, the easier it is for them to make connections and meaning. That means most of our work will be at the front end – just like in the Leigh and Greg example.

Notice that Leigh doesn't tell Greg which dots she sees unless she has to, and even then she only shares a few. Why might that be? Well, just as with the behaviour of empowering, we can't position someone for leadership if we're doing all the work. If we identified the dots and put them together ourselves, we'd be living a task and teach approach to strategy. And, as we know, that perpetuates the dependency cycle.

What we're doing instead is asking the same questions over and over again: "What dots do you see?", "What's the connection between those dots?", and "What does that connection mean?" Asking those questions consistently and repeatedly has the effect of reminding people that these are questions they could be asking of themselves. And over time, with our effort and practice, that's exactly what they'll do. Because they'll be asking themselves those questions, they'll begin to flex their strategic muscle, and grow as strategic thinkers.

The result? Our people will have more to say. Their actions will be guided by an awareness of the factors affecting the business. But it doesn't end there.

Trusted Advisors

Great as being a strategic thinker is, it isn't the end point. A trusted advisor is someone who can not only make meaning of the dots but can communicate that meaning to someone else in a way that gets them to hear and act on it. You won't be surprised to hear me say that we can grow that ability in people too. It involves a simple question that we can offer after someone has made meaning of the dots and landed on a recommendation or course of action. It could be something like, "How can you talk to Sarah about that, so she'll really understand your idea and act on it?" Once again, ask a question consistently enough and soon people will begin to ask it of themselves.

What might prevent people from becoming trusted advisors is their cherished idea that if they have a good strategic view, then it should be acted on immediately. If we notice team members becoming frustrated because their ideas aren't leading to action, it means we might have missed a step. And the step is this: helping them to see that to be a trusted advisor we need to further the agenda of the person we're looking to advise; we need to establish the trusted advisor relationship before we can expect our advice to be heeded. If they do gain that level of trust, it's because we've helped them to think it's a worthwhile strategic goal to be a trusted advisor. So rather than commiserate with our people when they fail to get others to act on their advice, we just help them see that the non-action is information: it's telling them that they're not speaking to the customer, stakeholder, or colleague in way that they can understand or act on. Non-action can also be an indication that the stakeholder doesn't perceive how our people are furthering their agenda. If that's the case, we can use purposeful mindfulness to help others see the effect of their communication, how they're coming across, or how they may really be trying to further their own agenda or cherished idea.

If any of this sounds tough, that's because it is. There's a reason why leaders adopt the task or teach approach: it's easier. But persevere and something almost magical happens. It'll begin slowly as perceptions of your team and your business area shift. People in and out of your business will hear your people talking and begin to see them differently. Stakeholders will appreciate your people's input; they'll begin to trust your people's take and like the way they express it. That might start as a stray conversation – a stakeholder commenting on how your people seem more vital to their strategies – then, over time, stakeholders will begin to seek your people out and ask for their advice. But the magical part is that this will begin to happen independently of you. When that happens, it's your clue that you're living this attribute of a leadership mindset: you've created leaders of others.

Action Teams

It's difficult to lead without having something to actually lead on. So if we really want to position others to lead, creating leadership opportunities is just as important. That's where something like an action team can help.

First, a definition: an action team is a team of people who are tasked with a specific project that addresses a core challenge in the team or business. It can be handed to them by saying, "Here's a thing we need you to implement", but the best way is if teams propose the solution to the challenge. Let's say Greg goes away and comes back with some ideas to create the leadership culture that will enable a cohesive approach throughout the leadership team. Leigh could take those ideas and develop a plan to action them. Then, armed with that plan, she could call a meeting with Greg and some others and nominate them to action her plan. That's OK, but if we're looking to create leaders – and, in this case, position others for leadership – it's a missed opportunity. And the opportunity is this: why not ask Greg to form a team to action his ideas? Leigh might need to have a conversation with Greg to make sure his ideas are on track, but if they are, why not allow him to lead on it?

Parameters: Taking Care of You

"Hold on." I recognize the voice right away: Ingrid InVolve.

She has a problem; I can tell from the frown on her face.

"I'm all for empowering people," she says thoughtfully. "But do you know what happens when you hand over the reins?"

I have an idea, but perhaps not what Ingrid's thinking.

She pulls up a chair and takes a seat at my writing desk. "Let me tell you," she says, settling down to what sounds like the start of a lecture. "With the greatest trust and desire to empower and position others for leadership, I hand over a task," she pauses to make sure I heard the "hand over" part. "I tell people to go ahead and put their plans into action," she's deliberate in her phrasing, so her point's airtight. "And I feel good about that because isn't that what creating leaders is all about?" She takes a breath and I hear the "but" coming. "But you know what happens when they put the plan into effect?" The question's rhetorical, even I know that. "Things go wrong. Simple things that I'd have thought about before I'd even taken a single step."

The thing is —

"And the plan doesn't just go wrong," she says, cutting me off, "it goes spectacularly wrong. And on top of that there's now the flack to deal with from my leader." She pauses. "When I'm talking to my boss, the last thing I want to say is that I handed the project over and didn't know what they'd be doing." Ingrid pauses to let her point sink in. "And who cleans it up?" she asks. "It's me. Cleaning up a mess I could have avoided to begin with."

It would be a mistake to dismiss what Ingrid's saying. It's a real fear for a lot of leaders. The last thing we want is for Greg to run off and do whatever he wants while Leigh sits in her office hoping it all pans out. What Leigh could do is take Greg's ideas, and — here's the crucial part — think them through and return them to him with clear parameters for him and his team to work within.

Those parameters could include anything from timescales and budgets to information they need in order to complete the project. If the team works within those parameters, they can go ahead. They'll need to update Leigh from time to time, but will mostly work on their own. If they're outside the parameters then they need to run the plan by Leigh before implementation and accept that it might get changed. If that happens Leigh would use the create and strategic thinking questioning approaches to help Greg and his team see the potential holes in their thinking.

The reason for parameters is twofold: the obvious one is that it allows space in which people can lead. In a chapter about creating leaders, that's probably a good idea. The other is more subtle: it gives us, as leaders, a chance to take care of ourselves. Like I've said numerous times, the attributes and behaviours described in this book are a challenge to live. Creating leaders is no exception. What Ingrid is highlighting is one of the hardest things about handing over the reins: the insecurity about whether it will go well.

As I'm sure you can see, parameters are our input. They define the playground for our teams to work within. If we ask create and strategic thinking questions when we brief the team, we can be sure that they're thinking in the kind of way that will help them land on a solution that will work. Within those parameters could be a reminder that they need to figure out how to keep their leader in the loop – not to ask permission, but rather to keep them updated. That way, at any point, the team can confidently fill the leader in on where the project sits. The job of parameters is to increase the probability of our teams succeeding in their project, and to alleviate the nervousness a leader may feel when delegating.

Before we leave parameters, one last thing: the easiest thing in the world is to offer parameters that are so airtight that they only leave room for one outcome. Of course, those are not the kind of parameters I'm advocating for. If we can create parameters that allow for more than one solution, we're giving our team a chance to make decisions, think things through, and, of course, lead.

Challenge: Making it Real

As the title of this challenge suggests, this is about taking the ideas in this chapter and putting them into practice. All you need to do is fill out the table that follows. Give each question some thought and write your answer in the middle column. All I'm asking you to write in the right-hand column is a date: the date when you'll put your answer into effect.

Question	Your answer	Date
In which areas can you use a task and a teach approach less?		
In which areas and with whom can you apply a create approach?		
Who might you grow as strategic thinkers and trusted advisors?		
Which areas of your team or business might benefit from action teams?		

Take your time with this challenge. It's deceptively simple.

Creating Leaders Reminders

♦ The behaviours of creating leaders are empowering others and positioning others for leadership.

♦ Our leadership world view informs whether we are task-, teach-, or create-focused.

♦ Empowerment is the by-product of involvement.

♦ Questions informed by a loose hypothesis are at the core of the create approach.

♦ Strategic thinking means being able to see the dots, connect the dots, and make meaning of the dots.

♦ Helping others to grow their strategic thinking muscles helps to position them as trusted advisors.

♦ An action team is a team of people who are tasked with a specific project that addresses a core challenge in the team or business. It empowers people because it involves them.

♦ Parameters are a way to take care of yourself while setting your people up for success.

Chapter 6
Enterprise Thinking

A Life on the Ocean Waves

There's a gust of wind and the sail bellows. The boat lurches and tips up on the starboard side – heeling, they call it. It's exhilarating if you know what you're doing, slightly terrifying if you don't. Right now Clara isn't feeling exhilarated. The North Sea is a rough, unpredictable body of water, and now Clara's wondering how good an idea this was. She looks at the skipper – tiller and mainsheet in hand – sitting at the back of the small sailing dinghy. His feet are tucked under straps and his thighs are on the edge of the boat as he leans out to steady the vessel. He's the picture of relaxed. She scans the four other crew members. Two are holding onto ropes; two are balancing precariously in the cockpit – relaxed isn't the word that comes to mind to describe them.

A wave hits and the dinghy crashes down on its hull, and almost immediately the wind follows and the boat heels again. The starboard side is almost directly above Clara's head. She feels the icy water on her hands before she sees it pouring into the port side. There's a scream from her fellow crew members.

"Let the jib out!" the skipper shouts.

Clara isn't sure anyone's heard him. The jib is just as tight as it was, adding speed to a boat that's already travelling faster than she'd like.

"Balance!" the skipper shouts.

She knows she's meant to let the two crew members in the middle lean overboard on the starboard side; she remembers that from the classroom. Any more than that and the boat will be overbalanced. So she stays where she is, but the others don't follow suit. All four crew members are heading starboard. They're soaked, each with the same panicked look, and each with the same thought – to get to the highest point of the boat and out of the water.

The captain sees it too. "No!" he shouts, but no one's listening. Everyone but Clara is scampering starboard. When the four crew members get there things change right away.

To Clara it feels like it happens slowly, but she knows it doesn't. One minute she's on the port side of the boat, looking up at her crew mates hanging over the starboard bow trying to level the boat. And then the boat crashes level, but it doesn't stop there. The port side raises – and not just a gentle tip. It swings upward. She's above the crew and skipper now, the port side heeling just like starboard was seconds ago. Except this time it doesn't crash; this time, as she sees the starboard bow fill with water, the skipper shouts, "Capsize drill!" and she hears screams.

It seems like it takes minutes for her to fall from her perch into the water. She lands on the sail, no crew members in sight.

They appear one at a time. Wet, cold, and still scared. They're bobbing together in the sea when the skipper appears. He's standing on the centreboard as the boat lies on its side in the water. "Throw me the mainsheet," he shouts to Clara. "And then climb into the boat as best you can. You'll need to pull me in when I right it."

He looks at the other four crew members and shakes his head, but doesn't say a word.

The Needs of the Individual

In a small sailing dinghy like that, the fate of each person is connected to the fate of everyone else. If you sail, I'm sure you saw that capsize coming. It was on the cards as soon as the crew gave up on balancing the boat and started focusing on keeping themselves out of the water. That's why they moved to the starboard side: in their panicked thinking that meant they'd be safe. Of course, if everyone does that, there's too much weight on one side of the boat. And that's what made capsizing inevitable. By doing what was best for them as individuals, they did the worst thing for the whole crew.

That dynamic plays out in life and in business more often than we may care to think about: leaders of business units might drive the agenda of their area, despite the wider interests of the whole business; product teams might do a great job of promoting their product, despite the strategic focus of the business being on something else; country units might focus on the needs of their market over the goals of the wider business. On a smaller scale it might mean leaders doing what's best for their team over what's best for the department. And, of course, individuals might do what's best for them without regard to its impact on the business.

What all of these challenges have in common is the basic human drive to put ourselves before a wider interest. And that makes sense. Unless we're extremely altruistic or looking out for our loved ones, it's normal and natural for us to do what's best for ourselves. Although that might have worked for our ancestors when they were faced with the choice of bringing meat home to the tribe or not jumping into the path of a woolly mammoth, that same self-interest is often less useful in the interconnected world we live in today. These days, enterprise leaders aren't just nice to have, they're the glue that makes companies – particularly those that are geographically disparate or product-diverse – succeed.

But before we start thinking that enterprise thinking is just something leaders do, let's not forget that the six attributes are useful no matter what level we are at in a company, and in both our work and personal life.

Enterprise Thinking as an Attribute of a Leadership Mindset

We all use enterprise thinking to some degree. If that sounds unlikely to you, consider this for a moment: what's your hope for your family? Is your goal for everyone to do their own thing, or is your hope that everyone will look out for each other – adults and children alike – and work in the best interests of all? Does that latter vision change the way in which you interact with your family? Affect what you'd be willing to personally sacrifice for them? Or how about being part of a movement or group that we believe in? Are we willing to canvass in the cold and rain? Are we talking about that cause every chance we get? Are we devoting our free time to it because we believe in the ideals it stands for? The same goes with our teams, departments, or business units: whoever our loyalties are with, we tend to promote their interests.

What's at the core of all these situations is what we see as the enterprise. So although we all naturally engage in enterprise thinking – thinking about a bigger unit beyond ourselves – that doesn't mean we all regard the same unit as enterprise. In all the examples I have given so far, what we consider to be the enterprise determines how we interact and, crucially, whose interests we promote.

"What are you saying?" Sidney Self-Interest says. "I shouldn't work to hit my numbers locally, but help the company internationally?" He shakes his head in disgust. "I don't get paid based on global numbers, my performance is based on me hitting my targets."

It's a refrain I've heard before.

"Look," Sidney says, only just on the calm side of angry, "I sell a local product here. It isn't available globally, so I can only make my numbers in this local market." He pauses for effect. "So why would I want to create inroads for my company's global products? So my local products can have a direct competitor?" If he had a mic he'd probably drop it.

A perspective like that means that rather than collaborate with the enterprise, Sidney is competing with it. So to make his numbers and grow his local business, he intentionally doesn't promote his company's global brands. Think about the consequences of that attitude if it isn't just Sidney who thinks that way but it's happening in the company's markets around the world. The end result is that it's impossible for the company to deliver on its global brand strategy.

In a situation like Sidney's you can bet that there are executives sitting in company HQ who either have developed or are developing a strategy to grow global brands in his local market. And will Sidney be viewed as an ally in that project, do you think? In fact, even though he's making his numbers now, how likely is Sidney to move up in the business? These are real problems for Sidney if he wants to grow as a leader. And for him, just like for all of us who share his perspective, the solution starts with a shift in thinking – a shift in what we see as the enterprise.

That's why enterprise thinking is one of the six attributes. At its core, a leadership mindset is a broad world view. In business, the broadest possible view is of the wider enterprise. Creating leaders, flexing our thinking, being curious: all these attributes draw on our willingness to look beyond our immediate world and see how it fits into a wider context. If we can do that as leaders, possibilities open up to us.

Compete Versus Cooperate

The first shift in enterprise thinking, then, is one that Sidney may have trouble with: it's the ability to move from seeing ourselves as being in competition with other teams, departments, business areas, or even the wider enterprise, to wanting to cooperate with them.

"Right," Sidney says, "and when I start missing my numbers because I'm trying to sell global products into a market that wants my local products ..." he pauses, and this time he's crossed over to the angry side of calm. "I can see it now, Cynthia CEO will fly out in the corporate jet to pat me on the back and say, 'Well done, thanks for your cooperation.'"

OK, that's a real objection. And it would be about as silly as Sidney makes it seem if that's what I meant. The shift from compete to cooperate isn't a grand gesture, it doesn't require a wholesale change in how we operate, and it doesn't mean jettisoning everything that's working for us in order to be subject to the whims of HQ. It means flexing our thinking to start wondering, with genuine curiosity, about how what we're doing can feed into our company's goals. We'll explore that in more detail later, but for now the point is a subtle one: are we willing to challenge the idea that working in the company's best interests means working against our own?

That's an important question, because the behaviours of enterprise thinking that we're about to explore take it as read that the answer is yes. Maybe you're not convinced yet. That's OK. Maybe you can recite lots of examples of a corporate view that doesn't see or understand the challenges of your team, department, or business unit. That's also valid. At the risk of annoying you, I wonder why your corporation doesn't know about those things. When I talk about compete versus cooperate, I'm not suggesting that it's a one-way street: that we cooperate and to heck with the cost to our teams, departments, or business units. What I'm wondering is what might happen if we, using all the six attributes, found a way to work with HQ – maybe by being a trusted advisor to them and giving them the information they don't have – so we're both cooperating with each other?

I encourage you to mull that one over as we explore enterprise thinking.

The Behaviours of Enterprise Thinking

So perhaps while you give that some thought, let's take a look at the behaviours of enterprise thinking:

Attribute of a leadership mindset	Behaviours
Enterprise thinking	Understanding our connection Living our place in the bigger picture

Before we jump into those, let's think about another possible objection to adopting the attribute of enterprise thinking. This one is a direct retort to the first behaviour: understanding our connection. And it goes something like this, "Why should I?"

Every business I've ever consulted for wants its people to be enterprise leaders. Every enterprise leader wants their team to be enterprise thinkers. That makes sense. After all, if leaders are working in the best interests of the business, business units will be joined up. It means that there will be cross-pollination of best practice, strategies that connect, and teams and business units working toward one goal. In fact, the president of one company I've worked with is fond of saying that what their competitors fear is the day their company works as one unit. So businesses definitely want enterprise thinkers. But back to that very valid objection: why should I? Why should the individual leader, middle manager, or front-line staff member work to hold an enterprise view? Typically, it means doing more. It means stretching their thinking to consider the wider implications of what they're doing. It means working across teams even though it could slow down a project. And it means doing the extra work of finding out what's happening in the rest of the company.

Sorry to be repetitive here, but with all that I've just said, why should I? Why would anyone? Well, enterprise thinking isn't something we demand of employees; it's something we give them a reason to have. That's why connection is the first behaviour. If we, as leaders, are looking for people to step up and hold an enterprise view, our job is to give them a reason to want to – something that connects them to the business. Because when they – and we – have that connection, they'll want to do everything that I listed in the last paragraph. And more. Connection is the driver of enterprise thinking. And it's connection that leads to the second behaviour: living our place in the bigger picture. That's because if we care, we want to know the scope, vision, and strategy of the business – and how we fit into it. And if we feel connected to the business and see the big picture, we want to make that picture happen.

So, before we start to look closely at the behaviours, I've got a challenge for you.

Challenge: Your Connection

A lot of this chapter will be about creating connection in your team or business. But before we get to that, we need to be connected to that business. After all, how can we model enterprise thinking if we're not connected to the enterprise? So the focus of this challenge is for you to find that connection for yourself. This isn't about connecting to the strategy of the business, or even to whatever it is the business does. It's about finding *your* connection with the business.

Grab a piece of paper and divide it in half. On one side write down the living, breathing values that you see in your workplace. I don't mean your published company values, and I don't mean the ones you see your friends at work living. I mean the ones your business really lives. For example, does the business support experimentation? Does it recognize and encourage cooperation? Does it seek out different points of view and encourage healthy debate? Is it inclusive? List all the values you can identify, using as much paper as you like.

If this sounds tough, and you're thinking something like, "I have no idea what values are living and breathing at work." I've got good news: it's easier than it seems. Start with the behaviours you see around you that are condoned by the business. Are people valued for being "professional" or "friendly" maybe? Of course, those are behaviours not values, but our behaviours are informed by our values. And that's also true in business because businesses tend to hire people who embody the qualities they prize. It's what we mean when we say a potential candidate is a good fit. The behaviours are manifestations of a company's true values.

To get to the value, ask yourself why it matters to the company that their staff are friendly. You might conclude that they value friendship, or maybe kindness. The specific value that underpins the behaviour is hard for me to guess – I don't know your business or the people in it, but you do. If you're seeing the people in your work being professional, is that because they value respect, or is it trustworthiness that's important to them? My point is, keep drilling down into and exploring the behaviours you're seeing until the value you come up with chimes with what you know of the people in your business.

Your page might look like this:

Living, breathing values in my business	
Dependability	
Efficiency	
Passion	
Truth	
Challenge	
Originality	

The next bit may be easier. On the other side of the page, write out your values. Just the top few will do. Here's an example:

Living, breathing values in my business	My values
Dependability	Family
Efficiency	Commitment
Passion	Freedom
Truth	Risk
Challenge	Winning
Originality	Courage

Now for the hard part: can you find connections between your values and the ones you see being lived in your business? It doesn't have to be an exact match. In the example I've given, commitment and dependability have flavours of each other even though they're not the same word. That's also true of courage and challenge. It may be that you want to drill down further into a value to get to its core. Freedom, for example, is a broad value – if you have something similar, think about what freedom means to you. Is it financial freedom, freedom from obligation, freedom to travel, or something else?

When you can see how your personal values and those of your business overlap, stop for a second. Think about what that means. Think about how your business reinforces those values in you. And think about how you can reinforce them in your business. That last point is important because it's the place of connection with your business. After all, if your business is helping you live your values and allowing you to bring those values into the world, to my mind, that's a powerful connection to a place. Having that connection is the difference between simply having a job and being involved in the mission of the business.

Take the time to notice what that connection means to you. Maybe you've been aware of that connection all along, maybe it's why you signed up to the company in the first place. Maybe you're realizing it for the first time. Either way, ask yourself, "In what way does consciously stating that connection change how I feel about the business?" And then ask yourself, "How can I inhabit that connection more? What can I do to explicitly live that connection at work?" If you're a senior leader, does that mean pivoting the business or your area to reflect that connection more? Does it mean reorganizing departments, or refocusing product lines? If you're not a senior leader, perhaps a middle or line manager, does it mean refocusing your team? Or being more transparent with them? If you're an individual contributor, does seeing that connection have any implications for what you want to do in the business?

My guess is that not everyone who tries this challenge finds the point of overlap with their business. It may be that, instead, as you worked through this challenge, you saw that your values and those of your business share no commonalities. If that's the case, I'd also guess you've been feeling restless there for a time. Maybe the wage, the pension, or the people have kept you in the role. And maybe they will continue to do so. That doesn't mean you won't do a good job, I'm sure you will. On a very basic level, enterprise thinking is about caring about the business and how the business operates. We care as enterprise leaders because we feel like the business is our own, or at least an extension of who we are.

If we don't feel that connection in ourselves it'll be hard to model it in our roles. I'm not saying that if we don't feel that connection it's time to move on – although it is true that when I've done this challenge during my consultancy work, some people realized just that. To be more precise, what they saw was that living their values both in and out of work was more important than the wage, the pension, or the people. They saw that they had something to contribute, and that where they were wasn't necessarily the best place to do that.

As you can imagine, finding a place of connection isn't just powerful as a leader, it's vital. It's only when we feel part of a business' purpose that we start to think broadly about what's in the best interests of that business, because a shared purpose means that what's in the best interests of the business is in the best interests of ourselves. And that realization is what enterprise thinking turns on. The ability to think broadly allows us to be enterprise thinkers.

Now that we know why connection matters to enterprise thinking, let's see how we can operationalize that connection in a team or business.

The Behaviours of Enterprise Thinking: Understanding Our Connection

I'm not suggesting we all have to sit down with our teams and do the challenge I just offered. But that doesn't mean connection is only important for some people in a business. Some senior leaders already have that connection – it may have contributed to why they've risen to the role. Business owners have that connection because the business they've started is often a direct reflection of their values. But here's the thing: enterprise thinking isn't a given at senior levels. For that reason, I'll explore connection from an organizational perspective. In doing so I'll offer an approach to enterprise thinking that helps create connection for staff while, at the same time, helping raise the level of thinking for senior leaders.

The premise is simple. In the last challenge, connection was based on an overlap of personal and company values. That overlap gives us a stake in the business, since furthering the company's values furthers our own. The reason we don't need to do that last challenge with our whole team or business is because there are other ways to give people a stake in a business. The easiest route of all is to draw on our old friend involvement. I talked a lot about involvement when discussing the create approach in Chapter 5. There, involvement was about empowering people. Here, we can operationalize connection by taking the idea of involvement further.

To do that, let's think about an equation that I think offers a framework for how we grow a connection to a business and cultivate enterprise thinking. Here it is:

collaboration + coordination = connection

In the equation, collaboration is the act of conversing with others to determine the best way of doing something. It works best when we have those conversations early. Coordination is the process of implementing the output of our collaborations. When we do those steps in that order it means we'll be working together seamlessly, and that creates connections across teams, departments, and countries.

Thought of like that, connection – like empowerment or employee engagement – is the by-product of two elements: creating an environment in which it's a functional requirement to collaborate, and easy to do so across teams, departments, business units, or countries, while at the same time creating processes to do something with the output of the collaboration. Do that and teams become invested in what's happening outside their teams because what happens outside their teams directly affects them. Creating connection means we want to think about how our actions impact and support other areas of the business – enterprise thinking, in other words.

Although it might not be apparent, that brings us back to involvement. Why? Because we can't make people collaborate or coordinate if they don't want to. So let's take a look at each element of the equation and see how involvement can help us to achieve our aims.

Collaboration

I think it's fair to say that just about every business I've consulted for has, at some time or another, tussled with the collaboration dilemma: how do you get a team of highly effective, type A personalities to work together?

"Well there's your strike one and two," Trisha Together says. Her accent makes her sound like she's in a western – it's the kind of Texan drawl that only exists in film directors' imaginations. "Highly effective people don't want to work together because they reckon they can handle the task better on their own; and type As, well, they're so driven they steamroller over anyone who might disagree. Not a lot of collaboration going on there."

Maybe it's the accent that throws me. I had a point, I just can't recall what it was.

"And they ain't the only problems," she says, filling the silence. "There's the fact folk don't want to collaborate because it takes too long, leads to talking shops where nothing's decided, creates endless meetings, and don't forget the egos and logistics that get in the way."

All valid points. The thing I'm wondering about is, does that mean collaboration doesn't work or does it mean how we're collaborating doesn't work?

Trisha stops dead like a freight train hitting a mountainside.

All of the points Trisha's raised can result from what I call false collaboration. You know what I mean: the meetings people go to or positions people might take when they feel expected to collaborate or forced to defend their perspective. It's the imposed nature of the collaboration that means conversations won't be dynamic or won't feature people bouncing ideas off each other, because they don't want to offend, or maybe even be there in the first place. And they don't want to be there because they don't feel there's anything to be gained for them or their area of the business. In fact, they might even think the conversations are pointless because people outside their teams don't know enough about their business unit to offer useful input. And when that happens, all of Trisha's points are true.

Collaboration isn't about putting people in a room and asking them to work together for the greater good of the business. If you've ever tried that you know how well it works. And if you haven't tried, save yourself the effort and don't. So what can we learn? More specifically, what can we learn about cultivating connection by imposing the need to collaborate? The answer is in the question: it's impossible to impose collaboration. That's why it can't be a top-down approach, no matter how good or well-thought-out the idea. Cultivating collaboration is often a culture change. And, like most culture changes, it's a systemic change where the people most affected by the change are in the best position to create it.

And that's where involvement takes centre stage. Our people already know the areas in which better collaboration will help them. That's a good place to start from because we already have buy-in to solve the problem; we can start creating connection through collaboration by asking our people where those pressure points are. You've probably spotted that this is consulting people, not involving them. The involvement takes place when we ask people what they need in order to allow the collaboration they're looking for to happen. And then give them the space and resources to make that happen.

The "space and resources" can be anything that creates team interconnectedness. It could involve formalized briefing sessions at the start of projects, which include multiple teams peripheral but relevant to the project; creating spaces for cross-functional conversations early on, so teams can input on a project; or any other helpful initiative.

One of my favourite collaboration processes is what I call break parties. Breaking ideas is an approach we first met in Chapter 1 and were reacquainted with in Chapter 3. Here, it's a chance for cross-departmental teams to break the idea by finding holes in an initiative and, of course, plugging those holes when they rebuild the idea. It could focus on looking for holes in early ideas, over-sights in an implementation plan, or new ways of working in a post-mortem. The point is, it gives teams a chance to share insights on a project or idea. Having cross-departmental eyes looking at an idea increases the chances of spotting what may be obvious challenges. What could a cross-departmental team bring to the party when they don't know the project or department they're providing feedback on? This unfamiliarity is precisely why they're so useful. It's their ability to look at the idea with fresh eyes – the beginner's heart we talked about in Chapter 2 – that allows them to see things experienced eyes may have missed.

Whatever the process of collaboration we adopt, it's important that both the avenues of collaboration identified and the way to collaborate come from our people. This isn't a process exercise; it's a mindset shift. Implementing the best process without a shift in mindset will have short-lived success. Allowing the avenues and the means of collaboration to come from our teams means that those teams are taking the first step toward enterprise thinking: they're beginning to connect with the business. If you've recognized some of the create approach from Chapter 5 in that, then congratulations – you're seeing the interplay between the six attributes.

Of course creating leaders isn't the only attribute at play, what I'm suggesting requires genuine curiosity to ask where improvements are possible; flexibility of mind to connect the strands of thinking and consider what could be done that hasn't been before; mindfulness to see and hear what people are really saying; and resilience, because creating a culture of collaboration doesn't happen overnight.

Crucial to this approach is that the avenue and the means of collaboration that people identify are useful to them and to the business. Asking questions helps people gain clarity about how the avenues of collaboration they've highlighted will do that. It's a chance to lay the foundations for the enterprise thinking we're seeking to cultivate. For example, if the shipping team thinks a collaborative channel with packaging design is a good idea, why is that? What would they collaborate on? If they're curious about how packages are designed, that's interesting for them to know, but it doesn't nurture the enterprise thinking we're looking for. If it's because they feel that working together to redesign product packs would mean they could get a greater number of products on each truck, that's the enterprise thinking we're looking for. It means that collaboration has resulted in lower costs for the business; interconnectedness between two departments; and a willingness in both departments to think outside of their immediate area for the betterment of the business. It also means that both teams feel invested in a business that is acting on their ideas. And that takes us to the second part of the equation: coordination.

Coordination

As I mentioned earlier, coordination means having a system in place to deal with the output of people's collaboration. It's at the coordination stage that the equation has the greatest chance of breaking down. Businesses are often very good at getting staff input – consulting. Sometimes they're good at creating forums where staff can share ideas – collaboration. The problem for many businesses is doing something with the tangible ideas that come from staff.

Think about that for a second. Do we nurture a connection to the business if we ask staff for their ideas, work with them to develop a system of collaboration, and then do little or nothing with the ideas they offer? As obvious as that question may be, the feeling that businesses have done enough by asking for ideas is common. That's fine if all we want as leaders is the ideas of our people. But what if we want something more? If we want our people to have a real connection to the business, then asking for ideas isn't enough. Asking for ideas without acting on them not only doesn't create connection, it actively disconnects people from the company as they see that it doesn't listen, isn't interested, or is too set in its ways – none of which nurtures connection or enterprise thinking.

That's why coordination is so important: it helps the teams that develop ideas to work together to implement those ideas for their own good, that of the teams they're collaborating with and the company. People in those teams have a connection to the business as they feel their input is valued. And that encourages them to look at the wider business rather than just at their own departments. But what coordination model can do all that?

I feel more than know that there's someone behind me, so I turn. And there's Trisha Together, her back resting against the frame of my office door, left leg curled up so she can rest her foot on the door frame too. She's looking at the floor like an indifferent gunslinger spoiling for a fight. "You asked a real question there," she says.

I nod because I did ask a question.

"Coordination is the opposite of the 'if you build it, they will come' philosophy," she says.

Her statement seems definitive, so I turn back to my computer.

"Buddy," she drawls, "you can build the greatest process this side of the Rockies to share and act on ideas, but that don't mean a single person'll use it."

Despite being a displaced character from a spaghetti western, Trisha isn't wrong: creating connection by decree can't work. Yes, as leaders, we carve out the space to make connection happen, but that's where the direction ends. Following Trisha's point, if we build it, they probably won't come. And we wouldn't really want our staff to come if they were only doing what we wanted them to, rather than being driven from a point of connection to the business.

So how do we help on the coordination side of the equation? We do what we've done on the collaboration side – we ask, and we create the space for it to happen.

"Wishful thinking," Trisha says.

But is it really? If our teams have gone to the trouble of identifying areas of collaboration; have spoken with the team they want to collaborate with; have been open to questions about how those areas benefit the enterprise; have adjusted accordingly and now have compelling answers to those questions; have actually collaborated with a team outside of their immediate circle to develop those answers; and, finally, have developed ideas to improve working practices for both teams that benefit everyone, how likely is it that those teams would want to put those ideas into practice?

That question is at the heart of this approach to connection. Because, in my experience, the answer to that question is "very likely", but with a caveat. The caveat in this case is that their leaders neither take their ideas and repackage them, nor change them until they are only a vague simulacrum of the original ideas and then ask them to put the leaders' ideas into effect. It's the leader's job to help teams create – to ask questions to help them hone their ideas at the collaborate stage to ensure those ideas will benefit all. We can sit in on break parties and help find holes in the ideas. We can talk with the teams and even offer input as they rebuild ideas. What we'd get from that is the reassurance that they are working on good ideas. Armed with that reassurance, we can then offer them implementation parameters, similar to the ones I talked about in Chapter 5. The teams can then design their own process of coordination, and, like all things we design ourselves, they will be invested in making it succeed. If that coordination process works, there's no reason why teams can't share it with others, who may adopt it wholesale or adjust as needed.

The end result is a coordination process that will be similar across an organization. One designed by teams who are not only rightly proud of their work, but also feel connected to a business that allowed that to happen. And that brings us full circle.

Connection

With the connection that results from collaboration and coordination comes something more: enterprise thinking. The process of collaboration saw people thinking beyond their teams to work in the best interests of all. And the process of coordination saw teams working together to implement their ideas in the best interests of all. What's implicit in the entire process is the willingness to think beyond the immediate team or business area concerns and connect team tactics to a bigger strategy. In short, we grow enterprise thinking because the process requires enterprise thinking in order to function.

If we were in the *Wizard of Oz*, this is the point where Toto tugs on the curtain to reveal the workings of the wizard. Except rather than the wizard's, "Pay no attention to that man behind the curtain!" in this case we will be paying close attention to the idea behind the curtain, which is at the heart of embedding the six attributes. It's an idea that I mentioned at the start of this book: that we can't embed a leadership mindset by simply learning about it. The six attributes are a way of looking at the world borne out of our experiences that ultimately leads to a set of behaviours. That means we can only embed the attributes by living them. What I've outlined over the last few pages is what's behind the curtain: in this case, a mechanism to grow enterprise thinking by giving people the experience of enterprise thinking.

Experience is as effective for senior leaders as it is for teams. If we don't already hold an enterprise view, actively looking for points of collaboration with other senior leaders is a good place to start. Acting on the ideas that the collaboration throws up helps us to create high-level processes of coordination across business or country units. Just as is the case for our teams, we get to grow and embed enterprise thinking by demonstrating it. The processes of coordination we uncover can then be used by our managers and team leaders to support their teams' processes. The effect is that we not only enhance enterprise thinking for ourselves, we also integrate strategies at the senior level and model that integration for our teams.

We'll explore that in a bit more detail when we look at the other behaviour of enterprise thinking – living our place in the bigger picture – but, for now, let's take a moment to think about how what we've just looked at can work in practice.

Challenge: Putting the Equation to Work

So we've explored how collaboration + coordination = connection.

This can work on a personal and professional level, as well as on an organizational one. We can pivot between the personal, professional, or organizational depending on what we're thinking of as the enterprise. Whatever it is, the principle of this challenge can be adapted to suit – it just requires a bit of flexibility of mind.

Unlike the other challenges so far, this one involves working with others. You can do it as a thought experiment if you like, but since we're looking to grow enterprise thinking, at some point we'll need to engage with the enterprise. If this is your first excursion into the equation, start small. If your organization is the focus of this challenge, choose to implement it with a team that's likely to be amenable to the ideas and one who you know will be keen to take on the challenge. If it's for you, then begin by approaching a peer in a different area who you feel would support the idea of collaboration. If it's a personal challenge, work with others who you feel will be receptive. To keep things simple, I'll be using an organizational application as the example. But, as I said, make any adjustments that make sense for whatever focus you have in mind.

Ready? Then let's go.

As a leader in your business, consider for a moment which teams or units you feel could benefit from a wider view of the company. The goal here isn't just to enhance performance, don't forget, the ultimate goal is enterprise thinking through connection. So although there may be lots of areas where you'd like to see improvement, for this challenge we're concerned only with those that require a cross-team, cross-department, or cross-unit solution. When you have those groups in mind, we're ready for the next step.

Ask the teams whether they share your view. It's a big step, I know, and that's why we're beginning with teams that we're reasonably confident will be open to the concept. To be clear, I'm not suggesting that you tell them what you feel they should collaborate on, or even that they should. Instead, you're asking whether they feel there are challenges they face as individual teams that could be helped by working with others. Because we're looking for connection, it's important that the ideas for collaboration come from the teams themselves. They may offer the area you thought of or it may be something different. When you have that, the next step is simple: give them space to collaborate. That may mean adjusting workloads. It may mean throwing a pizza party. Whatever you do, the goal is for the teams to feel that they're supported and that their ideas will be taken seriously.

When they share their ideas, you're stepping into the next part of the challenge. Use the create questioning that we talked about in Chapter 5 to help guide their thinking. Try questions like: "How will your idea help your two teams and the business?", "What can we expect to gain from implementing the idea?", and "In what way will the idea reinforce the business strategy?"

It may be that a break party is a good idea. When the teams have a solid idea that benefits each other and the business, offer them the parameters that we talked about in Chapter 5 to work within as they develop and execute their plan.

As you can probably see, the real challenge here isn't in helping the team to develop ideas or come up with a plan – it's not your job to direct or manage this process. Your real challenge is in helping the teams make connections with each other and with the wider business. That happens when they solve the challenge for themselves. The more you focus on the connection, the more successful this challenge becomes; because the greater the connection, the more likely teams are to develop ideas that support each other and the business.

Finally, to repeat a word of caution, it was easy to write this challenge and it's easy to read it. It's much tougher to do. If this is your first excursion into applying the six attributes in your business – at the risk of sounding like a broken record – start small. Start with teams who will likely be receptive; start on the periphery of your business if that feels better. Give yourself every chance to succeed, and mitigate as much as possible against those elements that might make it a struggle. After all, we're looking to build on success, not fall at the first hurdle.

The Behaviours of Enterprise Thinking: Living Our Place in the Bigger Picture

It's 3000 BC. A Neolithic man, let's call him Urgtal, crests a hillside in Pembrokeshire, Wales. It's wet, but not cold. His right hand clasps the wool fleece around his neck to keep the rain out. In the distance he can see a disused monument made of quarried stone. Thousands of years from now they'll call it bluestone and wonder how it came to form the outer ring of Stonehenge, but Urgtal doesn't know anything about that. His pace quickens as he heads toward the stone and then, without knowing why, he breaks into a run. He feels the wind rushing through his hair, the rain on his face, his heart beating in his chest. He's smiling as he runs. He throws his pack down on his approach to the monoliths – he wants his hands free to touch them.

The stone is smooth when he glides his palms across it. It's been quarried by experts, men far more talented than himself. He rests his right cheek against the wet stone, rain falling on his head. It's almost like he can feel the life of the stone, its formation over countless years, the way it has stood on an outcrop, probably not far from here, for countless more: a silent witness to the changing landscape. How it was pulled from its birthplace and hewn by careful hands; how it stood as their monument for years. But no longer. Now these stones will be brought to a new place to stand in the light. To be a beacon. Urgtal presses his ear against the rock like a doctor listening for a heartbeat. "There is a place for you, my friend," he says tenderly. "Not here anymore. Somewhere else where you will be loved."

It has always fascinated me why the Neolithic builders of Stonehenge brought the spotted dolerite bluestones 160 miles to erect them at Salisbury Plain. Maybe, like Urgtal, they stumbled on the remnants of an ancient monument in Wales and decided to move the stones. Maybe a Welsh tribe decided to take their monument with them. But what fascinates me even more is thinking about the conversations people might have had when moving them. Though the stones weigh less than two tons – light by Stonehenge standards – moving them on wooden lattices with ox and human muscle power was no small feat.

Did people complain about doing it, I wonder? Did they doubt the wisdom of whoever made the decision to bring the stones from Wales? Or did they understand why? Did they see moving the stones as their piece in a much larger project? Did seeing that bring them a sort of comfort? That there was a plan and this was their part to play? I'd like to think the latter was true. Because if it is, it means people can do amazing things when they see how their role makes something bigger possible. Although it's great for people to see the big picture, what I'm suggesting – through our Neolithic digression – is that it's not enough.

As well as seeing the whole picture of what a business is doing, we need to see how we are connected to that picture – that's what the story is really about. Equally important is seeing how the role that we're fulfilling day in and day out fits into that picture – that's what I mean by living our place in the bigger picture. Our Neolithic ancestors wouldn't have had many competing priorities when they were tasked with moving stone monoliths from Wales to Salisbury Plain. Nowadays we don't have that luxury. We're fielding emails, running with competing priorities, answering to several stakeholders, and maybe even working on several projects. So it's easy to focus on what's in front of us and lose sight of how what we're doing fits into a strategy. Even if a company does a good job of reminding their people of the overriding strategy, it doesn't make it any easier to see that strategy when we're in the trenches. That's true for leaders as much as for everyone else.

And that's why living our place in the big picture is a behaviour of enterprise thinking. Because as leaders it's self-evidently vital that what we're doing reinforces the business strategy, and it's also true that we need to help others to see their role in the same way. The way we do that is by connecting our actions and those of our teams to the strategy of the business. Before we think about how to do that, let's take a moment to remind ourselves of what we mean by strategy.

A Strategy Reminder

As we saw in Chapter 5, strategy is more than planning. What makes strategy difficult is navigating conflicting interests and an unpredictable business landscape. Strategies differ from objectives and plans. An objective is what we're looking to achieve, the plan is how we'll do it, and the strategy is how we'll make that plan work. Let's illustrate that with our Neolithic example of moving bluestones over a great distance.

Our objective, plan, and strategy might look like this:

- Objective: transport 80 bluestones from Wales to Salisbury Plain.

- Plan: assemble a wooden lattice, six oxen, and groups of 60 people to move each monolith.

- Strategy: cut and prepare trees in Wales, recruit oxen and people from nearby towns. Use incentives of food, tools, and the chance to be blessed by ancestors to gain a workforce.

Of course all of that is made up. But the principle is sound: our strategy feeds into our plan, which feeds into our objective. And that's how we get the holy grail of joined-up working in the Neolithic period. The same idea works in our world too.

Put simply, these days business objectives are broadly the same, with a few exceptions. What are those objectives? To make a return for shareholders and project a strong company image. That applies to the non-profit or charity sectors just as much as it does in business – all have to generate money to keep doing whatever they do. The plan is usually to sell our product, service, or cause while growing the business. The strategy for how to do that, while navigating uncertainty, is what makes each business different. Sometimes a business fails because the plan isn't great – relying on ice cream sales all year round, for example. More commonly, a business can run aground because its strategy is flawed.

Since the objective and plan are often givens, and because strategy is so important, most businesses talk mainly about strategy. And since most businesses have different teams, departments, and units, it also means talking about a central strategy, which, while important, isn't the whole story. In fact, for many businesses we can think about strategy as a flow that looks like this:

Corporate strategy

Departments/Units/Countries

Actions

In this flow the corporate strategy overarches the business. The departments, units, and countries support the corporate strategy. The actions are the things people do to make the strategy happen. The holy grail of joined-up working is for all of these to fit together. And that brings us to what makes it tough to see our place in that flow.

The Difficulty of Living Our Place in the Bigger Picture

It may be more precise to say that it's easy to see our place in the part of the flow that we're in. The hard part is seeing how our area connects back to the business unit, let alone the corporate strategy. Why might that be? To answer that question, take a look at the following strategic flow. It's a more detailed version of a strategy flow, this time for one business unit in a company:

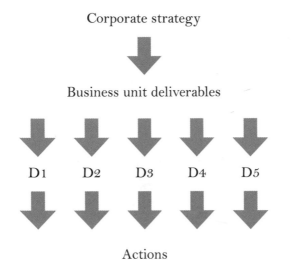

Corporate strategy

Business unit deliverables

D1   D2   D3   D4   D5

Actions

Before we look at this, let's define some terms. As before, the corporate strategy is the overarching strategy of the business. The business unit has deliverables it needs to achieve to support the corporate strategy. That's rarely one thing, so here I've just made up numbers (D1, D2, D3, etc.) to represent the various deliverables. The actions are just what they sound like: the actions that need to be taken or tactics that need to be employed to make good on the deliverables.

Now recall there's several teams in each business unit, each working on different actions. And recall too that there's several business units, and maybe a few functions too. Remember how I said that the hard part was to see how our part connects back to the business unit, let alone the corporate strategy?

"Look," Viola VP says, "thanks for the graphics and all that. I mean it must have taken ages to put together, but ..." she pauses and the look on her face says she's trying to find the right words.

"It's just much easier than all that. If your point is that sitting in the trenches of an operational strategy makes it hard to live the big picture, that's a given."

OK, so she didn't ignore me completely, she just thinks the answer's obvious.

"What we need as leaders is to have people see the overall strategy from where they sit in the business." She stops and I can see she's thinking. "Don't you think it's just as hard from the top of a business? From where I sit in the senior team, I need to make sure my business unit is working to the strategy too."

She sighs and lets the air puff up her cheeks on the way out.

Of course she's right. At all levels we need to be aware of what we're doing and how we enforce the corporate strategy. And, of course, that isn't easy. For a warehouse worker, let's say, it can seem like the job is simply loading and unloading boxes. How do we keep them aware that the efficiency with which they load a truck helps the logistical strategy of the commercial operations department? Or how, with the myriad of other things happening in a business unit, can we make sure we hit our numbers while supporting the wider business? After all, business units are called that for a reason: they're businesses within a business and that means they have all the challenges and complexities of their day-to-day operation with the added pressure of reporting to another business.

And that's the challenge: keeping ourselves and our people focused on the corporate strategy while we're inundated on a day-to-day basis with the tasks and challenges we face. That's Viola's point: how do we keep a group of diverse people focused on a corporate strategy which often feels remote? The answer to that? Make it less remote.

Strategy and Connection

When we were talking about connection, I said that for enterprise thinking to take hold we need people to feel that their values and ideas are reflected in the business. I suggested that action teams implement their own ideas. The goal of that is for people to see a direct cause and effect between what they say and its impact on their everyday world at work. That's how we get connection.

"Thanks for the recap," Viola says, "but we've moved on. You're saying that we make corporate strategy less remote through connection to strategy?" She stops and looks at me, a smile is maybe a second away.

Viola's got the point. In the same way that we can grow connection to the enterprise, we can grow connection to strategy. Do that and we have teams living their place in the bigger picture. That doesn't mean we need to create action teams; the idea we're borrowing is direct relevance. Think about why it works when a team sees their ideas being valued and implemented: because it matters and is relevant to them. Now think about why a team might not be connected to the corporate strategy: because they can successfully do their day-to-day role without giving the corporate strategy a moment's thought. If people aren't living their place in the strategy, the message they're sending to their leaders is that the strategy isn't relevant to them.

"Great," Viola says, "finally something helpful. So all I need to do is explain why the strategy is relevant to them and I'm off to the races."

Since Viola's in my imagination, I'll choose to imagine that she hasn't read Chapter 5, because if she had, she'd know that's exactly what I don't mean. If you haven't read the chapter yet, here's a synopsis: the shortest way to entrench apathy is to tell someone why they should care about something.

"Wow, OK," Viola says, "there's no need to be rude." She pauses so I'll get the message. When she feels her protest has landed she continues. "I can't change the corporate strategy to suit everyone, so what's the idea?"

Viola's right. We can't change the corporate strategy, not at our level of the business anyway. But our job isn't to rewrite the corporate strategy, it's to make sure that our area of the business reinforces it. And we can do that while making it directly relevant to our teams.

Nested Strategies

Since all business units are businesses in their own right, they have an objective and a plan too. Like I said before, the objective is, loosely speaking, to make a return. For a business unit the plan is to make that return by selling their products and services *and* support the corporation's strategy. So what's the business unit strategy? That would be how they plan on selling their products or services while supporting the declared strategy of the corporation. That means we can represent the business unit strategy like this:

business unit goals + corporate strategy = business unit strategy

The shift in mindset here is to see that a business unit doesn't just have to regurgitate the corporate strategy. Instead, it makes it relevant to its interests and its people by adding to it. "What does it add?" Viola might ask. The answer is its own business objectives.

Maybe now's a good time for an example. Let's say we work for a car manufacturer whose corporate strategy might be something like this:

Diversify and grow revenue streams and market share by providing reliable products and services that add value to our customers' lives.

Let's say we're the vice president of after-sales. We need to reinforce the corporate strategy, of course, but we also have plans of our own. We might want to: introduce more app-based technology so customers can track service intervals; offer best-in-class warranty extensions; provide the best customer service in the car industry; attract and hire technologists so we can develop automated warranty processes; and reduce staff turnover – and that might be just a few of our ambitions. The point is, although some of these things are covered in the corporate strategy, some aren't. As vice president, we want to incorporate the things that aren't into our business unit strategy. So our strategy might look like this:

Support the corporate strategy by researching and providing cutting-edge products and technology, offered by long-term staff who value providing best-in-industry customer service.

Now we have a strategy our business unit can relate to. From here we'd develop the areas we'd need to focus on to make the combined strategy happen: business unit strategic focus areas (SFAs). Then we'd look at the deliverables or strategic outcomes (SOs) and, lastly, at the operational strategies to make the deliverables happen. Put into our strategy flow, it would look like this:

Corporate strategy

Business unit strategy

Business unit strategic focus areas

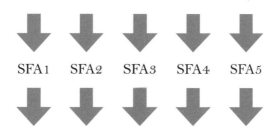

SFA1   SFA2   SFA3   SFA4   SFA5

Strategic outcomes (business unit deliverables)

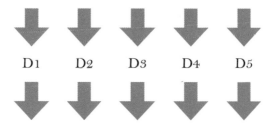

D1   D2   D3   D4   D5

Operational strategies (actions)

What this flow shows us is that we don't just swallow the corporate strategy wholesale; instead, we reinvent it for each level. That's why I'm referring to "*strategic* focus areas", and calling the deliverables "*strategic* outcomes" and the actions "operational *strategies"*. At each point we restate the strategy to support the one above and make it relevant to the people at that level.

Let's map an area in the car manufacturer's business unit to illustrate the point:

Corporate strategy:
Diversify and grow revenue streams and market share by providing reliable products and services that add value to our customers' lives.

Business unit strategy:
Support corporate strategy by researching and providing cutting-edge products and technology, offered by long-term staff who value providing best-in-industry customer service.

Business unit strategic focus area 1:
Warranty extensions that retain customers and build our reputation as the best in industry.

Strategic outcome 1 (the deliverable):
Offer competitive warranty products.

Operational strategy 1 (action): *Carry out competitive analysis.*

Operational strategy 2 (action): *Look for gaps in the warranty market.*

Operational strategy 3 (action): *Develop warranty products that surprise and delight customers.*

"Great," Viola says. Her voice comes out of nowhere.

I don't say anything because I'm trying to figure out if she's being sarcastic or not.

"I get it," she says, "but there's one thing. How does it get us living our place in the big picture? That's the point of all of this, right?"

There's no irony in her voice at all, so I take it for a real question. It's about connecting strategies. In this example we're connecting strategies vertically in a business – from the overarching corporate strategy to the actions in that business unit. At each point we're adapting the strategy for the audience that needs to implement it. That makes the strategy immediate and directly relevant to people's day-to-day work. If I'm doing the task of developing warranty products, I know my focus is on developing *competitive* warranty products. And I'm doing that so the company can offer *warranty extensions that retain customers and build our reputation as the best in industry*. And that matters because by offering great warranties the business unit is providing *cutting-edge products*. So I'm helping the business provide *reliable products and services that add value to our customers' lives*. The end result is being just as joined-up as the Neolithic monument-builders, without having to move a two-ton rock. Of course, alongside that one SFA are several others, but the principle of connecting them is just the same.

As you can probably already see, working vertically isn't the only way to connect strategies. We can also connect strategies horizontally. After-sales might share some common objectives with marketing – to get the message out about their warranties, for example. It may also share objectives with human resources, since after-sales wants to attract and retain top-notch customer service professionals to ensure they're delivering the best customer service possible. If that's the case, then those departments can reinforce aspects of each other's functional and business strategies, and in turn connect with the operational strategies that inform each other's actions.

That's what I mean by nested strategies – strategies that fit together: each reinforcing the other, and each meaningful for its audience. Do that and we don't have to ask people to memorize or be invested in a remote corporate statement; instead, we're making it easier for them to care about the things they do every day.

By helping people connect to a meaningful strategy on their level that reinforces the ones above, all the way back to the corporate strategy, we're doing something else. We're growing enterprise thinkers. How? Because when we connect to a local strategy, it's easier to see how we fit into the overall agenda.

Have you ever been lost in a shopping mall and used one of those store maps? If you're anything like me, you'll look for the big red arrow that says "you are here", then look in the index for the store you're after. Then you look around to check off the stores around you on the map. When you have a handle on where you're at, you plot a course to where you want to go. That's exactly the same function connecting strategies does: a strategy that's directly relevant to me is that arrow; the nearby stores are the other local strategies; and the map itself? Well, that's the company strategy.

Being able to see my company like that means I see how all the teams, departments, and units fit together. Not only does that provide a sort of comfort, it also means it's easy to see my role reflected in the strategies around me – and that makes it easier to work in the best interests of the bigger picture.

Challenge: Recognizing Your Strategies

This challenge could be one you take on with your leadership team. Whether you're a small business with just a few departments or a multinational with country divisions, the principle is the same. Of course, your leadership team doesn't have to do all of the work – we'll get to why not at the end of the challenge.

For the purposes of this challenge I'll be thinking about a leadership team in a department, let's say human resources. That means I'm assuming that there's already a corporate strategy in place. As always, feel free to draw on flexibility of mind to adapt and adjust to make the scenario more meaningful for you.

One way to begin this challenge is with a conversation. This can be with yourself or with your leadership team. Let's say it's with your team. My guess is that your leadership team knows the corporate strategy well. Most can probably recite it word for word, and those who can't can offer an accurate synopsis.

Now ask the team: "What are our goals as a human resources department?" What we're getting at is what we're trying to do in the business that isn't covered by the corporate strategy but is vital to our own success.

The answer to that question is your department's objective. Keep this clear but broad. We're building a functional strategy, not a list of what you want to do. We're looking for a couple of lines, no more. It may be things that your team is already doing but that aren't stated in a strategic statement. If there's confusion, don't be put off by it. Often leadership teams feel that working to the corporate strategy makes sense and doesn't need more elaboration. But that doesn't make it so. If we want connected, nested strategies, the second level down isn't the place to let the thread break. So, in as broad a statement as possible, see if you can capture the essence of your department. Ask yourself, "Why does the department exist at all?" Human resources' strategic statement might be something like: "Support the corporate strategy by being sought out to develop and advise on human resources policy across all areas of the enterprise."

Notice the length of the strategic statement. Notice that although it's broad, it's also directly relevant to human resources. And notice how it's suggesting some things your leadership team needs to focus on to make that strategic statement a reality. What might those things be? Well, that's the next part of the challenge.

Now ask the team: "What does the department need to focus on for that strategic statement to be everyone's lived experience?" In our example that might be: (1) positioning human resources leads as trusted advisors to the wider enterprise; (2) offering cutting-edge advice on attracting and retaining the best staff; (3) assisting in succession planning for management and leadership; and (4) ensuring all departments seek out advice from the department rather than adopt "shadow human resources" operations. Those and any other ideas the team may think of are your department's SFAs. This time, notice that from a broad strategic statement you developed targeted areas to focus on. Of course we don't know how we'd do these things yet, and right now that doesn't matter. What SFAs do is provide a target. And we know that by hitting that target we move the needle on the functional strategy, and that helps us support the corporate strategy.

Of course, you already know the next step. Now ask your team: "What deliverables do you want to see from each focus area?" That's what I've been calling SOs, and the point is to unpack what the team hopes to achieve from focusing on these areas. Take them one at a time, and take them slow. In our example the first SFA has the strategic outcome of being invited to offer strategic insight on all human-resources-related matters. The third SFA might have two outcomes: offering a company-wide succession-planning and training program for managers and leaders; and establishing human resources as the focal point of leadership development. Notice how this second outcome also reinforces the first SFA. Nested strategies have a habit of doing that.

I'm sure you've seen the last stage in this challenge coming a mile away: it's to build operational strategies or actions for each SO – actions for each deliverable, if you prefer. In all probability, there'll be more than one action – that's no problem. Our job is to make sure that the action directly relates to the strategic level.

Let's take the first SO of the third SFA: offering a company-wide succession-planning and training program for managers and leaders. A few operational strategies here might be: to understand the mindset that company leaders of the future might need; to complete a needs-analysis; to develop manager and leader development pathways; and so on.

Notice how each of the operational strategies contributes toward delivering the SO – which, in turn, delivers on the SFA; which delivers on the departmental strategy; which helps the department support the business as a whole.

I mentioned at the start of this challenge that your leadership team doesn't have to do all of the work. And, of course, you don't need to do this on your own. If the goal were just to develop nested strategies, you and the team could do that quickly – that would be an example of the task and teach approaches from Chapter 5. But speed isn't the goal: our aim is to help people connect to the strategy and live their place in the bigger picture. That takes time, and it takes a willingness to involve people in the process of this challenge.

Practically, it's a good idea for you and your fellow leaders to develop the departmental strategy, SFAs, and SOs. It may be that you want to think those things through before you bring the idea to the wider team, so you can help guide them through the process. If the department is large, each leader on the team might develop their own strategy to promote their particular objectives, while reinforcing the departmental and corporate strategies. Either way, when it comes down to SOs and operational strategies, we want our teams to be involved too. And their involvement will mean everyone, at all levels, will need to think about how what they're doing fits into the wider business (enterprise thinking), and that necessarily creates strategic levels that reinforce each other (strategic connection).

The truth is this isn't a one-off challenge; it's something we keep doing. That's also true of helping people connect to and live strategy. To be clear, I'm not saying the strategy needs to keep changing – no one likes a business that's changing direction with the wind. What I mean is that the work of making that strategy relevant doesn't end.

If strategy is about navigating an ever-changing landscape, one of the elements that keep shifting underfoot is the connection our people have with our business. If we assume that everything is fine, or fail to survey the territory around us, we may be walking into danger. Enterprise thinking is a willingness to act in the best interests of the business because we care about it. Do that and our businesses are more than simple revenue-generating machines: they become a conglomeration of values, ideas, connections, and, yes, vision. When we have those elements, and apply the six attributes, a business becomes a change agent in the world as it seeks to make its vision a reality.

Enterprise Thinking Reminders

♦ The behaviours of enterprise thinking are understanding our connection and living our place in the bigger picture.

♦ Seeing ourselves as being in competition with other teams, departments, or business areas is an obstacle to enterprise thinking.

♦ Involving people helps them to feel connected to your business.

♦ Collaboration + coordination = connection.

♦ Nested strategies reinforce the corporate strategy while making that strategy relevant at every level of the business. Strategies can be nested vertically, horizontally, or both.

Epilogue 1:
Applying the Six Attributes of a Leadership Mindset in Business

The Mindset Panacea

"I've been looking forward to this epilogue," Phil Follower says from the doorway. He seems relaxed; he's even smiling slightly. "I get it, you know. If I'm looking at the world in a certain way, my mindset," he drops in the word proudly, "could create problems in a team. I see things one way; others see it their way. There are arguments and disagreements."

He walks into my office and leans against the glass desk. It shifts under his weight. "Before you know it, people don't want to walk down the hallway to talk to each other. Leaders block each other, maybe even stop their people working across teams. Shift that mindset and everything changes." He stops and looks at me. "That's some shift, that mindset shift."

It must have been months since I wrote the introduction because Phil was big then but now he's gained about twenty pounds of pure muscle.

"That's true and not true," I say, remembering his fist of a couple of hundred or so pages ago.

Phil doesn't say anything but his relaxed demeanour gives way to the beginnings of a snarl.

It's tempting to see mindset as the answer to everything. Shift a mindset and we shift a problem, or so the thinking goes. But here's the thing: if we accept that a leadership mindset is way of looking at the world borne out of our experiences that leads to a set of behaviours, we have to accept that's true for how all mindsets are formed.

"So what are you saying?" Phil says, "That my idiot colleague has a point?" He's rolling up his shirt sleeves. I choose to believe he's hot and not considering thumping me again.

Let's say a team doesn't support or actively fights an idea we've hatched. It's true we could see that as an inflexibility of mind and proof they're not living the six attributes. What's also true is that their experiences led them to hold that mindset. It could have been formed in a business that showed them that changes don't stick; that management doesn't listen; that when changes do happen they don't address any of the real issues. We can dismiss their concerns as evidence that the person simply can't be pleased, doesn't try, or always complains. Or we can entertain the idea that their objections all point to systemic challenges in the business. In fact, their lived experience may drive people to lose connection with the business, as their worst fears are reinforced with every pep talk, every failed change initiative, and every new process. If we allow those systemic challenges to continue, they'll actively prevent people from thinking differently, which means their current mindset becomes even more entrenched.

That's why the six attributes of a leadership mindset aren't a panacea: even if we could shift mindset in an environment like I've just described, it would be a temporary shift. If a team chooses to adopt the six attributes and to trust that things can be different, they'll give up on it as soon as they go back to a workplace that's exactly the same as before. An environment where their ideas aren't acted on, and where changes that are made fail to address the issues they've pointed out. And if that happens the company in question is worse off than it was before. And it may not get another chance. Why would the team believe that anything would be different the second time around?

Phil unrolls his sleeves and turns. As he approaches the door, this muscle-bound figment of my imagination veers toward the bookcase. He pulls an imaginary copy of this finished book off my bookshelf. "Fine," he says, "I'll read the epilogue."

The Two-Stage Approach

I turn back to my computer. At Innate Leaders, my business consultancy, we've found that a two-stage approach to mindset works well. The subject of this epilogue is to highlight how that two-stage approach can work in a range of business challenges.

I'm sure you can see that approach in play throughout the book: first, develop the six attributes, second, apply that shift in thinking to real-world challenges. That doesn't mean a team or person needs to develop all the attributes. Everyone I've met has some of the attributes, but the key question is: which are needed in the current challenge? That way rather than helping people think differently in a void, we can build on existing strengths. We embed strengths and shifts in perspective as systemic challenges are addressed. The result is a self-sustainable solution because that shift in mindset stays with your business, which means you can use it to solve the challenges of today and tomorrow.

So now let's take a brief look at the kind of challenges where that two-stage approach might apply.

Building Cohesive Teams

If teams are struggling, part of the challenge could be that the team members just don't like each other. Working on the six

attributes can help individuals to see themselves and their colleagues for what they are: no better or worse than anyone else.
Building that shift in thinking into a team charter can help create
a common purpose for the team, and consolidate the gains from
their shift in perspective. If lived, the charter also offers a means
of accountability. That might be stage one.

There's also a good chance that the operational model of the
business makes it tough for teams to truly collaborate and build
esprit de corps. If you're thinking that our connection equation
(collaboration + coordination = connection) might be a useful
way to think about addressing systemic obstacles to team cohesion, I'd be inclined to agree. If there's no need for people to
work together, it means a team can't really be a team; instead,
they're a group of people loosely organized around a common
area in a business. Does that sound like fertile ground to grow
indifference to what teammates are doing, or resentment at having to attend meetings that aren't helpful? I think so too.

This isn't a mindset challenge; it's a systemic one that can be
worked on as a team once a shift in mindset has taken place. That
would be stage two. Because although growing the six attributes
can produce insights and shifts in perspective, just like any other
experience in life, it stands a chance of fading if it isn't culti-
vated. And that brings us back to the connection equation.
Because only when the team shifts its way of thinking will it be
able to design a system of collaboration that will last. It's only
when people see each other as trusted advisors with shared challenges that they'll be willing to develop long-term processes to
implement their joint ideas.

Throughout the book you've probably noticed another theme:
the process of developing the process *is* the process of embedding the attributes. (Sorry about that sentence; the awkwardness
doesn't diminish the real-world effect, though.) In order for that
to work, the team in which you're looking to grow cohesion
needs to develop those systems themselves. Anything else is an

imposition, which is the best way to make sure a system fails. I understand that imagining an un-cohesive team working alongside each other to develop those systems seems like a fantasy now. That's the value of the six attributes: growing them means the team sees each other as colleagues. Seeing that, they spot how their colleagues can help make their lives easier, and that's what makes working together possible.

Leadership

I'll keep this brief because leadership has been at the core of the whole book. I find it useful to think of leadership as a verb. Thought of like that, conscious awareness of how we're leading matters. Stage one in leadership development could begin by exploring the limits and opportunities of leaders' current perspectives. What does leadership mean? To manage the business? To guide? To set the direction? To grow other leaders? As stage one continues we could deep dive into the attributes to come up with a shared vision of leadership and a shared set of leadership behaviours.

The real value of the six attributes is their ability to be operationalized – that's what the attributes and behaviours give us. We can not only identify the attributes that will benefit the business and help our leaders grow, we can also have a list of behaviours we can measure that growth against. That's the focus of stage two: to operationalize the shared leadership culture.

Why would we want that? Perhaps you've worked in a business where the senior leaders had a clear view of leadership. Let's say it was to empower, to listen to other points of view, to create staff involvement wherever possible – the six attributes. And let's even say that front-line staff saw and bought into that vision. The only thing is that when those staff interacted with middle managers they bumped up against a different vision of leadership. Then leadership was about being told what to do, being performance-tracked, maybe even continuing with outdated processes because "it's always been done that way". An extreme example, perhaps, but hopefully I'm making the point.

That's why stage two seeks to operationalize the culture. Because great though it is that the behaviours of the six attributes live at the top of a company, what matters is that every employee has direct experience of them. Not only because that means we have joined-up leaders, but also because, by operationalizing a shared vision of leadership, we're also creating the leaders of the future in our business as front-line staff learn what it means to lead from people who represent the leadership vision of the company.

Strategic Direction

Have you ever been to a strategic planning session where you hear great ideas, ones that herald a new dawn for your company? I think most executives have. And then what happens to those ideas? Of course sometimes they're implemented. But often they're not. Why is that? Well, it could be because in the comfort of the conference room – with its leather chairs, snacks on tap, and freedom from the everyday – our ideas feel real, and the possibilities limitless. When we head back to the office and the strains and demands of our roles press upon us, the ideas become humdrum or pipe dreams. Or maybe something else happens. Maybe those strategy sessions aren't all that strategic at all. Maybe they would be better named planning meetings because that's what we do: plan the actions of the year to come. Either way, those meetings can be a wasted opportunity.

My guess is there are two possible reasons why outputs from these sessions end up in the strategy graveyard: they're regarded as nice-to-have, or they feel uninspired. A two-stage approach here might focus on honing all six attributes, not in depth, but as more of an *amuse-bouche* that stirs the creative juices and whets the appetite for a different way of working.

Unlike the strategy work of Chapter 6, strategic direction is about understanding where the business is at and what's possible in the future. Are we hunkering down to ride out a bad year? Are we looking to expand? Are we focusing on culture? Is new business the goal? Is there a need for diversification? Whatever the central issue, mindset work that encourages new perspectives is our stage one.

Stage two could focus on honing the ideas that emerge from strategy planning. That could mean converging on a few ideas that address the current issues. We don't need details yet, just ideas. The bulk of the work at stage two is in honing those ideas to become real, actionable, and revolutionary. We could do that by settling on our top five strategic options, and then break and rebuild each. It may be that some ideas don't stand the break test. If that happens, we let the idea go. We keep breaking and rebuilding the remaining ideas, perhaps discarding more. And we do that until we're left with one or two ideas that leave us feeling excited *and* nervous. We want both those feelings because both are the barometers of a revolutionary idea.

Change Management

We've talked about change situations a fair amount in this book. The big shift in thinking here is from consulting with people to involving them. I know that sounds like a simple thing to say, and one that most businesses will say they do already. My experience is that most businesses do a great job of consulting teams, without really involving them. So stage one in this case might focus on enterprise thinking, creating leaders, and resilience. We need enterprise thinking for the leadership team to see the value of involving people who are affected if the change is to be sustained over years not months. Involving people means creating leaders. And we'll need resilience because cultures don't change overnight, or even over months. Although we'll see the shoots of change soon, we'll only be able to say the culture has changed some way down the road.

So at this stage, we might concentrate on the first two of these attributes. As perspectives begin to shift, we'd explore the effect on the whole enterprise. Is this the right change? How do we know? Would people affected by the change agree that it's the right one? Two crucial questions to ask are: "How do we involve them in the change process?" and "Where can people lead in that process?"

These are the kinds of questions people ask when they are looking out for the enterprise. Built in is the willingness to do what's best for the business versus what's expedient, and the ability to see change as a chance to grow the next generation of leaders. When your leadership team asks questions like these, we know we're coming to the end of stage one.

From there stage two kicks in and we begin to create systems to involve the staff. Now we define the change by asking those most affected what they'd like to see; we take those ideas onboard and allow them to inform our thinking. Then we give the ideas back to the team to allow them to implement the changes, within parameters that include a mechanism to feed back to the leadership team. The goal isn't to create followers of new systems and processes. As you can see, the focus is on creating leaders of the change outside of the leadership team.

Unique Business Challenges

Here's a real question: "Is it possible to address a challenge we've never come across before using the same way of thinking that we always have?" Framed like that it feels like the answer's obvious. When a unique challenge arrives and we see it for what it is, we know it's time for a different approach. In that case stage one might focus on two attributes: genuine curiosity and flexibility of mind. Genuine curiosity to learn as much as we can about the challenge, and flexibility of mind to put that learning together in an interesting way and arrive at a revolutionary idea. Then we'd implement that idea at stage two, informed by our shift in thinking.

Now here's another question: "How often does a unique challenge look that way when we first encounter it?" If your answer is often, then we can use the approach I just outlined. But if your answer is rarely or never, then it can take money, time, and effort before we realize that our usual approach won't work. And when we get to that point, we're so time-crunched that we need to arrive at an answer now. In that case, we don't know we're dealing with a unique challenge. The question now is: "How do we flex quickly?" Because what do we tend to do when we see that an approach isn't working? That's right, we try variations on a theme, or push the square peg into the round hole, only this time harder.

What I'm suggesting is that our usual ways of working can be cherished ideas. So stage one in this case is about enhancing the mindset of our teams before we're faced with challenges that necessitate new approaches. Stage one is about growing our flexibility of mind and genuine curiosity muscles. But this time our stage two is different: this time it's about creating working practices that question themselves. That's only possible if we're armed with genuine curiosity – a mindset that asks why. Why do we do X that way? Is there a better way of doing it? What are the limits of organizing ourselves in this way? We combine that with flexibility of mind to find ways to keep asking ourselves those questions and doing something with our answers. Because we've completed stage one, we'll be able and willing to develop new ways of working that are self-reflective and changeable as needed.

The learning culture of genuine curiosity gives us our safety net against approaching all challenges in the same way. The ability to flex our thinking means we don't attach ourselves to one way of doing things. That isn't just a culture that can exist in a leadership team; it's possible to cascade that perspective out to the wider company.

Epilogue 2:

Applying the Six Attributes of a Leadership Mindset in Life

A Leadership Rug

The challenge of writing a book describing the six attributes of a leadership mindset is that there's a risk that we come to see those attributes as separate, or perhaps even contingent on each other. We can't have genuine curiosity, the thinking might go, unless we have flexibility of mind. That's a risk I've been willing to take.

You see, a leadership mindset isn't "made up" of its attributes; it's more like we know we're living the six attributes when our actions and thinking are infused with them. The attributes are a rug woven with six coloured strands – mindfulness, genuine curiosity, flexibility of mind, resilience, creating leaders, and enterprise thinking. Just like we can only see the pattern by looking at the whole rug, we live the attributes when we allow those strands to weave together. Each influencing the other; dependent on the others to reveal the pattern.

The fun part is weaving our own rug: putting emphasis on the strands that matter most to us. It's the particular mix that means the six attributes look different on everyone. And so they should. How can flexibility of mind look the same, for example? So feel free to take these ideas and create your own leadership mindset

– weave a rug, a carpet, a coaster. What we create doesn't matter. It just matters that we're at the loom.

The Promise of the Six Attributes of a Leadership Mindset

If you've read this book in order, you may have noticed a theme running through these pages. Yes, the six attributes are a useful thing to have as a business leader, but that's not the only application you noticed.

You, Diligent Reader, have seen something else. I said at the start that, as well as a business book, I'm also offering a way to navigate ourselves through life.

"I'm glad you mentioned that," Diligent Reader says, "because, yes, I remember you said that. I can get behind that if we're talking about resilience and mindfulness."

Your eyes scan the ceiling of my office and I can see that you're pondering the other attributes. You tilt your head from side to side. "Yes, I can give you mindfulness." You think about that for a second and then nod your head.

It's a fair point, and I'm not just trying to flatter you because you bought the book. Yes, resilience is a useful life skill. And, for some, mindfulness as a way to de-stress works a treat.

You nod as if to say, "I just said that."

I can see I'm losing you, so I make it snappy.

Ideas like genuine curiosity, flexibility of mind, creating leaders, and enterprise thinking all have their use in life as well. Yes, they're just as difficult to apply, and just as hard to live consistently. But if we're willing to take on the mantle of personal leadership in our everyday lives, the effects can be profound.

Honestly, I mean it. Imagine what the world would look like if we were all willing to entertain the notion of being wrong. In a flexibility-of-mind world it would be impossible to have polarized points of view, for the simple reason that we'd know our view was one of many valid ideas. What would that do to our politics I wonder? Or to how disagreements are handled on a personal or global scale? What would the world look like if we welcomed challenges to our ideas, rather than argued tooth and nail for our perspective? And what if we flexed our thinking as we saw our cherished ideas for what they are? And what about if we all held genuine curiosity – a willingness to learn just for the sake of learning? What might we discover? Not just in science or business, but personally? What might we learn about the big ideas that divide our societies? Climate change, inclusion, the growing divide between the rich and the poor, and religious conflict? And what if we married our new-found learning with flexibility of mind to combine all that we encounter into a bigger idea? One that we could put into effect?

What would the world be like, I wonder, if – as we developed that bigger idea – we began to see our fellow humans as the enterprise? And because of that we seek strategies to reinforce the well-being of the human enterprise. Not for the benefit of some, but for all of us. What would our world look like then?

Diligent Reader taps on the door frame, not a *can I can come in?* knock but more a *hey I'm still here* knock.

When I turn from my laptop, your mouth is already open, just about to speak, "You don't think that's maybe taking things a bit too far?" Your voice is kind; the tone you might use with a child who wants to eat a whole chicken.

Maybe. So how about if we didn't apply these ideas on a world level? What if we saw each moment in which we interact with someone else as a chance to grow them and, in the process, grow ourselves? What if we asked questions with genuine curiosity to understand other people's world view? What, if when friends and family asked for help, we applied flexibility of mind to their challenges to help them arrive at a bigger idea? One they never dared to dream was possible?

Along with a shift in thinking, the six attributes mean a change in the way we behave. That change in behaviour leads to different ways of doing things. It means we don't tend to rely on the same approach and the same solutions we've always tried, and that means coming up with revolutionary approaches to the challenges we face on a personal, professional, and world stage. For my money, in an uncertain economic climate and a fast-changing world, we need leaders who can adapt quickly, who can innovate, and who can grow leaders of others, and we need those leaders to be everywhere.

Like I've said repeatedly, none of this is easy. It begins, Diligent Reader, when we realize that our views and ideas are just that: ours. It continues when we challenge our perspective. It grows as we allow people to surprise us with their ideas and we admit that we'd never have seen it that way without them. It grows further when we use those moments of surprise to open ourselves up to being surprised even more and encourage others to lead in their own life. It deepens when we allow that to become a self-evidencing cycle, as we see others as leaders rising to the challenges in their own lives.

In life, those people could be our partners, our kids, our friends, a group we're part of, or, of course, our colleagues. The promise of the six attributes is that as we grow them we necessarily help to grow the mindset of others. It's like a contagion that spreads – each leadership mindset giving rise to another. And another. And another. And who knows where that might lead?

Take care,

j.

Bibliography

Atlantic, The (2008 [1963]). "Martin Luther King Jr.'s 'Letter from Birmingham Jail'". Available at https://www.theatlantic.com/magazine/archive/2018/02/letter-from-birmingham-jail/552461/.

Bach, Richard (1977). *Illusions: The Adventures of a Reluctant Messiah* (London: William Heinemann Ltd).

Beck, Aaron T. (1967). *Depression: Clinical, Experimental, and Theoretical Aspects* (New York: Harper & Row).

Biko, Steve (1987 [1973]). Black Consciousness and the Quest for a True Humanity. In Aelred Stubbs (ed.), *Steve Biko: I Write What I Like* (Oxford: Heinemann Educational Publishers), pp. 87–98.

Carnegie, Dale (2006 [1936]). *How to Win Friends and Influence People* (London: Vermilion).

Carter, Elizabeth (tr.) (1910). *The Moral Discourses of Epictetus* (London and Toronto: J. M. Dent & Sons).

Duckworth, Angela, Christopher D. Peterson, Michael Matthews, and Dennis R. Kelly (2007). "Grit: Perseverance and Passion for Long-Term Goals", *Journal of Personality and Social Psychology*, 92(6): 1087–1101.

Gwilt, Joseph (tr.) (1826). *The Architecture of Marcus Vitruvius Pollio in Ten Books* (London: Priestley and Weale). Available at: https://archive.org/details/architectureofma00vitr/page/n7.

Hamilton, Edith and Huntington Cairns (eds) (1961). *The Collected Dialogues of Plato*, tr. Lane Cooper (Princeton, NJ: Princeton University Press).

Kübler-Ross, Elisabeth (2009 [1969]). *On Death and Dying: What the Dying Have to Teach Doctors, Nurses, Clergy and Their Own Families*, 40th anniversary edition (Abingdon: Routledge).

Mednick, Sarnoff A. and Martha T. Mednick (1967). *Examiner's Manual: Remote Associates Test: College and Adult Forms 1 and 2* (Boston, MA: Houghton Mifflin).

Michelson, A. A. (1903). *Light Waves and Their Uses* (Chicago, IL: University of Chicago). Available at: https://archive.org/details/lightwavestheiru00mich_0/page/n9.

Milgram, Stanley (1963). "Behavioral Study of Obedience", *The Journal of Abnormal and Social Psychology*, 67(4): 371–378.

Milgram, Stanley (1974). *Obedience to Authority: An Experimental View* (New York: Harper & Row).

Quiller-Couch, Arthur (1916). *On the Art of Writing: Lectures Delivered in the University of Cambridge, 1913–1914* (Cambridge: Cambridge University Press). Available at: https://www.bartleby.com/190/12.html.

Ritter, Simone M., Simone Kühn, Barbara C. N. Müller, Rick B. van Baaren, Marcel Brass, and Ap Dijksterhuis (2014). "The Creative Brain: Corepresenting Schema Violations Enhances TPJ Activity and Boosts Cognitive Flexibility", *Creativity Research Journal*, 26(2): 144–150.

Rotter, Julian B. (1966). "Generalized Expectancies for Internal Versus External Control of Reinforcement", *Psychological Monographs: General and Applied*, Vol. 80(1) (Washington, DC: American Psychological Association): 1–28.

Schultz, Kathryn (2010). *Being Wrong: Adventures in the Margin of Error* (London: Portobello Books).

Watson, Burton (tr.) (1993). *The Zen Teachings of Master Lin-Chi: A Translation of the Lin-Chi Lu* (New York: Columbia University Press).